Language and Literacy Beyond Decoding

Also Available

Developing Vocabulary and Oral Language in Young Children
Rebecca D. Silverman and Anna M. Hartranft

Language and Literacy Beyond Decoding

Evidence-Based Instruction in Grades PreK–6

edited by

Rebecca D. Silverman

Kristin Keane

Foreword by Catherine E. Snow

THE GUILFORD PRESS
New York London

A Division of Guilford Publications, Inc.
www.guilford.com

Printed in the United States of America

This book is printed on acid-free paper.

For product and safety concerns within the EU, please contact *GPSR@taylorandfrancis.com*, Taylor & Francis Verlag GmbH, Kaufingerstraße 24, 80331 München, Germany.

Last digit is print number: 9 8 7 6 5 4 3 2 1

Library of Congress Cataloging-in-Publication Data is available from the publisher.

ISBN 978-1-4625-5959-6 (paperback) — ISBN 978-1-4625-5960-2 (hardcover)

To E, whose endless curiosity, love of reading, and ability to comprehend beyond her years give me hope for the future

—RDS

For the card, the keys, and the books:
To my mother, Mrs. Acorn, and the Salvio Street branch librarian

—KK

About the Editors

Rebecca D. Silverman, EdD, is the Judy Koch Professor of Education in the Graduate School of Education at Stanford University. A former elementary school teacher, Dr. Silverman's research focuses on language and literacy development and instruction in early childhood and elementary school. In particular, her work has contributed to the research base on (1) supporting vocabulary and other aspects of language that are critical to reading and writing, and (2) using multimedia and educational technology to facilitate literacy. At Stanford, she leads The Language to Literacy Research Lab (*https://langlitlab.stanford.edu*) and teaches in the Stanford Teacher Education Program. She also engages in research–practice partnerships with school districts and provides professional development to teachers seeking to support language and literacy throughout elementary school. Dr. Silverman has served on the Board of Directors for the International Literacy Association and is the current editor-in-chief of *The Elementary School Journal.* Her research has been published in numerous journals of education research and practice.

Kristin Keane, PhD, is Assistant Professor of Reading Development at the University of California, Berkeley. She uses mixed-methods approaches to study literacy development and instruction in elementary schools, paying special attention to the ways multimodal and digital literacies—including technological approaches—can enhance engagement, comprehension, and dialogic discussion of varied types of text. Previously, Dr. Keane was Director of Research and Partnerships at The Language to Literacy Research Lab at Stanford University. Her school-based work has included leading a network of literacy coaches, serving as a literacy staff developer, and teaching in various contexts in California. She has published a number of articles on literacy practice and development in leading education journals.

Contributors

Phoebe J. Ahn, MEd, Peabody College, Vanderbilt University, Nashville, Tennessee

Doris Luft Baker, PhD, College of Education, The University of Texas at Austin, Austin, Texas

Gina Biancarosa, EdD, Department of Special Education and Clinical Sciences, Center on Teaching and Learning, College of Education, University of Oregon, Eugene, Oregon

Sonia Q. Cabell, PhD, School of Teacher Education and Florida Center for Reading Research, Florida State University, Tallahassee, Florida

Philip Capin, PhD, Harvard Graduate School of Education, Harvard University, Cambridge, Massachusetts

Eunsoo Cho, MEd, School of Education, University of California, Riverside, Riverside, California

C. J. Espittia, PhD, School of Teacher Education and Florida Center for Reading Research, Florida State University, Tallahassee, Florida

Javier Garza, MEd, Department of Teaching, Learning, and Culture, College of Education, Texas A&M University, College Station, Texas

Cinthia Berenice Herrera, BS, College of Education, The University of Texas at Austin, Austin, Texas

Yixian Huang, MEd, College of Education, The University of Texas at Austin, Austin, Texas

Bhabika Joshi, MEd, Peabody College, Vanderbilt University, Nashville, Tennessee

Kristin Keane, PhD, School of Education, University of California, Berkeley, Berkeley, California

Hyejin Kim, MA, Crane Center for Early Childhood Research and Policy at the Schoenbaum Family Center, The Ohio State University, Columbus, Ohio

Young-Suk Grace Kim, EdD, School of Education, University of California, Irvine, Irvine, California

Kacee Lambright, PhD, Department of Teaching, Learning, and Culture, College of Education, Texas A&M University, College Station, Texas

Molly Leachman, MEd, MA, School of Education, University of California, Irvine, Irvine, California

Endia Lindo, PhD, Department of Teaching and Learning Sciences and ANSERS Institute Faculty, Texas Christian University, Fort Worth, Texas

Yeqing Liu, MS, Crane Center for Early Childhood Research and Policy at the Schoenbaum Family Center, The Ohio State University, Columbus, Ohio

Jeannette Mancilla-Martinez, EdD, Peabody College, Vanderbilt University, Nashville, Tennessee

Whitney N. McCoy, PhD, Center for Child and Family Policy, Duke University, High Point, North Carolina

Sholeh Moradibavi, MA, College of Education, The University of Texas at Austin, Austin, Texas

Emily Phillips Galloway, EdD, Peabody College, Vanderbilt University, Nashville, Tennessee

Shayne B. Piasta, PhD, Crane Center for Early Childhood Research and Policy at the Schoenbaum Family Center, The Ohio State University, Columbus, Ohio

Ramona T. Pittman, PhD, Department of Teaching, Learning, and Culture, School of Education, Texas A&M University, San Antonio, San Antonio, Texas

C. Patrick Proctor, EdD, Carol A. and Peter S. Lynch School of Education and Human Development, Boston College, Chestnut Hill, Massachusetts

Sarah Reiley, MA, Department of Counseling, Educational Psychology, and Special Education, Michigan State University, East Lansing, Michigan

Jasmine Rogers, EdD, School of Education, American University, Washington, DC

Hanyue Sha, MA, College of Education, The University of Texas at Austin, Austin, Texas

Pilar Sierra, BS, Department of Teaching, Learning, and Culture, College of Education, Texas A&M University, College Station, Texas

Rebecca D. Silverman, EdD, Graduate School of Education, Stanford University, Stanford, California

Ashley Stack, PhD, Department of Teaching, Learning, and Culture, College of Education, Texas A&M University, College Station, Texas

Kausalai Kay Wijekumar, PhD, Department of Teaching, Learning, and Culture, College of Education, Texas A&M University, College Station, Texas

Tricia A. Zucker, PhD, Children's Learning Institute, University of Texas Health Science Center at Houston, University of Texas, Houston, Texas

Foreword

In 2000, the National Reading Panel (NRP) Report delivered to American educators the myth that word reading accuracy and fluency would, with the addition of a bit of vocabulary teaching and a reading strategy or two, solve the national reading challenge. That challenge—that far too many children in the United States were unable to read with the level of comprehension needed in the 21st century—was not resolved by the inoculation approach the NRP promoted. It persists into 2025, and some would argue it has gotten worse. Making sure that phoneme awareness and phonics are delivered early and intensively may have produced schoolchildren with adequate second-grade oral reading fluency but those children have evidently had little silent reading experience. So, we now have a generation of children who are able to read words but are uninterested in reading books. If they have neither the skills nor the experience of reading texts longer than the passages on end-of-year exams, then they are very unlikely to be able to read well enough to allow them to integrate new learning into their cognitive schemes or to question the truth of what they are learning or to engage in critical analysis.

Hypotheses about the sources of poor comprehension skills are numerous. Can they be explained by poor oral language skills, by gaps in background knowledge, by the absence of motivation, or by the lack of the stamina needed to manage longer texts? All these are credible contributors to disappointing comprehension outcomes after third grade. And each of them might itself be the result of teaching that, unwittingly, conveys the message that reading is about the accurate pronunciation of words rather than about the construction of meaning and the possibility of being enchanted by the worlds that books open up for readers.

The chapters in this book help those of us who recognize that comprehension of content and learning through literacy are the real site of failure for American schools. They offer evidence that illuminates the current challenge, emphasizing the role of oral language development and authentic literacy encounters in explaining later obstacles. Support for oral language, knowledge building, and motivating interactions with text ideally starts in early childhood, going parallel to instruction in the code, and continues through the elementary school years, until students' comprehension skills are sufficiently developed that they are acquiring language, knowledge, and motivation to read through the act of reading. That is the prerequisite to a truly literate society for the 21st century.

Catherine E. Snow, PhD
John H. and Elisabeth A. Hobbs Professor of Cognition and Education
Harvard Graduate School of Education

Acknowledgments

To all of the teachers and students from Louisiana to Massachusetts and from Maryland to California with whom we have worked on research over the years, thank you for your engagement in the research process. You have taught us so much about teaching and learning and language and literacy.

To all of the current and former project officers at the Institute of Education Sciences, thank you for your guidance and support in the critical work of conducting research to understand how to best support teachers and students in developing language and literacy throughout school. Your commitment to research and education over the years is deeply appreciated.

Contents

1

From Language to Literacy

The Critical Role of Language Comprehension in Reading Comprehension

Rebecca D. Silverman and Kristin Keane

Guiding Questions

1. What is language comprehension, and why is it important?
2. How do students develop language comprehension?
3. What is the role of instruction in supporting language comprehension?

THE WHAT AND WHY OF LANGUAGE COMPREHENSION

Every few years, the U.S. Department of Education releases *The Nation's Report Card for Reading* based on the National Assessment of Educational Progress (NCES, 2024b). When these reports are released, news outlets publish headlines indicating that substantial numbers of U.S. students are not proficient in reading. These headlines cause panic among policymakers, educators, and parents and reignite the "Reading Wars," a decades-long debate over how to teach reading. The debate continues and has been exacerbated by recent reports that NAEP Reading scores declined in the wake of the COVID-19 pandemic and have yet to recover (e.g., Belsha & Meltzer, 2025; Schwartz, 2025).

The debate in the "Reading Wars" is mostly focused on whether and how much to use phonics instruction to teach students to decode words. Research from fields such as neuroscience, psychology, and education, commonly referred to as the Science of Reading, has established that direct and systematic phonics instruction is important and has positive effects on decoding and reading comprehension outcomes (National Institute of Child Health and Human Development, 2000).

The focus on phonics is important, but attention to phonics has overshadowed attention to other aspects of reading comprehension that are necessary for students to meet the high standards set by the NAEP, which expects proficient fourth graders to be able to "integrate and interpret texts and apply their understanding of the text to draw conclusions and make evaluations" (NAEP, 2024a).

Many educators are familiar with the Simple View of Reading, which suggests that reading comprehension is a product of decoding and linguistic comprehension, or Scarborough's Rope, which portrays skilled reading as a rope with interwoven strands of skills related to word recognition and language comprehension. (See Box 1.1.) As these models and other newer models of reading comprehension, such as the direct and indirect effects model of reading (DIER) discussed by Kim et al. in Chapter 4 of this book, suggest, reading comprehension requires students to decode words *and* to understand what words mean and how they work together to convey meaning across sentences, paragraphs, and texts. Shining the spotlight on decoding leaves language comprehension in the shadows. In this book, we seek to broaden the focus of the spotlight and highlight the importance of language comprehension in reading comprehension.

Box 1.1. Language Comprehension Terminology

Note that researchers have used different terminology in reference to language comprehension, sometimes referring to this construct as listening comprehension or linguistic comprehension. These terms may be used interchangeably in this book, but they all refer to the ability to understand or make meaning of language.

As noted in a recent National Academy of Education report, it is incredibly difficult to "move the needle" in reading comprehension (Pearson et al., 2020). Research suggests it can be done (Silverman et al., 2020), but it requires focusing on language comprehension in addition to decoding throughout early childhood and elementary school. The chapters in this book by leading researchers in the field provide background information and practical recommendations for supporting language comprehension to facilitate reading comprehension. In this chapter, we provide an overview of the research on language comprehension development and instruction and share major themes that have emerged from our research and research by other authors featured in this book. We hope these themes will be instrumental to educators as they consider how to apply the Science of Reading beyond decoding.

THE DEVELOPMENT OF LANGUAGE COMPREHENSION

While learning to decode is not a natural process and usually requires explicit and systematic instruction, the development of language comprehension is a natural process, and it occurs through everyday interactions that children have with caregivers and others in their environment. Children attend to the sounds their caregivers make and, through joint attention, learn to associate words and their referents and add them to their *vocabulary knowledge.* In English, children's first words are typically related to their immediate wants and needs (e.g., *no, more, baba* for bottle). They learn to distinguish words that sound similar (e.g., *ball* and *book*) and, thereby, develop *phonological awareness,* which is a core component of both decoding and language comprehension. Over time, they learn that smaller parts of words matter (e.g., if they hear /s/ at the end of the word *cookie,* that means more than one) and that the order of words matters (e.g., *Dad hit the ball* and *The ball hit Dad* mean different things) and, thereby, develop *morphological awareness* and *syntactic awareness.* They also learn that several words can refer to one thing (e.g., *woman* and *lady* could be used interchangeably) and one word can refer to many things (e.g., *bat* can refer to something used in baseball or a type of animal), and thereby develop their *semantic awareness.* Additionally, they learn abstract words that refer to concepts that are not tangible (e.g., *happy* or *sad*), and they learn words that refer to concepts that may be beyond their immediate environment or experience (e.g., *jungle* or *safari*), growing their vocabulary to include knowledge of more than 1,000 words before they enter prekindergarten.

While the development of language comprehension is considered a natural process, it depends on language exposure. In fact, there is a robust research base on how caregivers and teachers can ensure children are provided with robust exposure to language that can facilitate language development. For example, in this book, Cabell and colleagues (Chapter 2) describe an approach they have developed called Strive-for-Five. Meant for teachers of students in prekindergarten through first grade, the approach can be used to foster back-and-forth conversations about text that support language development. A common interaction between a teacher and student in these grades entails the teacher asking a closed-ended question (e.g., "What was the boy doing?"), the student responding (e.g., "Riding a bike"), and the teacher evaluating that response (e.g., "Yes, that's right."). Using the Strive-for-Five approach, which calls for at least five back-and-forth exchanges with a student, teachers support and extend students' language and comprehension. For example, in a Strive-for-Five interaction, the teacher asks an open-ended question (e.g., "Why was the boy riding his bike?"), the student responds (e.g., "He wanted to visit his friend."), the teacher asks a follow-up question (e.g., "Why did he want to visit his friend? How was he feeling that day?"), and the student responds with additional information (e.g., "He was having a bad day and was lonely."). The multiple back-and-forth exchanges in Strive-for-Five support children in interpreting and using language to a greater extent, which can facilitate their language comprehension.

While children's language development evolves rapidly in early childhood and elementary school, even adults are still developing their language comprehension. There are over a million words in the English language alone, and new words are being created every day. Thus, developing language comprehension is a substantial endeavor. Given the vast number of words to be learned and the various ways they could be affixed or combined, scholars have come to see language comprehension as an unconstrained skill that continues to develop across the lifespan (Paris, 2005). While decoding is critically important because children will not be able to access written words without the ability to decode, scholars view decoding as a much more constrained skill than language comprehension. For example, there are only 26 letters and 44 sounds in the English language, and though there are many sound-symbol correspondences children need to learn, the task of decoding is still much more constrained than the task of comprehending the thousands of words needed to understand language across contexts. Notably, for multilingual learners who are developing language comprehension across languages, the endeavor is even more formidable.

Given the scope of the development of language comprehension, scholars have recently stopped using the old adage used to describe reading development as the process of first learning to read and then reading to learn across the elementary school grades. Using this adage seemed to suggest that the focus of instruction in early elementary school should be decoding and the focus of instruction in later elementary school should be comprehension. Since language comprehension develops across the lifespan and children understand more than they can read for much of elementary school, scholars have begun to emphasize the importance of supporting language comprehension from the time children enter school in prekindergarten or kindergarten throughout elementary school; by the end, the goal of instruction is that children are able to decode and comprehend at a level that allows them to acquire new knowledge of concepts and content through reading.

Importantly, to prepare children to be able to comprehend text once they are able to access it on their own, children should have lots of experience with book language, which is often more formal or less familiar than the language used in everyday conversations at home and in school. Even though we rarely, if ever, say "once upon a time" in real life, children should know what this means because they have heard it from books read to them by their caregivers and educators. Exposure to the more rare vocabulary, morphology, and syntax in books will enable children to understand what they are reading when they have developed the ability to accurately and automatically read the words in texts on their own. There has been debate in the field about whether to refer to what we call "book language" as "academic language" because the term academic language seems to suggest that the language used in school settings is superior to nonacademic language or the language used at home or in the community, creating a hierarchy of language that implies that one language is better or more important than the other. By using "book language," we hope to move away from any hierarchy of language and suggest that there are different types of language that are all equally important. For example, being able to communicate with family and friends at home is at least as important as, if not more important than, being able to access books, but, to do both, children must have comprehension of both types of language. This knowledge of how to use language across different contexts is called *pragmatic awareness.* While pragmatic awareness is often not mentioned in discussions of language comprehension, it is important to remember that different kinds of language are useful in different kinds of settings, and books often use language that is different from language we use in everyday life. (See Box 1.2 for definitions of terminology about language comprehension used in this section.)

Box 1.2. Definitions Related to Language Comprehension

Phonological Awareness—The ability to recognize and manipulate the sound structures of spoken language, including syllables, rhymes, and individual phonemes (sounds).

Vocabulary Knowledge—The understanding and use of words in a language, including their meanings, usage, and relationships to other words.

Semantic Awareness—The ability to understand and interpret meanings in language, including word meanings, relationships (synonyms, antonyms, homonyms), and how words contribute to the meaning of sentences and discourse.

Morphological Awareness—The understanding of the structure of words and how morphemes (the smallest units of meaning, such as prefixes, suffixes, and root words) contribute to word formation and meaning.

Syntactic Awareness—The understanding of sentence structure and grammar, including how words and phrases are arranged to create meaningful sentences.

Pragmatic Awareness—The ability to understand and use language appropriately in different social and cultural contexts, including understanding tone, conversational rules, and nonverbal communication cues.

INSTRUCTION FOR SUPPORTING LANGUAGE COMPREHENSION

Though, as suggested by the National Academy of Education report mentioned earlier (Pearson et al., 2020), it can be hard to "move the needle" in reading comprehension, research suggests that there are instructional methods focused on language comprehension that can make a difference in reading comprehension. In fact, one of the main findings of that report was that "Language drives every facet of reading comprehension" and educators should focus on "redoubling our efforts to enhance language development, both oral and written, for students across the age-span" (Pearson et al., 2020, p. 3). The research reviewed in the National Academy of Education report, the research we reviewed in our own meta-analysis of studies of language comprehension-focused instruction, and the research by authors of chapters in this book suggest several themes that can guide educators on implementing instruction to support language comprehension. We review these themes, depicted in Box 1.3, in the following sections.

Box 1.3. What the Research Says about Supporting Language and Reading Comprehension

- Instruction should focus on multiple components
- Instruction should be engaging and content-rich
- Instruction should leverage the linguistic knowledge of multilingual and multidialectical students
- Instruction should be guided by assessment and progress monitoring
- Technology can be used to facilitate language comprehension
- Professional development should focus on supporting teachers' knowledge of language comprehension

Instruction Should Focus on Multiple Components

As noted, there are many components of language comprehension, including vocabulary knowledge and semantic awareness, morphological awareness, and syntactic awareness. Language comprehension-focused instruction that focuses on multiple components rather than just one is more likely to move the needle in reading comprehension. One of the programs reviewed in the National Academy of Education report, in our meta-analysis, and in a chapter in this book (Piasta et al., Chapter 3), the Let's Know program for prekindergarten (PreK) through grade 3 students includes attention to vocabulary knowledge and semantic awareness in addition to inference-making, which relies heavily on syntactic awareness, comprehension monitoring, and use of text structure to support comprehension (LARCC, Jiang, & Davis, 2017; LARRC, Jiang, & Logan, 2019). This program showed positive effects on measures of vocabulary, which indirectly affected reading comprehension and comprehension monitoring. Another program for PreK-3 reviewed in the National Academy of Education report, in our meta-analysis, and in a chapter in this book (Kim et al., Chapter 4) is called COMPASS, which stands for Comprehension Monitoring and Providing Awareness of Story Structure. This program addresses the same language skills (vocabulary knowledge and semantic awareness) as well as attention to text structure and comprehension monitoring and has also been shown to have positive effects (Connor et al., 2018; Noble et al., 2019; Phillips et al., 2021). In their chapter, Kim et al. discuss a new program derived from COMPASS called Story Detective that also includes attention to syntax and inferencing.

Other programs reported on in our meta-analysis that showed positive effects on language and/or reading comprehension outcomes include the Morphological Awareness Intervention Program (Apel et al., 2013), RAVE-O (Morris et al., 2012), the CLAVES program (Proctor and Silverman, Chapter 11), and Word Generation (Jones et al., 2019). The Morphological Awareness Program was developed for and implemented with kindergarten through second-grade students from low socioeconomic backgrounds and included attention to inflectional and derivational affixes and semantic awareness (i.e., words that are related by meaning). RAVE-O, implemented with first- and second-grade children described as "struggling readers," included systematic emphases on phonological decoding processes, orthographic knowledge (i.e., knowledge of the writing system), and semantic, syntactic, and morphological awareness. The CLAVES program focuses on vocabulary, morphology, and syntax in a program developed to support multilingual learners in upper elementary school. Finally, Word Generation, studied with fourth and fifth graders as well as middle schoolers in high-poverty schools, included attention to vocabulary, unpacking morphologically or syntactically dense text, and text organization.

What is common across all of these instructional programs is that they do not focus on just one facet of language comprehension and, instead, support children in multiple aspects of language comprehension. Interestingly, together, these studies show positive effects of a multicomponent approach across grades PreK-5 (and beyond), with multilingual learners, with students from low socioeconomic backgrounds, and with students who are considered "struggling readers," suggesting that multicomponent instruction to support language comprehension is relevant for all students in elementary school. Since Let's Know, COMPASS, and CLAVES are discussed in other chapters in this book, let's take a look at how this multicomponent approach is enacted in RAVE-O. In a sample lesson sequence in RAVE-O, which has lessons appropriate for first to fourth graders and students with or without dyslexia, students are introduced to a core vocabulary word and participate in a brief activity to support awareness of multiple meanings of the word. In one example, students are introduced to the word *track* and are shown illustrated cards representing running on a track, a train track, tracks in the snow, and a detective tracking a suspect. RAVE-O lessons also include intentional focus on the sounds and spellings of words (e.g., a focus on *tr*). Next, students discuss syntax and morphology as they read sentences and spell words. For example, they read the following sentences: "Sam can brush the tracks with sand. Then he can track the little sandy tracks. Sam is quite the tracker." Then, they discuss how the word track is used across different parts of speech to serve different functions in the sentence and how different morphemes are used to convey parts of speech and meaning. At the end of a lesson, students typically read and reread passages using the skills they have learned to build fluency. Focusing on many aspects of words and how they are used to convey meaning in text provides students with a solid foundation of language comprehension skills that enable them to read with comprehension.

Though RAVE-O focuses primarily on vocabulary knowledge, semantic awareness, morphological awareness, and syntactic awareness, many of the other programs mentioned above included attention to other skills related to language and reading comprehension, including the use of comprehension strategies such as inferencing and monitoring and attention to text structure. As discussed in a chapter in this book by Biancarosa (Chapter 7), inferencing is a critical skill necessary for reading comprehension. Inferencing is highly related to syntactic awareness in that, in order to infer meaning across sentences, attention to how grammar conveys meaning is needed. For example, to understand what *it* is referring to in the following sentence, it is necessary to understand how syntax affects meaning: "My book was wet, though I could still read *it*." However, inferencing goes beyond syntactic awareness and involves linking ideas across larger sections of text and understanding the broader theme or purpose (e.g., inferring the main idea of a passage based on multiple details). In this way, inferencing is related to other comprehension strategies such as monitoring, which includes tracking understanding while reading, and using text structure to support comprehension. In this book, Wijekumar and colleagues (Chapter 5) discuss how knowledge about text structure can enable students to generate main ideas, extend main ideas to summaries, and leverage main ideas to extrapolate inferences. Therefore, multicomponent instruction to support language and reading comprehension should integrate a focus on components of language, including vocabulary knowledge, semantic awareness, morphological awareness, and syntactic awareness, with attention to comprehension strategies such as inferencing and monitoring and the knowledge of text structures.

Instruction Should Be Content-Rich and Support Motivation and Engagement

Instruction to support language and reading comprehension should not only focus on multiple components, but it should also be content-rich and engaging. Though not a feature of the Simple View of Reading, other models of reading, such as Scarborough's Rope and the direct and indirect effects model of reading (DIER), include background knowledge, also referred to as content knowledge. When children are engaged in conversation, listen to books read aloud to them, or read on their own, they bring all of their knowledge of whatever the topic is to the experience. This background or content knowledge provides a schema (i.e., a framework or blueprint) for understanding the topic and includes knowledge of vocabulary and concepts related to the topic that help support comprehension of new information about the topic. O-Reilley et al. (2019) found evidence of a knowledge threshold, suggesting that students need a baseline of knowledge about a topic to comprehend a text on that topic. In fact, some of the instructional programs found to have positive effects on language and reading comprehension discussed above focused on building content knowledge as a critical aspect of the program. For example, the Let's Know program taught information and vocabulary related to animals and earth materials (LLRC et al., 2017); the CLAVES program supported content knowledge related to topics such as rights and freedoms (Proctor, 2020); and Word Generation included texts to build background knowledge on such topics as the role of government and education in society (Jones, 2019).

Content-rich instruction is important not only for building background knowledge but also for facilitating motivation and engagement. While motivation refers to the desire to read, engagement refers to active participation in the reading process. Whether and why a student is motivated to read will influence the extent to which they are engaged in reading. In a prominent line of work on what they referred to as concept-oriented reading Instruction (CORI), Guthrie (1993) found that concept-oriented instruction that highlights real-world connections to what students are learning and doing in school leads to greater motivation to read and more active engagement in the reading process, which, in turn, leads to greater reading comprehension. As Cho et al. discuss in Chapter 6 in this book, researchers have identified several instructional practices to facilitate motivation and engagement in reading. Specifically, they discuss the importance of scaffolded instruction, which, by providing incremental support, fosters perceived competence, an important component of motivation. They also suggest that, to promote motivation and engagement, teachers should promote growth mindset, reframe mistakes as opportunities, and acknowledge effort and strategy use. Additionally, they note that leveraging interest, offering choice, and encouraging independence can support motivation and engagement. Finally, Cho et al. advise teachers to create learning environments in which students feel they belong and are valued.

Instruction Should Acknowledge and Leverage the Linguistic Knowledge of Multilingual and Multidialectical Students

While attention to motivation and engagement is important for all learners, it is essential to recognize that multilingual and multidialectal learners often do not feel they belong and are valued in schools that do not acknowledge and leverage their full linguistic repertoire, especially when they are in classrooms with teachers who do not share their linguistic background. Given the vast number of multilingual and multidialectical learners in elementary schools in the United States, researchers have focused on identifying practices that are supportive of these learners. As discussed in Chapter 8 in this book, Baker et al. conducted a review of research and analyzed effects of interventions focused on supporting language and reading comprehension for culturally and linguistically diverse students (i.e., students who come from a variety of cultural, social, and economic backgrounds and who speak a language other than English at home). These authors found that, as mentioned earlier, interventions that focus on multiple components of language are important. In particular, they found that shared book reading, with attention to vocabulary and other aspects of language, is productive, especially in prekindergarten and kindergarten. Additionally, they found that interventions that facilitate active engagement, include structured dialogue and feedback, and encourage students to use and make connections to their native language are effective for culturally and linguistically diverse students in elementary school.

Two of the chapters in this book discuss particular programs shown to be effective with multilingual learners. In Proctor and Silverman (Chapter 11), the authors describe CLAVES, a program focused on Cultivating Linguistic Awareness for Voice and Equity in Schools, particularly for multilingual learners in grades four and five. This program is multicomponent, as mentioned earlier, but it also focuses on multilingualism, highlighting comparisons or contrasts with other languages and encouraging students to share how to translate words into languages they know.

In Phillips Galloway's chapter (Chapter 12), the author describes work with teachers to develop a four-phase approach to supporting the comprehension of multilingual learners in upper elementary school. The approach includes teaching students the language of books and school, engaging students' translingual funds of knowledge (i.e., the knowledge they have about the languages they speak), fostering students' metalinguistic knowledge (i.e., knowledge of how languages work), and supporting students' application of new language knowledge in discussion and text reading. Importantly, both of these approaches center students' multilingualism as an asset students can use to support their comprehension and learning in school.

Similarly, Pittman et al. (Chapter 9) discuss the importance of an asset-based approach for African American students who speak African American English (AAE) as well. Also known as African American Vernacular English (AAVE) or Black English, AAE is a rich variation of English spoken by many African Americans in the United States. It has its own unique grammar, vocabulary, and pronunciation patterns and is intricately connected to African American culture. Just as multilingual learners are often expected to use only English at school, African American children are often told not to use AAE at school. This approach results in a mismatch between what teachers are teaching and what students bring to school, making it unnecessarily difficult for children to access content and instruction. Pittman and colleagues argue that a much more productive approach is to validate the dialect children speak (e.g., by sharing texts with AAE in shared reading) and to engage students in critical conversations about how languages and dialects are similar or different and how and why they are used across cultural contexts.

Instruction Should Be Guided by Language and Reading Comprehension-Focused Assessments

While recent trends related to the Science of Reading have focused on the importance of screening and progress monitoring for phonological and phonemic awareness, decoding, and fluency, there has been much less attention to the assessment of language comprehension. Yet, as we found in a study of the beginning of first-grade predictors of third-grade reading comprehension difficulties, screening that includes measures of both decoding and language comprehension is more effective at identifying students who may need additional support than screening that includes only measures of decoding (Silverman et al., 2021). In fact, Catts et al. (2016) have described students who they refer to as having late-emerging reading difficulties—reading difficulties that do not emerge until students are expected to read and comprehend complex text in upper elementary school—and explain that many of these students could have been identified and provided with support for language comprehension, which could have prevented later reading comprehension difficulties. As Mancilla-Martinez and colleagues suggest (Chapter 10), there should be screening and progress monitoring focused on language comprehension for all students, and, as Piasta et al. indicate (Chapter 3), supplemental intervention should be provided to students who have difficulty in aspects of language comprehension.

Currently, in most districts, assessment of language skills is only implemented for multilingual learners who speak a language other than English at home. Mancilla-Martinez et al. point out in Chapter 10 that measures used with multilingual learners are often not appropriate because they do not consider children's language skills across languages. Such assessments may lead to over- or under-identification of multilingual students who need additional support through special education. Mancilla-Martinez et al. suggest that educators need to acknowledge the limitations of current assessments, encourage the development and validation of more appropriate assessments, and use alternative assessment practices such as those that focus on conceptual knowledge and take into account that multilingual learners may experience a different developmental trajectory than their monolingual peers.

As Phillips Galloway suggests (Chapter 12) suggests, language and reading comprehension-focused assessments need to hone in on features of language that are overrepresented in book or school language to guide instruction that supports this kind of language, which may be more or less familiar to students depending on their background knowledge or knowledge of language. Often, language comprehension measures focus on vocabulary to the exclusion of other aspects of language, such as morphology and syntax; however, using measures that disentangle vocabulary knowledge, morphological awareness, and syntactic awareness may be more useful in guiding instruction to support language and reading comprehension. Biancarosa (Chapter 7) suggests that measures that provide more detailed information on students' comprehension-related strengths and needs (e.g., in regard to inferencing) might lead to more targeted instruction. Assessment that provides this level of detail could be used to guide whole-class instruction as well as supplemental instruction focused on language and comprehension for those who need more support.

Technology Can Be Used to Facilitate Language Comprehension

In the chapter by Biancarosa, the author suggests, citing evidence from McMaster et al. (2019), that one way to support inferencing for young students is through the use of video. While there is much more research on the use of technology to support decoding, we found in a meta-analysis that we conducted (Silverman et al., 2024) that there is evidence that technology can supplement (though should never supplant) instruction in supporting language comprehension as well. Videos that leverage verbal and visual pathways for learning have been shown to be useful in supporting vocabulary and language comprehension, and e-books with features such as text-to-speech, definitions of words, and animation of key concepts have been shown to support language and reading comprehension. Such technology can facilitate access to content above students' reading levels, which can support background knowledge, vocabulary, and concept learning. Additionally, programs that include additional practice, support, and feedback with aspects of language may serve as a helpful addition to teachers' instruction in school.

One program that was included in our meta-analyses that used technology was a cross-age peer learning program in which fourth-grade "older buddies" and kindergarten "younger buddies" experienced print text, videos, and e-books on topics such as animal habitats and talked about these texts together (Silverman et al., 2017b). This approach was effective at supporting the language and comprehension of both the older and younger buddies. Another program featured in our meta-analysis that used technology was called Improving Comprehension Online (ICON, Proctor et al., 2011). In this program, students read text with a variety of features, including Spanish translations of texts and directions; human read-alouds of each text in English and Spanish; English monolingual and Spanish–English bilingual pedagogical "coaches" who provided assistance with using the system and responding to prompts; a revisable electronic worklog that collected student responses; a multimedia glossary; and pictures illustrating the narrative and informational text content. Bilingual and monolingual fifth graders who used the program gained more in vocabulary compared to their peers. A third program that was covered in our meta-analysis was the Intelligent Tutoring for Text Structure Strategy (ITSS), which Wijekumar and colleagues discuss in Chapter 5. ITSS provides web-based instruction to students in grades four to eight that focuses on using text structures to select important ideas, generate a logically connected main idea, extend the main idea to a summary, and extrapolate inferences to promote a coherent representation of text in memory. ITSS features a pedagogical agent that provides scaffolding and support throughout the program. This program has been shown to be effective across numerous studies. Together, these programs show the promise of using technology to support language and comprehension. However, much more research on the role of technology in supporting language and reading comprehension is needed, especially as new technologies (e.g., programs using artificial intelligence) become available in schools.

Professional Development Should Focus on Supporting Teachers' Knowledge of Language Comprehension

As mentioned at the beginning of this chapter, it is incredibly difficult to "move the needle" in reading comprehension, in part because of the complexity and unconstrained nature of language comprehension. One of the main conclusions from the National Academies of Education report (Pearson et al., 2020) was that the success of efforts to improve language and reading comprehension depends on strong and supportive professional learning, including coaching and communities of practice (p. 286). Indeed, many of the chapters in this book talk about the importance of teacher professional development. For example, Piasta et al. (Chapter 3) discuss the critical role of teacher knowledge of language comprehension in efforts to support students. These researchers call for professional learning opportunities for teachers to develop explicit knowledge of language development and research-based instructional practices to support language comprehension skills in their classrooms. Importantly, this professional learning should also address supporting language comprehension for children experiencing language difficulties, those newly learning English, and those who may be less familiar with the vocabulary and syntax of book and school language. Phillips Galloway (Chapter 12) provides a promising model for professional learning. Working with teachers of multilingual learners who were not multilingual learners themselves, the research team first provided background information on how language works and on collaborative translating. Then, they collaborated with teachers to develop an instructional routine to use across short texts. This model of providing teachers with a grounding in the research base and then working with them to apply research-based practices for lessons to use with their own students may help bridge the gap between research and practice.

CONCLUSION

In this chapter, we reviewed what language comprehension is and why it is important to reading comprehension. Specifically, we noted that language comprehension is the ability to understand or make meaning of language, and we suggested that understanding language is critical to reading comprehension because, once students learn to decode, they need to know how to make meaning from the words, phrases, sentences, or paragraphs they are reading. We also reviewed how students develop language from early interactions with caregivers and continue to build language comprehension through instruction in school and, eventually, texts they read on their own. Finally, we reviewed the role of instruction in supporting language comprehension, highlighting that research on language comprehension indicates the following: (1) instruction should focus on multiple components; (2) instruction should be content-rich and engaging; (3) instruction should leverage the linguistic knowledge of multilingual and multidialectical students; (4) instruction should be guided by assessment and progress monitoring; (5) technology can be used to facilitate language comprehension; and (6) professional development should focus on supporting teachers' knowledge of language comprehension. We hope this review of the literature and the information provided by the leading scholars in the field in the chapters in this book will help teachers as they endeavor to move the needle on language and reading comprehension throughout elementary school.

Reflection Questions

1. How do you already incorporate what the research says about supporting language comprehension into your own instruction?
2. What additional ways can you incorporate what the research says about supporting language comprehension into your own instruction?
3. How will you know whether changes you make to your own instruction to support language comprehension are having a positive impact on your students?

REFERENCES

Apel, K., Brimo, D., Diehm, E., & Apel, L. (2013). Morphological awareness intervention with kindergartners and first-and second-grade students from low socioeconomic status homes: A feasibility study. *Language, Speech, and Hearing Services in Schools, 44*(2), 161–173.

Belsha, K., & Meltzer, E. (2025, January 28). *NAEP scores show disheartening trends for the lowest-performing students.* Chalkbeat. *www.chalkbeat.org/2025/01/29/naep-reading-scores-decline-and-struggling-students-fall-behind*

Catts, H. W., Nielsen, D. C., Bridges, M. S., & Liu, Y.-S. (2016). Early identification of reading comprehension difficulties. *Journal of Learning Disabilities, 49*(5), 451–465.

Connor, C. M., Phillips, B., Kim, Y.-S. G., Lonigan, C. J., Kaschak, M. P., Crowe, E., et al. (2018). Examining the efficacy of targeted component interventions on language and literacy for third and fourth graders who are at risk of comprehension difficulties. *Scientific Studies of Reading, 22*(6), 462–484.

Guthrie, J. T. (1993). *Concept-oriented reading instruction.* National Reading Research Center.

Jones, S. M., LaRusso, M., Kim, J., Yeon Kim, H., Selman, R., Uccelli, P., et al. (2019). Experimental effects of Word Generation on vocabulary, academic language, perspective taking, and reading comprehension in high-poverty schools. *Journal of Research on Educational Effectiveness, 12*(3), 448–483.

Language and Reading Research Consortium, Jiang, H., & Davis, D. (2017). Let's know! Proximal impacts on prekindergarten through grade 3 students' comprehension-related skills. *The Elementary School Journal, 118*(2), 177–206.

Language and Reading Research Consortium, Jiang, H., & Logan, J. A. R. (2019). Improving reading comprehension in the primary grades: Mediated effects of a language-focused classroom intervention. *Journal of Speech, Language, and Hearing Research, 62*(8), 2812–2828.

McMaster, K., Kendeou, P., Bresina, B. C., Slater, S., Wagner, K., White, M. J., et al. (2019). Developing an interactive software application to support young children's inference-making. *L1-Educational Studies in Language and Literature, 19*(4), 1–30.

Morris, R. D., Lovett, M. W., Wolf, M., Sevcik, R. A., Steinbach, K. A., Frijters, J. C., & Shapiro, M. B. (2012). Multiple-component remediation for developmental reading disabilities: IQ, socioeconomic status, and race as factors in remedial outcome. *Journal of Learning Disabilities, 45*(2), 99–127.

National Center for Education Statistics. (2024a). *NAEP reading achievement levels*. U.S. Department of Education, Institute of Education Sciences. *https://nces.ed.gov/nationsreportcard*

National Center for Education Statistics. (2024b). *The Nation's Report Card*. National Assessment of Educational Progress.

National Institute of Child Health and Human Development. (2000). *Report of the National Reading Panel: Teaching children to read: Reports of the subgroups (00-4754)*. U.S. Government Printing Office.

Noble, C., Sala, G., Peter, M., Lingwood, J., Rowland, C., Gober, F., & Pine, J. (2019). The impact of shared book reading on children's language skills: A meta-analysis. *Educational Research Review, 28*, 100290.

O'Reilly, T., Wang, Z., & Sabatini, J. (2019). How much knowledge is too little? When a lack of knowledge becomes a barrier to comprehension. *Psychological Science, 30*, 1344–1351.

Paris, S. G. (2005). Reinterpreting the development of reading skills. *Reading Research Quarterly, 40*(2), 184–202.

Pearson, P. D., Palincsar, A. S., Biancarosa, G., & Berman, A. I. (Eds.). (2020). *Reaping the rewards of the reading for understanding initiative*. National Academy of Education.

Phillips, B., Kim, Y.-S. G., Lonigan, C. J., Connor, C. M., Clancy, J., & Al Otaiba, S. (2021). Supporting language and literacy development with intensive small-group interventions: An early childhood efficacy study. *Early Childhood Research Quarterly, 57*, 75–88.

Proctor, C. P., Dalton, B., Uccelli, P., Biancarosa, G., Mo, E., Snow, C., & Neugebauer, S. (2011). Improving comprehension online: Effects of deep vocabulary instruction with bilingual and monolingual fifth graders. *Reading and Writing, 24*(5), 517–544.

Proctor, C. P., Silverman, R. D., Harring, J. R., Jones, R. L., & Hartranft, A. M. (2020). Teaching bilingual learners: Effects of a language-based reading intervention on academic language and reading comprehension in grades 4 and 5. *Reading Research Quarterly, 55*, 95–122.

Schwartz, S. (2025, January 29). *Reading scores fall to new low on NAEP, fueled by declines for struggling students: Math scores slightly up in grade 4, stagnant in grade 8*. Education Week. *www.edweek.org/leadership/reading-scores-fall-to-new-low-on-naep-fueled-by-declines-for-struggling-students/2025/01*

Silverman, R., Kim, Y., Hartranft, A., Nunn, S., & McNeish, D. (2017a). Effects of a multimedia enhanced reading buddies program on kindergarten and grade 4 vocabulary and comprehension. *The Journal of Educational Research, 110*(4), 391–404.

Silverman, R. D., Martin-Beltran, M., Peercy, M. M., Hartranft, A. M., Artzi, L., Nunn, S. J., & McNeish, D. (2017b). Effects of a cross-age peer learning program on the vocabulary and comprehension of ELs and non-ELs in elementary school. *Elementary School Journal, 117*, 485–512.

Silverman, R. D., Johnson, E. M., Keane, K., & Khanna, S. (2020). Beyond decoding: A meta-analysis of the effects of language comprehension interventions on K–5 students' language and literacy outcomes. *Reading Research Quarterly, 55*(S1), S207–S233.

Silverman, R. D., McNeish, D., Speece, D. L., & Ritchey, K. D. (2021). Early screening for decoding- and language-related reading difficulties in first and third grades. *Assessment for Effective Intervention, 46*(2), 99–109.

Silverman, R. D., Keane, K., Darling-Hammond, E., & Khanna, S. (2024). The effects of educational technology interventions on literacy in elementary school: A meta-analysis. *Review of Educational Research, 20*(10), 1–41.

2

Content-Rich Classroom Conversations That Improve Language Comprehension in the Early Grades

Sonia Q. Cabell, C. J. Espittia, and Tricia A. Zucker

Guiding Questions

1. Why does building oral language and content knowledge early in schooling matter for later reading comprehension?
2. How can content-rich conversations promote all areas of language comprehension?
3. How can teachers build language comprehension using the Strive-for-Five framework during interactive read-alouds?

Typical instruction in the early primary grades in the United States tends to silo instruction into separate subjects: English language arts, science, social studies, and so forth. And these areas don't tend to *speak* to one another. The topics that students read about during English language arts (ELA) aren't typically connected to the topics they learn about in other parts of the school day. So students might read or listen to a story about whales in ELA while learning about weather patterns in science and local communities in social studies, with no explicit connection made among the topics. This assumes that science and social studies are taught on a regular basis to students in the primary grades; however, research shows that there is a lack of adequate content-area instruction for young students (Cox et al., 2017; Tyner & Kabourek, 2020).

There has been a push in the past decade or so to integrate content-area instruction (science, social studies) into ELA (i.e., *content-rich ELA instruction,* Cabell

& Hwang, 2020). The interest in integration is not about eliminating science and social studies instruction as subjects but rather about promoting a more coherent learning experience for students. Content-rich ELA instruction doesn't hop from topic to topic within a unit as traditional ELA instruction does (Paige et al., 2021). Rather, content-rich instruction is driven by units that focus on specific science and/or social studies topics, with texts that support incremental learning of these topics (Cabell & Hwang, 2023).

In the early grades (PreK–1), since the materials that students are reading during this period are linguistically simple (e.g., decodable texts), content-rich ELA instruction typically involves interactive read-alouds of texts that are more complex than what students are able to read on their own. In this way, the integration is usually between the oral language components of instruction (i.e., listening and speaking) and content-area instruction (i.e., science or social studies).

The focus on oral language and content-area instruction is a timely one. A recent report on U.S. state legislation about the Science of Reading identified both of these areas as needing more attention in the early grades (Neuman et al., 2023). Content-rich ELA instruction offers teachers a way to simultaneously support learning in the content areas and in literacy (Cabell & Hwang, 2020). The content-rich conversations that drive this type of instruction can be leveraged to promote all areas of language comprehension.

In this chapter, our goal is to provide an understanding of how classroom conversations during content-rich ELA instruction can support students' language comprehension. We first discuss the importance of building language comprehension during the early grades. Then, we describe the research on content-rich ELA instruction and where content-rich conversations fit in. Finally, we show how teachers can use the Strive-for-Five framework for classroom conversations to promote language comprehension in preschool through first-grade settings by modeling vocabulary and scaffolding students' responses during interactive read-alouds. We define important terms in Table 2.1.

THE IMPORTANCE OF BUILDING LANGUAGE COMPREHENSION

Language comprehension refers to both the comprehension and production of spoken language. It includes children's understanding of words (vocabulary), how words form sentences (language structures), inferencing (verbal reasoning), how text works (literacy knowledge), and content knowledge (background knowledge) (Scarborough, 2001). Language comprehension is indispensable to skilled reading

TABLE 2.1. Definitions of Key Concepts

Concept	Definition
Language comprehension	The ability to comprehend what we read or what is read to us, such as during a read-aloud, and what is spoken to us, such as during a conversation
Content knowledge	Knowledge of the social and/or natural world
Schema	The way our brains organize the knowledge that we acquire about a particular topic or domain
Conceptually coherent text set	A group of texts that deepen content knowledge over successive readings
Formal language	The language of books and of school
Conversation	A series of turns that stay on a given topic between two or more speakers
Contingent	In a conversation, a response that is directly related to what the prior speaker said
Scaffolds	Hints, explanations, or follow-up questions to simplify (downward) or add challenge (upward) for the student

comprehension, and research shows that accelerating language development during the early childhood years is essential to later reading ability (Hjetland et al., 2020). The more quickly students can develop language comprehension, the more that they can use that knowledge for subsequent learning (Cabell et al., 2022; Cunha & Heckman, 2007)

Oftentimes, educators think of each area of language comprehension as separate from one another. That is, they may spend one lesson teaching vocabulary and another lesson focused on inferencing. Much of the time, building background knowledge is viewed separately from ELA instruction entirely. Instead, it is in the purview of content-area instructional time, which may not occur as frequently in the early grades. This creates an inefficient system where time is spent on discrete skills that may not readily connect in the child's mind. During content-rich ELA instruction, all of the language comprehension areas can be combined through the use of interactive read-alouds (Cabell et al., 2025; Cabell & Hwang, 2020; Silverman et al., 2020).

WHERE CONTENT KNOWLEDGE FITS INTO LANGUAGE COMPREHENSION

Content knowledge, or knowledge of the social and natural world (Connor et al., 2017), is often viewed as unrelated to learning to read. Yet, what we already know about a topic is central to being able to understand it (Anderson & Pearson, 1984). Take, for example, the following passage:

> The observational discipline of ornithology, particularly within the avian field-identification, necessitates a sophisticated comprehension of avifaunal taxonomy, phenotypic variation, and migratory phenology. Enthusiasts must navigate a confluence of environmental factors—such as altitudinal gradients, photoperiodic shifts, and biotic interactions—that influence species distribution and behavior. Differentiating between morphologically cryptic species often requires acute perceptual acuity, integrating auditory cues from species-specific vocalizations with minute morphological distinctions, such as wing bar patterns, primary feather lengths, or subtle color differentials across plumage spectrums. Moreover, the observer must possess an understanding of ecological niches and microhabitats, as the presence of indicator species often suggests underlying trophic dynamics and vegetative composition within a particular biogeographic zone. Further complexity arises in identifying migratory species during transitional periods, when non-breeding plumages and juvenile morphs deviate from established field guides, complicating identification. Thus, the practice extends beyond mere visual acuity into a deeper cognitive synthesis of ecological, geographical, and behavioral variables. (text derived from ChatGPT)

Did you understand the passage? You might have known most of the vocabulary, but if you didn't have background knowledge of birds, you would have had trouble understanding that it is about birdwatching. As readers, we combine what we already know about a given topic with what the text says to create an overall mental representation (Kintsch, 2013). Our existing content knowledge helps us to make inferences to fill in the missing pieces (Ozuru et al., 2009). For example, if a reader has some knowledge of birds, the words *avian, species, wing,* and *feather* may clue the reader in that the passage relates to birds. In addition, the words *observational, visual,* and *identification* clue the reader in that the passage has to do with looking for something. Anyone with prior knowledge of birdwatching as an activity or hobby—whether from personal experience, a book they've read, or a show they've watched—will be able to recognize that the passage is about birdwatching.

And the more we know about a topic, the more we can learn from reading about it (Willingham, 2017). For instance, if a reader's background knowledge helps them quickly recognize that the passage is about birdwatching, they may also gain new knowledge about the topic, such as the importance of listening to "species-specific vocalizations" and an understanding of "microhabitats" to become a successful birdwatcher.

Although they bring unique funds of knowledge to the classroom, often students don't have sufficient background knowledge of the topics of the texts that they read for academic purposes. They haven't had enough exposure to a broad range of science and social studies topics in the earlier grades (Cox et al., 2017; Tyner & Kabourek, 2020). This becomes particularly clear when they are in the upper elementary grades, and they struggle to understand the textbooks across subjects that require increased content knowledge. So our instruction must be more than simply activating content knowledge before reading a topic. We *must* build in our students a broad knowledge base systematically, right from the beginning.

CONTENT-RICH ELA INSTRUCTION

Content-rich ELA instruction is one avenue for infusing more science and social studies instruction into the school day in the early grades. It is important to restate that we advocate for this instruction to complement, but not replace, science and social studies instruction. Reviews of research demonstrate that content-rich ELA instructional approaches show promise for improving students' vocabulary and comprehension during the elementary school years, along with enhancing content knowledge (Hwang et al., 2022, 2023). Emerging research points to the long-term effects of content-rich ELA instruction on later reading comprehension (Grissmer et al., 2023; Kim et al., 2023, 2024).

What does content-rich ELA instruction look like? In the primary grades, content-rich ELA instruction invites teachers to systematically build science and/or social studies knowledge through interactive read-alouds on specific topics, while repeatedly exposing students to semantically related words and ideas. Specifically, instruction is logically organized within and across grades around content topics, with knowledge building serving as a major goal of instruction and not just a secondary goal. This knowledge building over time in a connected fashion can help to develop students' schemata about specific topics, which can lead to not only better understanding the given topic but also transferring knowledge to other related topics (Kim & Burkhauser, 2022). A *schema* is the way our brains organize the knowledge that we acquire about a particular topic, and it changes as we learn new things. Schemata can be thought of as our knowledge structures. For example, a young child's schema of weather may grow and change over time. They may start out knowing that *sunny*, *windy*, and *rainy* relate to weather because during circle time, the teacher often asks, "What is the weather like outside?" Over time, with exposure from real-life weather events or knowledge from books, concepts like *overcast*, *humidity*, *fog*, *tornado*, and *hurricane* may be organized into their weather schema. Furthermore, organization could occur when enough knowledge is acquired to begin sorting these concepts into categories like *climate*, *natural disasters*, and *the water cycle*.

To develop students' knowledge structures, interactive read-alouds feature *conceptually coherent text sets,* which are collections of texts that deepen content knowledge over successive readings, with vocabulary words and concepts that may repeat across texts (Cervetti et al., 2016; Wright et al., 2022). Conceptually coherent text sets may use a range of genres, including narrative, informational, and dual-purpose (mixed genre) texts (Neuman & Kaefer, 2018). Narrative texts are written to entertain or share an experience in a story-like format, informational texts convey information about the natural or social world, and dual-purpose texts include elements of both informational and narrative texts (Duke & Tower, 2004). Exposing students to a range of genres enhances the literacy knowledge related to language comprehension, as different text types feature different text structures. In addition, building content knowledge using conceptually coherent text sets can help students not only learn words that are directly taught by teachers but also incidentally learn words to which they are exposed and that are related to ideas they have been learning about (Cervetti et al., 2016; Neuman & Kaefer, 2018; Wright et al., 2022). For example, during a unit that focuses on how different animals and insects survive, a teacher may read the book *Ladybugs* (Gibbons, 1966). When reading, students may incidentally learn the word *defend* when hearing, "It has three major ways to defend itself. Its bright color is nature's warning to others that this insect may be poisonous or just taste bad." They may use their knowledge of words like *survive* and *protect* to understand the word *defend*. As students' knowledge structures grow, it becomes easier to learn new words and ideas related to the given topic (Steyvers & Tenenbaum, 2005). This, in turn, makes it easier for students to understand, talk about, and write about topics.

During interactive read-alouds, research has shown that open-ended questions, language models, and scaffolds can improve students' oral language (Gonzalez et al., 2014; Wasik & Hindman, 2015; Zucker et al., 2021). Combining these interactive read-alouds with conceptually coherent text sets focused on science and social studies topics can enrich conversations in ways that elevate students' oral language growth further (Cabell et al., 2013; Kook & Greenfield, 2021; Wright & Gotwals, 2017).

HOW CONTENT-RICH CONVERSATIONS HELP BUILD LANGUAGE COMPREHENSION

The conversations that happen in content-rich ELA instruction are crucial to students' language comprehension growth (Cabell & Hwang, 2023). Although strategic conversations can happen throughout the school day, we focus attention on interactive read-alouds because they provide a facilitative context in which teachers and students have meaningful conversations that promote *formal language,* or the language of books and of school (Hadley et al., 2022). Formal language typically includes more complex language structures and rarer vocabulary than those in everyday spoken language (Snow, 2010). Classroom conversations can serve as a bridge for students who cannot yet read fluently to provide exposure to this academic language register (Wasik & Hindman, 2015). Through classroom conversations that feature contingent back-and-forth exchanges, teachers can scaffold students' language skills to extend what they say by providing additional information and vocabulary. These types of classroom conversations can benefit students' understanding and use of oral language (Farrow et al., 2020; Huttenlocher et al., 2002; Kim et al., 2020). Simply put, language growth depends on the chances students have to practice and receive feedback (e.g., MacWhinney, 2015).

A *conversation* is a series of turns that stay on a given topic between two or more speakers. In a conversation, a turn is *contingent* on the other speaker's turn; it is related to what the other speaker just said and continues the flow of the conversation. Contingency has been extensively studied in young children and is essential to oral language development (Hirsh-Pasek et al., 2015). The back-and-forth exchange has been referred to as the *conversational duet* and it plays an essential role in providing both the quantity of input and quality of interaction for optimal language growth (Hirsh-Pasek et al., 2015, 2018). The conversational duet in the classroom offers students chances to contingently respond to teacher elicitations (open-ended questions), allows teachers to provide advanced vocabulary, syntax (language structures), and new information (content knowledge) that relate to the joint focus of attention (conversational topic), and encourages students to practice their growing language skills. Students' active participation in content-rich conversations can also help them not only to grow their oral language but also to glean more content knowledge from conversations.

FEATURES OF CONTENT-RICH CONVERSATIONS

There are three important types of features of conversations: interactive, linguistic, and conceptual (Rowe & Snow, 2020). We highlight a few features from each type that can be used during an interactive read-aloud session.

Interactive features promote multi-turn conversations, are responsive to students, and support their active participation. Open-ended questions, which require more than a one-word response, are a key interactive feature that allows students to enter into conversations (Cabell et al., 2015). For example, "How do our five senses keep us safe?" is an open-ended question. Questions that are responsive to students' talk can keep conversations going and serve to scaffold students' learning. Within a conversation, teachers can ask questions to provide additional challenge for students (scaffold upward) or to provide additional support for students (scaffold downward) (Zucker & Cabell, 2023).

Linguistic features provide students with opportunities for language development, including vocabulary development. Explicit vocabulary-focused conversations during interactive read-alouds relate to students' word learning (e.g., Neuman & Kaefer, 2018; Zucker et al., 2013). In addition, teachers can linguistically extend the language structures that students use, providing models of more complex language. Consider a teacher asking, "What does precipitation mean?" and a child responding, "rain." The teacher may extend this by saying, "Yes, precipitation is rain, but it is also snow or hail. It is any form of water that falls to the earth's surface." The vocabulary and the language structures that teachers use in response to students' talk help students to grow in their language comprehension (Huttenlocher et al., 2002). Students may repeat or mirror back the language that teachers use, thus facilitating their language growth through ongoing conversations (Justice et al., 2013).

Conceptual features include topics of conversation that provide cognitive challenge for students and build verbal reasoning and background knowledge. Students, beginning in preschool, benefit from conversations that are abstract or decontextualized (Rowe, 2012), which are related to language comprehension both early in school and longitudinally (Demir et al., 2015; Uccelli et al., 2019). During interactive read-aloud, teachers' use of more cognitively demanding (or inferential) questions elicits more inferential responses from children (Zucker et al., 2010). For instance, a teacher's question of "how does the amount of sunlight a plant gets affect its growth?" may elicit answers like "sunlight makes it grow faster and stronger" or "too little sunlight makes the plant stop growing." These answers were not necessarily explicitly in the text and needed to be inferred by combining background knowledge with the new knowledge learned from the text. This differs from one-word responses that may be given when students are simply asked to name the things that plants need to grow.

All three of these sets of features—interactive, linguistic, and conceptual—can be woven into conversations that improve language comprehension. For example, when teachers read about and discuss content-area topics with students (conceptual), the back-and-forth conversations (interactive) are more likely to have advanced language models (linguistic) than when they engage in other classroom activities (Cabell et al., 2013; Kook & Greenfield, 2021). Giving teachers and students something meaningful to talk about is important to language growth.

THE STRIVE-FOR-FIVE FRAMEWORK

The Strive-for-Five framework can be used by prekindergarten through first-grade teachers to improve content-rich conversations in the classroom (Zucker & Cabell, 2023). Although we know that conversations are essential for students' language comprehension, it can be challenging for teachers to have strategic multi-turn conversations with students in bustling classroom environments. Oftentimes, classrooms are characterized by conversations with only three turns: (1) the teacher asks a question and calls on a student; (2) the student responds correctly; and (3) the teacher says "Good job" and moves on to the next conversation with another student. Or (1) the teacher asks a question; (2) the student responds incorrectly; and (3) the teacher says "Not quite" and looks for someone else to answer the question.

The Strive-for-Five framework can help teachers think about how to have conversations with their students that go beyond this typical pattern and stretch for at least five conversation turns with a given student. It is a marginal shift that can make a big difference. A key distinguishing factor in a Strive-for-Five conversation is staying with one student at a time to scaffold his/her learning, which can be seen in Figure 2.1.

There are three important teacher moves in a Strive-for-Five conversation: Turns 1, 3, and 5. In Turn 1, the teacher asks an open-ended question. This question sets the stage for a series of Strive-for-Five conversations the teacher can have with multiple students. For example, the teacher may provide a guiding question that students think about before reading aloud a text and then ask the guiding question to start a conversation after reading aloud. Depending on whether the text is a first read or a reread, teachers can increase the level of conceptual challenge by moving from concrete questions to abstract questions. In any event, the question requires a student to respond by using more than one word.

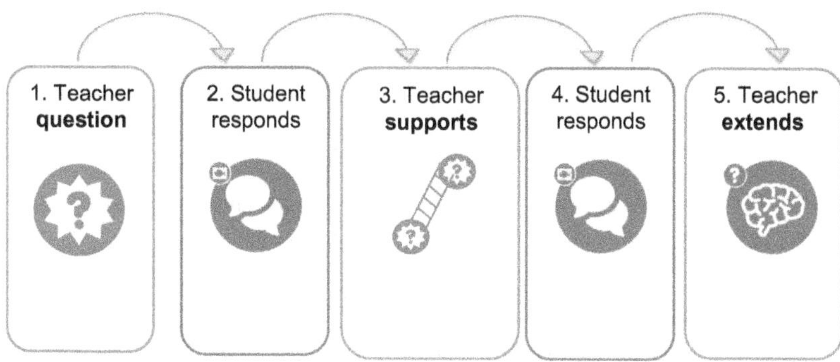

FIGURE 2.1. READ conversation—downward scaffold.

The key decision point for the teacher is in Turn 3, where the teacher scaffolds upward or downward. A *scaffold* is the support or guidance provided by the teacher based on a student's level of understanding. If a student answers the open-ended question correctly, the teacher provides an *upward scaffold* by asking a question that challenges the student. If a student answers the open-ended question partially correctly or incorrectly, the teacher provides a *downward scaffold* by providing a supportive question that helps the student move toward a correct response. Both types of scaffolds can be minimal, moderate, or intense (van Kleeck et al., 2003), as shown in Table 2.2 for upward scaffolds and Table 2.3 for downward scaffolds.

TABLE 2.2. Upward Scaffolding Strategies

Challenge level	Scaffold	Example
Minimal	*Extra facts:* Ask questions (what, where, when, or how) about related facts, ideas, or meanings.	"Yes, animals need food to survive. What else do they need to survive?"
Moderate	*Make inferences:* Prompt inferences or insights about the feelings, emotions, or desires of oneself or a character in a book.	"What do you think she is feeling when she has to leave?"
Intense	*Explain cause and effect:* Encourage the student to explain or infer the sequence of events or the causes behind them.	"What happens to your heart when you exercise?" "Why do you think the character did that?" "How did that happen? Can you tell me the steps?"

TABLE 2.3. Downward Scaffolding Strategies

Challenge level	Scaffold	Example
Minimal	*Reframe question:* Modify the original question into a simpler form, such as an either/or question, or one with limited response choices.	"Do plants absorb water through their leaves or their roots?" "Are hummingbirds or cats pollinators?"
Moderate	*Cloze technique:* Use a fill-in-the-blank technique with a rising intonation to prompt the child to complete the sentence	TEACHER: We use our sense of touch to . . . STUDENT: Feel. TEACHER: That's right. We use our sense of touch to feel.
Intense	*Model and repeat:* Model response explicitly and encourage the child to repeat the correct response.	STUDENT: He mad. TEACHER: He is frustrated. Can you say "frustrated"? STUDENT: Frustrated

As teachers move from minimal to intense in upward scaffolds, they push for higher-level conversations without stretching students too far beyond their abilities. The most common type of minimal upward scaffold that teachers use is asking for extra facts (Deshmukh et al., 2022). A moderate scaffold may be talking about feelings or emotions. An intense scaffold that stretches students further may be asking students to explain cause and effect.

It is particularly important to use downward scaffolds along a continuum of difficulty, providing the least amount of support needed for a student to be successful. Starting with a minimal scaffold allows students to continue to engage in thinking about the answer as well as offers them additional opportunities to use their language skills before the teacher simply provides the answer and language for them. The teacher might begin with a minimal scaffold that reframes the question into a yes/no or either/or type of question. If needed, the teacher might increase the intensity by using the fill-in-the-blank or cloze technique. At the most intense level, the teacher may ask the student to repeat the correct response after the teacher.

Turn 5 finishes the conversation as the teacher expands what the student says. Specifically, the teacher might rephrase, or grammatically *recast,* what the student says and add more information. This not only provides affirmation to the student but also provides an important advanced language model that *extends* what students are saying.

In the next section, we illustrate Strive-for-Five conversations within the context of content-rich ELA instruction using interactive read-alouds. We show how prekindergarten through first-grade teachers can have back-and-forth conversations with students that promote language comprehension. The examples are provided at each grade level to highlight the increasing complexity of topic knowledge (background knowledge), syntax/grammar (language structures), abstract language (verbal reasoning), and vocabulary that occur as students progress through the early grades. Each example describes the direction of the scaffold (upward or downward), level of support or challenge given (minimal, moderate, intense), and additional features that bolster language comprehension.

CONTENT-RICH INTERACTIVE READ-ALOUDS

During an interactive read-aloud session, once teachers have finished reading a content-rich text, ripe opportunities to engage in Strive-for-Five conversations emerge. In this "after" section of the content-rich read-aloud, students' language can be scaffolded upward or downward in ways that strengthen their language comprehension. This is accomplished through modeling complex syntax and/or grammar (language structures), challenging their thinking (verbal reasoning), extending knowledge of a subject (background knowledge), and explaining or defining new words (vocabulary). Each component of language comprehension used in these content-rich Strive-for-Five conversations relates to the interactive (i.e., open-ended questions, multi-turn), linguistic (i.e., syntax, vocabulary), and conceptual (i.e., building background knowledge, inferential questions) features that strengthen the quality of conversations.

Science: The Five Senses

Let's begin by considering how teachers might interact with students after a read-aloud focused on the science topic of the Five Senses. Notice how all examples are focused on the topic of Five Senses, but the substance of the conversation grows in complexity and length at each grade level. Starting with a 5-turn conversation on the identification of what body parts relate to a particular sense (prekindergarten), to a 7-turn conversation on knowledge of concrete facts related to a particular sense (kindergarten), to a 9-turn conversation about understanding how our body interprets the senses (first grade).

Prekindergarten: After reading *Cold, Crunchy, Colorful: Using Our Senses* (Brocket, 2014)

1. Teacher: So what do our eyes tell us? (open-ended question)
2. Student: smell

3. Teacher: What do our eyes tell us? Do our eyes tell us about colors or smells? (downward scaffold)
4. Student: Colors
5. Teacher: That's right! Our eyes help us to see colors (extension)

The teacher starts by asking an open-ended wh- question (first turn). Because the student offers an incorrect response, the teacher uses a minimal support downward scaffold by reducing the answer to an either/or question (third turn). The student chooses the correct response and then the teacher attempts to reinforce knowledge as well as extend the student's language by modeling a more syntactically advanced sentence (fifth turn). In this example, the teacher is providing foundational content knowledge (background knowledge) and modeling complex syntax (language structures).

Kindergarten: After reading *Look, Listen, Taste, Touch, and Smell* (Nettleton, 2004)

1. Teacher: We just learned we have taste buds on our tongues. What do they help us do? (open-ended question)
2. Student: They say if something is yummy or gross.
3. Teacher: Exactly! They help us know when something tastes good or bad. (extension) Do you remember how many taste buds we have in our mouths? (upward scaffold)
4. Student: *shakes head no*
5. Teacher: Do we have 10,000 taste buds or 100 taste buds? (downward scaffold)
6. Student: 10,000!
7. Teacher: Nice job. We have 10,000 taste buds in our mouths that work together to help us know if something tastes good or not. (extension)

The teacher begins by asking an open-ended wh- question (first turn). Since the student responds appropriately, the teacher extends the student's response to model a more complex sentence as well as provides an upward scaffold with minimal challenge (extra facts) in the third turn. The student has some difficulty answering the challenge question, so the teacher offers a minimal support either/or question to help them (fifth turn). The student makes the correct choice, so the teacher responds by extending their response (seventh turn). In this example, the teacher is providing knowledge about taste buds (background knowledge) and modeling more sophisticated syntax (language structures).

First grade: After reading *The Five Senses* by (Prior, 2012)

1. Teacher: How does the nervous system work in our body? (open-ended question)

2. Student: It works like . . . what's it called . . . the things in our brain.
3. Teacher: The neurons? (vocabulary definition)
4. Student: Yeah!
5. Teacher: And neurons send the information where? (upward scaffold)
6. Student: To our brain.
7. Teacher: Exactly! And then what happens? (upward scaffold)
8. Student: Our brain sends a message back to our body.
9. Teacher: Nice job! The nervous system is like a telephone, they send signals to each other to communicate. (extension)

The teacher begins with an open-ended how question (first turn). The student attempts to respond correctly but has difficulty identifying the correct vocabulary word. The teacher proceeds by clarifying the vocabulary word for the student (third turn). She then uses an upward scaffold with minimal challenge (extra facts) to get the student to answer the original question fully at both the fifth turn and the seventh turn. The student responds appropriately, so she then extends the student's answer by offering an additional analogy to think about how our brains and neurons communicate (ninth turn). In this example, the teacher is providing vocabulary to add to the child's schema of the nervous system (background knowledge & vocabulary). In addition, she is assisting the student in integrating ideas within the text (verbal reasoning). She also engages the student in a longer back-and-forth conversation that finishes with an extension of the student's language (language structures).

Social Studies: Native Americans

Now let's consider how teachers might interact with students after a read-aloud focused on the social studies topic of Native Americans. Notice how all examples are focused on the topic of Native Americans, but the substance of the conversation grows in complexity and length at each grade level. Starting with a 5-turn conversation on basic facts of Native American food sources (prekindergarten), to a 9-turn conversation on Native American clothing (kindergarten), to a 9-turn conversation about the migration of a particular Native American tribe and inferences about how people of the tribe may have felt (first grade).

Prekindergarten: After reading *The Very First Americans* by (Ashrose, 1993)

1. Teacher: Long ago, how did Native Americans get their food? (open-ended question)
2. Student: At the store.
3. Teacher: Remember, this was a very long time ago when there were no grocery stores. Instead, they hhh____. (downward scaffold)

4. Student: Hunted!
5. Teacher: Yes they hunted for things like buffalo and fish and then cooked them on the fire. (extension)

The teacher begins by asking an open-ended "how" question (first turn). Since the student answered incorrectly, she uses a downward scaffold with a moderate support fill-in-the-blank question (third turn). The student correctly fills in the response, so the teacher then extends the student's response by adding additional facts about how the Native Americans cooked their food (fifth turn). In this example, the teacher is assisting in developing the student's schema around Native Americans through scaffolding and extension (background knowledge).

Kindergarten: After reading *Buffalo Bird Girl: A Hidatsa Story* (Nelson, 2015a)

1. Teacher: What kind of clothes did Buffalo Bird Girl and her family wear? What did you notice? (open-ended question)
2. Student: Um they made out of buffalo.
3. Teacher: Their clothes are made of buffalo skin. (recast and extension) What did they look like? Tell me about them. (upward scaffold)
4. Student: like . . . um . . .
5. Teacher: Do you remember what their shoes are called? (downward scaffold)
6. Student: *no response*
7. Teacher: /mmmm/ (downward scaffold)
8. Student: moccasins!
9. Teacher: Good, they were wearing moccasins. (extension)

Here, the teacher begins with an open-ended wh- question (first turn). She then extends the student's answer to clarify which part of the buffalo was used to make clothes and then uses an upward scaffold with minimal challenge extra facts (third turn). In the same turn, she also recasts the student's response by providing a model of conventional grammar. When the student has trouble responding to the challenge question, she employs two downward scaffolds that increase in intensity to provide more support for the student. She starts by using minimal support by reframing the question (fifth turn). The student is still unsure of the answer, so the teacher then uses a moderate support cloze prompt (seventh turn). Then, once the student produces the correct response, the teacher extends the response by modeling a more syntactically complex sentence (ninth turn). In this example, the teacher expands the student's schema of Native American clothing (background knowledge), provides a definition for the name of the shoes they wear (vocabulary), and extends the student's language (language structures).

First grade: After reading *The Cheyenne People* (Saxena, 2014)

1. Teacher: What type of house did the Cheyenne people live in? (open-ended question)
2. Student: I don't remember
3. Teacher: Ti-_____? (downward scaffold)
4. Student: A tipi!
5. Teacher: Yes, a tipi. A tipi was a type of home that could easily be packed up and moved. (extension) Why did the Cheyenne need homes like this? (upward scaffold)
6. Student: So they can follow the buffalo!
7. Teacher: You are right! So they could follow the buffalo herds, which was one of their main food sources. (extension) How do you think the Cheyenne people felt about packing up and moving all of time? (upward scaffold)
8. Student: They probably felt tired.
9. Teacher: Yeah, I am sure it was extremely tiring for the Cheyenne to constantly move their whole village from place to place. (extension)

The teacher begins by asking an open-ended wh- question (first turn). Since the student needs assistance remembering, she offers a downward scaffold moderate support cloze prompt (third turn). When the student answers the fill-in-the-blank question correctly, she responds on the fifth turn by providing an extension that includes further definition of a tipi as well as offers an upward scaffold with intense challenge level (cause and effect). Because the student offers an appropriate response at the seventh turn, the teacher extends the student's response by including information about the buffalo being the Cheyenne's main source of food as well as provides an additional upward scaffold with a moderate challenge level (inferences or emotions). The student responds appropriately, so she finishes by extending the student's response by modeling a more syntactically complex sentence (ninth turn). In this example, the teacher helps the student arrive at the correct vocabulary word (vocabulary), assists the student in making the connection between the type of home and how the Cheyenne people survived (background knowledge), promotes inferring the emotions of the Cheyenne people (verbal reasoning), and models more complex syntax and grammar (language structures).

In the following section, we offer guidance in what features to consider when building conceptually coherent text sets as well as examples of text sets that relate to the topics above (The Five Senses and Native Americans). For each topic, there is a text set for both prekindergarten and kindergarten/first grade.

BUILDING TEXT SETS TO PROMOTE CONTENT KNOWLEDGE

As previously described, conceptually coherent text sets are collections of texts that deepen content knowledge over successive readings, with vocabulary words and concepts that may repeat across texts (Cervetti et al., 2016; Wright et al., 2022). Conceptually coherent text sets address the literacy knowledge strand of language comprehension. Literacy knowledge includes understanding print concepts, genres, text structures, and text features, so students can use them for a variety of purposes (Scarborough, 2001). One way to build students' literacy knowledge is to read aloud conceptually coherent, content-rich text sets that motivate students, systematically build knowledge, provide access to challenging language and/or ideas, and expose children to a variety of genres (Lupo et al., 2020). When considering what types of texts to use in a read-aloud text-set, both text complexity and genre should be considered. Remember that these texts are not ones that students will be able to read themselves but rather are at a complexity beyond students' current reading levels, exposing them to advanced language.

When identifying the complexity of a text, there are four text elements to consider: (1) topic familiarity, (2) relative abstractness or concreteness of words and ideas, (3) formality of language, and (4) cohesiveness (Lupo et al., 2020). Topic familiarity has to do with the amount of background knowledge students have on a topic and the amount of vocabulary they know in a text. Evaluating abstractness or concreteness of words and ideas means looking at whether the words and ideas in the text can elicit mental images (i.e., the word *cup* is concrete; the word *truth* is not). The formality of language relates to whether the book is written in academic *textbook* language or if it is written in a conversational tone. Lastly, cohesiveness relates to how closely tied are the ideas presented in a text. For example, an easier text will contain vocabulary and topics students are familiar with, concrete words and ideas that easily produce a mental image, more conversational language, and few cohesive ties (i.e., elements that link ideas together). On the other hand, a more complex text will contain vocabulary and topics that the reader may not be familiar with, more abstract words and ideas that are difficult to visualize, more academic language, and numerous cohesive ties that explain how ideas in the text relate to one another. When building text sets, teachers can use a variety of genres ranging from easy to complex. Each text set can have at least one of each genre (information, narrative, dual-purpose). For example, for the topic of Five Senses, prekindergarten teachers could use the narrative *The Listening Walk* (Showers, 1993), the informational text *Cold, Crunchy, Colorful: Using Our Senses* (Brocket, 2014), and the dual-purpose text *I Hear a Pickle (and Smell, See, Touch, and Taste It, Too!)* (Isadora, 2017), and for the topic of Native Americans they could use the narrative *Fry Bread: A*

Native American Family Story (Maillard, 2020), the informational text *The Seminoles of Florida: Culture, Customs, and Conflict* (Conklin, 2016), and the dual-purpose text *This Land* (Fairbanks, 2024). Using text sets such as these, teachers can help children deepen their vocabulary through exposure to words and concepts across contexts.

SUMMARY

Instruction is most effective for students when multiple components of language comprehension (background knowledge, vocabulary, language structures, verbal reasoning, and literacy knowledge) are synchronously addressed (Silverman et al., 2020). High-quality conversations—conversations about texts that include interactive, linguistic, and conceptual features—are one way to incorporate all components of language comprehension during instructional time. Strive-for-Five conversations incorporate each feature through strategic upward and downward scaffolds that help students grow in their language comprehension. Content-rich interactive read-alouds serve as a catalyst for these types of conversations since they systematically build knowledge through developing students' schemata and engage children in topics about the natural and social world around them.

As seen in the examples of Strive-for-Five conversations about science (The Five Senses) and social studies (Native Americans), teachers (1) provided information about foundational content knowledge (background knowledge), (2) explained or reinforced new words (vocabulary), (3) modeled complex syntax by recasting and extending children's responses (language structures), and (4) promoted abstract thinking (verbal reasoning). The conceptually coherent text sets provided demonstrate how teachers can utilize books of various genres to both teach literacy knowledge (e.g., genre and text features) as well as give teachers the opportunity to engage in these rich conversations in their own classrooms.

Reflection Questions

1. Examine your current English language arts curriculum to see how the interactive read-aloud is conceptualized. Are there text sets on science and/or social studies topics that incrementally build knowledge? Does the curriculum suggest open-ended questions that can be used to encourage conversation about the texts?
2. Select or create one conceptually coherent text set focused on a topic. For each text, write an open-ended guiding question that can serve as a starting point for your Strive-for-Five conversations.

3. Consider recording yourself facilitating a conversation about a text after a read-aloud. What do you notice about your conversations with your students? When are you scaffolding upward? When are you scaffolding downward?

ACKNOWLEDGMENTS

The work presented here was funded by the Institute of Education Sciences, U.S. Department of Education, through Grants R305A170635 (PI: Sonia Cabell) and R305A210157 (PI: Tricia Zucker), awarded to Florida State University and the University of Texas Health Science Center at Houston, respectively; and by the Office of Special Education Programs, U.S. Department of Education, through Grant H325D210062 (PI: Laura Steacy), awarded to Florida State University. The opinions expressed are those of the authors and do not represent the views of the Institute, Office, or the U.S. Department of Education.

REFERENCES

Anderson, R. C., & Pearson, P. D. (1984). A schema-theoretic view of basic processes in reading comprehension. In P. D. Pearson, R. Barr, M. L. Kamil, & P. Mosenthal (Eds.), *Handbook of reading research* (1st ed., pp. 255–291). Longman.

Ashrose, C. (1993). *The very first Americans.* Grosset & Dunlap.

Brocket, J. (2014). *Cold, crunchy, colorful: Using our senses.* Lerner Publishing Group.

Cabell, S. Q., DeCoster, J., LoCasale-Crouch, J., Hamre, B. K., & Pianta, R. C. (2013). Variation in the effectiveness of instructional interactions across preschool classroom settings and learning activities. *Early Childhood Research Quarterly, 28*(4), 820–830.

Cabell, S. Q., Gerde, H. K., Hwang, H., Bowles, R., Skibbe, L., Piasta, S. B., & Justice, L. M. (2022). Rate of growth of preschool-age children's oral language and decoding skills predicts beginning writing ability. *Early Education and Development, 33*(7), 1198–1221.

Cabell, S. Q., & Hwang, H. (2020). Building content knowledge to boost comprehension in the primary grades. *Reading Research Quarterly, 55,* S99–S107.

Cabell, S. Q., & Hwang, H. (2023). Leveraging content-rich English language arts instruction in the early grades to improve children's language comprehension. In S. Q. Cabell, S. B. Neuman, & N. Patton Terry (Eds.), *Handbook on the science of early literacy* (pp. 175–185). Guilford Press.

Cabell, S. Q., Justice, L. M., McGinty, A. S., DeCoster, J., & Forston, L. (2015). Teacher-child conversations in preschool classrooms: Contributions to children's vocabulary development. *Early Childhood Research Quarterly, 30,* 80–92.

Cabell, S. Q., Kim, J. S., White, T. G., Gale, C., Edwards, A., Hwang, H., Petscher, Y., & Raines, R. (2025). Impact of a content-rich literacy curriculum on kindergarteners' vocabulary, listening comprehension, and content knowledge. *Journal of Educational Psychology, 117*(2), 153–175.

Cervetti, G. N., Wright, T. S., & Hwang, H. (2016). Conceptual coherence, comprehension, and vocabulary acquisition: A knowledge effect? *Reading and Writing: An Interdisciplinary Journal, 29*(1), 1–19.

Connor, C. M., Dombek, J., Crowe, E. C., Spencer, M., Tighe, E. L., Coffinger, S., et al. (2017). Acquiring science and social studies knowledge in kindergarten through fourth grade: Conceptualization, design, implementation, and efficacy testing of content-area literacy instruction (CALI). *Journal of Educational Psychology, 109*(3), 301–320.

Conklin, W. (2016). *The Seminoles of Florida: Culture, customs, and conflict.* Teacher Created Materials.

Cox, S., Parmer, R., Strizek, G., & Thomas, T. (2017). Documentation for the 2011–12 Schools and Staffing Survey (NCES 2016-817). National Center for Education Statistics, Institute of Education Sciences, U.S. Department of Education.

Cunha, F. & Heckman, J. (2007). The technology of skill formation. *American Economic Review, 97*(2): 31–47.

Demir, Ö. E., Rowe, M. L., Heller, G., Goldin-Meadow, S., & Levine, S. C. (2015). Vocabulary, syntax, and narrative development in typically developing children and children with early unilateral brain injury: Early parental talk about the "there-and-then" matters. *Developmental Psychology, 51*(2), 161–175.

Deshmukh, R. S., Pentimonti, J. M., Zucker, T. A., & Curry, B. (2022). Teachers' use of scaffolds within conversations during shared book reading. *Language, Speech, and Hearing Services in Schools, 53*(1), 150–166. https://pubs.asha.org/doi/full/10.1044/2021_LSHSS-21-00020

Duke, N. K., & Tower, C. (2004). Nonfiction texts for young readers. In J. Hoffman & D. Schallert (Eds.), *The texts in elementary classrooms* (pp. 125–144). Mahwah, NJ: Erlbaum.

Fairbanks, A. (2024). *This land.* Crown Books for Young Readers.

Farrow, J., Wasik, B. A., & Hindman, A. H. (2020). Exploring the unique contributions of teachers' syntax to preschoolers' and kindergarteners' vocabulary learning. *Early Childhood Research Quarterly, 51*, 178–190.

Gibbons, G. (1966). *Ladybugs.* Holiday House.

Gonzalez, J. E., Pollard-Durodola, S., Simmons, D. C., Taylor, A. B., Davis, M. J., Fogarty, M., & Simmons, L. (2014). Enhancing preschool children's vocabulary: Effects of teacher talk before, during and after shared reading. *Early Childhood Research Quarterly, 29*(2), 214–226.

Grissmer, D., White, T., Buddin, R., Berends, M., Willingham, D., DeCoster, J., et al. (2023). *A kindergarten lottery evaluation of Core Knowledge charter schools: Should building general knowledge have a central role in educational and social science research and policy?* (EdWorkingPaper: 23–755).

Hadley, E. B., Barnes, E. M., Wiernik, B. M., & Raghavan, M. (2022). A meta-analysis of teacher language practices in early childhood classrooms. *Early Childhood Research Quarterly, 59*, 186–202.

Hirsh-Pasek, K., Adamson, L. B., Bakeman, R., Owen, M. T., Golinkoff, R. M., Pace, A., et al. (2015). The contribution of early communication quality to low-income children's language success. *Psychological Science, 26*(7), 1071–1083.

Hirsh-Pasek, K., Alper, R. M., & Golinkoff, R. M. (2018). Living in Pasteur's quadrant: How conversational duets spark language at home and in the community. *Discourse Processes, 55*(4), 338–345.

Hjetland, H. N., Brinchmann, E. I., Scherer, R., Hulme, C., & Melby-Lervåg, M. (2020). Preschool pathways to reading comprehension: A systematic meta-analytic review. *Educational Research Review, 30*, 100323.

Huttenlocher, J., Vasilyeva, M., Cymerman, E., & Levine, S. (2002). Language input and child syntax. *Cognitive Psychology, 45*(3), 337–374.

Hwang, H., Cabell, S. Q., & Joyner, R. E. (2022). Effects of integrated literacy and content-area instruction on vocabulary and comprehension in the elementary years: A meta-analysis. *Scientific Studies of Reading, 26*(3), 223–249.

Hwang, H., Cabell, S. Q., & Joyner, R. E. (2023). Does cultivating content knowledge during literacy instruction support vocabulary and comprehension in the elementary school years? A systematic review. *Reading Psychology, 44*(2), 145–174.

Isadora, R. (2017). *I hear a pickle: And smell, see, touch, & taste it, too!* Nancy Paulsen Books.

Justice, L. M., McGinty, A. S., Zucker, T., Cabell, S. Q., & Piasta, S. B. (2013). Bi-directional dynamics underlie the complexity of talk in teacher-child conversations. *Early Childhood Research Quarterly, 28*, 496–508.

Kim, J. S., & Burkhauser, M. A. (2022). Teaching for transfer can help young children read for understanding. *Phi Delta Kappan, 103*(8), 20–24.

Kim, J. S., Burkhauser, M. A., Relyea, J. E., Gilbert, J. B., Scherer, E., Fitzgerald, J., et al. (2023). A longitudinal randomized trial of a sustained content literacy intervention from first to second grade: Transfer effects on students' reading comprehension. *Journal of Educational Psychology, 115*(1), 73–98.

Kim, J. S., Gilbert, J. B., Relyea, J. E., Rich, P., Scherer, E., Burkhauser, M. A., & Tvedt, J. N. (2024). Time to transfer: Long-term effects of a sustained and spiraled content literacy intervention in the elementary grades. *Developmental Psychology*. Advance online publication.

Kim, Y.-S. G., Petscher, Y., Uccelli, P., & Kelcey, B. (2020). Academic language and listening comprehension—Two sides of the same coin? An empirical examination of their dimensionality, relations to reading comprehension, and assessment modality. *Journal of Educational Psychology, 112*(7), 1367–1387.

Kintsch, W. (2013). Revisiting the construction–integration model of text comprehension and its implications for instruction. In D. E. Alvermann, N. J. Unrau, & R. B. Ruddell (Eds.), *Theoretical models and processes of reading* (6th ed., pp. 807–839). International Reading Association.

Kook, J. F., & Greenfield, D. B. (2021). Examining variation in the quality of instructional interaction across teacher-directed activities in head start classrooms. *Journal of Early Childhood Research, 19*(2), 128–144.

Lupo, S. M., Berry, A., Thacker, E., Sawyer, A., & Merritt, J. (2020). Rethinking text sets to support knowledge building and interdisciplinary learning. *The Reading Teacher, 73*(4), 513–524.

MacWhinney, B. (2015). Language development. In L. S. Liben, U. Müller, & R. M. Lerner (Eds.), *Handbook of child psychology and developmental science: Cognitive processes* (pp. 296–338). John Wiley & Sons.

Maillard, K. N. (2020). *Fry bread: A native American family story*. Dreamscape Media.

Nelson, S. D. (2015a). *Buffalo bird girl: A Hidatsa story*. Abrams Books for Young Readers.

Nettleton, P. H. (2004). *Look, listen, taste, touch, and smell: Learning about your five senses.* Picture Window Books.

Neuman, S. B., & Kaefer, T. (2018). Developing low-income children's vocabulary and content knowledge through a shared book reading program. *Contemporary Educational Psychology, 52,* 15–24.

Neuman, S. B., Quintero, E., & Reist, K. (2023). *Reading reform across America: A survey of state legislation.* Albert Shanker Institute. *www.shankerinstitute.org/read*

Ozuru, Y., Dempsey, K., & McNamara, D. S. (2009). Prior knowledge, reading skill, and text cohesion in the comprehension of science texts. *Learning and Instruction, 19*(3), 228–242.

Paige, D. D., Wong Fillmore, L., Cabell, S., Goldenberg, C., & Griffin, A. (2021, July 12). *Comparing reading research to program design: An examination of McGraw Hill Education's Wonders, an elementary literacy curriculum.* Student Achievement Partners. *https://achievethecore.org/page/3364/comparing-reading-research-to-program-design-an-examination-of-mcgraw-hill-education-s-wonders-an-elementary-literacy-curriculum*

Prior, J. (2012). *The five senses.* Teacher Created Materials.

Rowe, M. L. (2012). A longitudinal investigation of the role of quantity and quality of child-directed speech in vocabulary development. *Child Development, 83*(5), 1762–1774.

Rowe, M. L., & Snow, C. E. (2020). Analyzing input quality along three dimensions: Interactive, linguistic, and conceptual. *Journal of Child Language, 47*(1), 5–21.

Saxena, S. (2014). *The Cheyenne people.* Gareth Stevens.

Scarborough, H. S. (2001). Connecting early language and literacy to later reading (dis) abilities: Evidency, theory, and practice. In S. B. Neuman & D. K. Dickinson (Eds.), *Handbook of early literacy research* (pp. 97–125). Guilford Press.

Showers, P. (1993). *The listening walk.* HarperCollins.

Silverman, R. D., Johnson, E., Keane, K., & Khanna, S. (2020). Beyond decoding: A meta-analysis of the effects of language comprehension interventions on K–5 students' language and literacy outcomes. *Reading Research Quarterly, 55*(S1), S207–S233.

Snow, C. E. (2010). Academic language and the challenge of reading for learning about science. *Science, 328*(5977), 450–452.

Steyvers, M., & Tenenbaum, J. B. (2005). The large-scale structure of semantic networks: Statistical analysis and a model of semantic growth. *Cognitive Science, 29,* 41–78.

Teale, W. H. (2003). Reading aloud to young children as a classroom instructional activity: Insights from research and practice. In *On reading books to children* (pp. 123–147).

Tyner, A., & Kabourek, S. (2020). *Social studies instruction and reading comprehension: Evidence from the early childhood longitudinal study.* Thomas B. Fordham Institute. *https://fordhaminstitute.org/national/resources/social-studies-instruction-and-reading-comprehension*

Uccelli, P., Demir-Lira, Ö. E., Rowe, M. L., Levine, S., & Goldin-Meadow, S. (2019). Children's early decontextualized talk predicts academic language proficiency in midadolescence. *Child Development, 90*(5), 1650–1663.

Wasik, B. A., & Hindman, A. H. (2015). Talk alone won't close the 30-million word gap. *Phi Delta Kappan, 96*(6), 50–54.

Willingham, D. T. (2017). *The reading mind: A cognitive approach to understanding how the mind reads.* Josey-Bass.

Wright, T. S., Cervetti, G. N., Wise, C., & McClung, N. A. (2022). The impact of knowledge-building through conceptually-coherent read alouds on vocabulary and comprehension. *Reading Psychology, 43*(1), 70–84.

Wright, T. S., & Gotwals, A. W. (2017). Supporting kindergartners' science talk in the context of an integrated science and disciplinary literacy curriculum. *The Elementary School Journal, 117*(3), 513–537.

Zucker, T. A., & Cabell, S. Q. (2023). *Strive-for-five conversations: A framework that gets kids talking to accelerate their language comprehension and literacy.* Scholastic Inc.

Zucker, T. A., Cabell, S. Q., Justice, L. M., Pentimonti, J. M., & Kaderavek, J. N. (2013). The role of frequent, interactive prekindergarten shared reading in the longitudinal development of language and literacy skills. *Developmental Psychology, 49*, 1425–1439.

Zucker, T. A., Cabell, S. Q., Petscher, Y., Mui, H., Landry, S. H., & Tock, J. (2021). Teaching together: Pilot study of a tiered language and literacy intervention with Head Start teachers and linguistically diverse families. *Early Childhood Research Quarterly, 54*, 136–152.

Zucker, T. A., Justice, L. M., Piasta, S. B., & Kaderavek, J. N. (2010). Preschool teachers' literal and inferential questions and children's responses during whole-class shared reading. *Early Childhood Research Quarterly, 25*(1), 65–83.

3

Gaps and Opportunities for Supporting Language and Comprehension in Early Childhood Classrooms

Shayne B. Piasta, Hyejin Kim, and Yeqing Liu

Guiding Questions

1. Are we sufficiently supporting language learning for young children?
2. What challenges exist and need to be overcome to better support language learning?
3. What can we do to improve language instruction—and thus comprehension—in early childhood classrooms?

Language—including vocabulary, morphology, syntax, and oral comprehension—is not only foundational for children's literacy development (Hjetland et al., 2020) but also for positive cognitive development, socioemotional development, and learning across various domains (Hentges et al., 2021; Kent & Wanzek, 2016; Peng et al., 2020; see Box 3.1 to learn more about language development and components). We know that children's language develops most rapidly during early childhood and that trajectories are relatively stable as children move into upper elementary and middle school (Schmitt et al., 2017). This suggests a critical need to support children's language learning early on, during the early childhood years.

Box 3.1. Language Is the Ability to Produce and Understand Speech

What are the components of language and how do these develop in children? Check out Crash Course Linguistics from PBS Digital Studios—a series of brief, engaging, and easy to understand webinars about language and language learning: *www.pbs.org/show/crash-course-linguistics*.

In this chapter, we address these guiding questions as we consider the gaps and opportunities to build children's language in classroom settings. We specifically focus on preschool through grade 1 classrooms within the United States or similar educational contexts. We also focus on general language supports used in classrooms. These general supports provided to the overall class also benefit children who are multilingual/multidialectal, newly learning English, or identified as having communication- or language-related disabilities, alongside additional supports that are tailored to these children's specific needs.

ARE WE SUFFICIENTLY SUPPORTING LANGUAGE LEARNING FOR YOUNG CHILDREN?

One way to gauge how much language learning is happening is to benchmark children's change on standardized language assessments, such as those listed in Table 3.3 (see page 62). These assessments use normative samples to establish expectations for "typical" language scores and change in scores over time. Often, these changes over time are measured in standard deviation (*SD*)[1] units as a consistent metric that can be compared across studies. Compiling information across multiple language assessments and normative samples, Schmitt et al. (2017) found that children ages 3–7 years should gain between 0.60 to 0.82 *SD*s in their language skills per year. We can examine whether children met these benchmarks in longitudinal studies. In one study, 420 children enrolled across five different U.S. states completed standardized language assessments in preschool, kindergarten, and grade 1 (Language and Reading Research Consortium et al., 2018). Per year, these children gained an average of 0.68 to 1.21 *SD*s in their language skills. These children were predominantly from homes where English was the primary language and had parents with college degrees (65%); only 15% qualified for the federal free or reduced-price lunch program.

In a second longitudinal study, a nationally representative sample of preschool children enrolled in the federal Head Start program (i.e., predominantly from low-income homes) completed standardized vocabulary assessments in the fall and spring. These children gained an average of 0.51 to 0.57 *SD*s in their vocabulary skills. In a third study involving 724 children enrolled in preschool classrooms across one state in 2010–2013, Logan et al. (2024) reported an average gain of 0.46 *SD*s in language skills over one year of preschool programming. These children reflected a range of socioeconomic backgrounds; for example, 22% of their parents had a high school diploma as their highest degree with others holding college (28%) and graduate (13%) degrees. Thus, although some studies indicate that young children are making sizeable language gains, data also indicate that some children—particularly those from marginalized backgrounds—are not exhibiting the 0.60 to 0.82 *SD* gains expected. Recent data for children matriculating from one state's public prekindergarten program into grade 1 suggest that the COVID-19 pandemic may have particularly affected language and comprehension learning, as opposed to code-focused literacy skills (Hadley et al., 2024).

SUPPORTING LANGUAGE AND COMPREHENSION IN EARLY CHILDHOOD CLASSROOMS

Why might this be? Children's language is affected by a variety of cognitive and experiential factors, including the language environments to which they are exposed at home and at school (Rowe & Snow, 2020). Given that 57% of children ages 3–5 years attend center-based early childhood programs outside of the home (Hanson & Bobrowski, 2024), and kindergarten and grade 1 are compulsory in the United States, early childhood classrooms are key for language learning. Teachers can support early language learning by providing rich classroom language environments and implementing various research-based practices (see Table 3.1). These practices can take place spontaneously (e.g., in-the-moment recasting of a child's statement that they "go-ed to the store" as "Yes, you *went* to the store!") or be structured and intentionally integrated into lesson plans and instruction (e.g., preplanning vocabulary instruction and child-friendly definitions based on the concepts, themes, or books introduced to the class). Teachers can use these practices to support children's development of both lower-level (foundational skills such as vocabulary and syntax) and higher-level (more sophisticated skills that are required for comprehension, such as inferencing, comprehension monitoring, and text structure knowledge) language skills (Hogan et al., 2011). To support the latter,

TABLE 3.1. Research-Based Classroom Practices to Facilitate Language and Comprehension

	Explicit guidance and opportunities to practice	Cohesively integrate concepts and provide cognitive challenge	Adaptive and responsive to children's interests and needs
Increase children's opportunities to hear and use language (e.g., through multi-turn conversations, open-ended questions) especially in authentic activities	√	√	√
Model and provide repeated exposure to complex and varied language (e.g., use recasts and expansions, conjunctions, embedded clauses, diverse and sophisticated vocabulary, book language)	√		
Engage in shared/dialogic book reading and discussion using a variety of genres		√	
Define and explain vocabulary (e.g., via child-friendly definitions, examples, antonyms/synonyms)	√	√	
Expand children's conceptual knowledge and higher-order thinking (e.g., teaching content in addition to skills, asking "how" and "why" questions)		√	
Engage in responsive language exchanges (e.g., respond to children's talk, follow the child's lead, ask follow-up questions)	√		√
Model and encourage decontextualized, inferential, and abstract language (i.e., language removed from the here and now used for predicting, explaining actions and emotions, metaphorical language)	√	√	

(continued)

TABLE 3.1. *(continued)*

	Explicit guidance and opportunities to practice	Cohesively integrate concepts and provide cognitive challenge	Adaptive and responsive to children's interests and needs
Teach text structures along with key/clue words signaling the structures and use graphic organizers	√		
Encourage narrative language (i.e., orally convey a sequence of events through storytelling, using wordless picture books, retelling stories)	√		√
Link concepts and language to children's knowledge and experiences		√	√
Give corrective feedback (e.g., recasts, explanations)	√		√
Encourage peer-to-peer talk (e.g., turn-and-talk)	√		√
Engage in cognitively challenging talk		√	
Provide application and practice opportunities throughout the day (e.g., using new words and syntactic structures)	√		
Provide verbal descriptions and explanations, including think-alouds	√		
Encourage children to think critically or reflect on meaning		√	
Model and encourage checking for understanding (e.g., asking "Does this make sense?" using a think-aloud to connect ideas)		√	
Provide differentiated language supports/scaffolds based on children's needs	√		√

early childhood teachers might model inferencing and teach story grammar and expository text structures.

Yet, similar to the longitudinal findings shared above, observational studies of early childhood classroom practices signal room for improvement in supporting language within early childhood classrooms. For example, studies using a general measure of teacher-child interactions, the Classroom Assessment Scoring System (CLASS; Pianta et al., 2004, 2006), consistently report low quality of interactions that afford higher-level thinking, promote language use, and feature teacher feedback (Schachter et al., 2022; Weiland et al., 2023). In fact, quality is often below the threshold at which children show improvements in their language and literacy learning (Burchinal et al., 2010). More nuanced observations indicate limited structured opportunities for language and comprehension learning in early childhood classrooms (Capin et al., 2024; Cutler et al., 2022; Phillips et al., 2020). For example, children in preschool and kindergarten classrooms spend approximately 8% to 12% of their day (i.e., 7 to 25 minutes on average) involved in language exchanges or other learning opportunities to build language and comprehension (Bratsch-Hines et al., 2019; Weiland et al., 2023), with considerable variability among and within classrooms. Structured language and comprehension instruction in grade 1 classrooms appear to be similarly limited (Connor et al., 2009). Together, these findings indicate a need to better support early childhood teachers in providing high-quality language and comprehension learning opportunities.

LET'S KNOW! LANGUAGE-FOCUSED INSTRUCTION

Language-focused curricula are one way to support early childhood teachers and their students. From 2010 to 2015, the Language and Reading Research Consortium (LARRC)—along with its advisory board comprised of teachers, language and literacy specialists, and administrators—developed and tested Let's Know! as a whole-class/Tier 1 supplemental curriculum for preschool through grade 3. Let's Know! was designed to improve children's lower- and higher-level language skills and, thus, comprehension. Language skills are explicitly taught via research-based instructional strategies as teachers and children read narrative and expository texts on the topics of fiction, animals, earth materials, and folktales. Let's Know! follows a scope and sequence across its 85 lessons meant to be taught in 30-minute sessions. Key features of Let's Know! are presented in Figure 3.1 and unit and lesson structure are presented in Figure 3.2. Details regarding the

Key features
Supplemental to core literacy program
Scope and sequence of language-focused learning objectives for prekindergarten–3
Lower-and higher-level language targets
Explicit instruction coupled with guided and independent practice opportunities
Incorporation of authentic narrative and expository texts
Language targets
Text structure (narrative, compare-contrast, sequences and cycles, description, cause-effect)
Integration (synthesis, inferencing, prediction, comprehension monitoring)
Word knowledge
Grammar
Research-based language teaching techniques
Focused stimulation (repeated exposure)
Cloze procedures
Rich, extended instruction
Modeling
Dialogic reading
Discussion
Questioning
Think aloud
Key/clue words
Graphic organizers

FIGURE 3.1. Key features, language targets, and teaching techniques of Let's Know!

development and scope/sequence of Let's Know! are presented in LARRC (2016), and the Let's Know! lessons are available for free at *https://larrc.ehe.osu.edu.*[2]

LARRC tested Let's Know! in a large randomized controlled trial spanning 6 states involving 315 prekindergarten through grade 3 classrooms and 1,732 children (LARRC, 2017, 2019, 2022; Piasta et al., 2016). Results were mixed as to the impact of Let's Know! on children's lower- and higher-level language and

Whole-class 30-minute lessons	
4 topical units (2 narrative, 2 expository)	
Within-unit lesson routine	***Within-lesson routine***
Hook (unit overview to generate interest and set purpose(s) for reading/learning	Set (overview and goal)
Read to Me (exposure to rich text and opportunities to teach/apply learning)	I do (modeling)
Words to Know (vocabulary)	We do (guided practice)
Text Mapping (grammar)	You do (independent practice)
Integration (higher-level language skills)	Close (review)
Read to Know (independent practice)	
Stretch & Review (review and deepen learning)	
Close (end-of-unit, hands-on experience to consolidate knowledge and skills)	

FIGURE 3.2. Unit and lesson structure of Let's Know!

comprehension skills, relative to business-as-usual instruction. Across all grades, Let's Know! positively impacted children's understanding of vocabulary words taught within lessons and their ability to monitor their comprehension when reading or listening to text. There was some indication of positive impacts on prekindergarteners' oral comprehension of expository text and third graders' reading comprehension of narrative text. Let's Know! did not impact children's understanding of story grammar or oral comprehension as assessed by standardized measures. For first through third graders, Let's Know! indirectly impacted their reading comprehension because of its impacts on learning vocabulary. These findings echo other studies in showing that language and comprehension skills can be improved through classroom instruction, particularly when assessed by study-specific measures, but that current classroom curricula do not necessarily achieve large improvements on standardized measures of language and comprehension (Rogde et al., 2019; Silverman et al., 2020).[3]

CHALLENGES IN SUPPORTING LANGUAGE AND COMPREHENSION IN EARLY CHILDHOOD CLASSROOMS

Ongoing research provides insight into several challenges that may limit the impacts of language and comprehension instruction in early childhood classrooms. As indicated, many current classroom curricula may not sufficiently support language and comprehension learning. Such curricula may need to be more targeted or intensive or better supported by accompanying professional development; for example, researchers are currently developing and testing a small-group, Tier 2 version of Let's Know! (Bridges et al., 2023). The Tier 2 intervention, Let's Know!2, is specifically targeted toward grade 1 children who are at risk of comprehension difficulties due to low language skills. It intensifies language instruction via simplifying language input, increasing scaffolding, and attending to distributed practice (see Figures 3.3 and 3.4). The impacts of Let's Know!2 are being tested in a two-state randomized controlled trial involving 36 elementary schools and 245 first-grade children (Piasta, Hogan, et al., 2024). Updates on this work will be posted to *https://crane.osu.edu/our-work/lets-know2*. Other research groups are also working to develop more effective classroom curricula and interventions for supporting language and comprehension (e.g., Baker et al., 2020; Kelley et al., 2020; McMaster et al., 2019; Neuman et al., 2021; Petersen et al., 2022; Phillips et al., 2024; Snowling et al., 2022; Zucker et al., 2019).

AVAILABILITY AND USE OF CLASSROOM CURRICULA AND INTERVENTIONS THAT IMPROVE LANGUAGE

Despite ongoing efforts to develop and test language-focused classroom curricula and interventions, at present, teachers have access to relatively few curricula or intervention programs with evidence of positive effects on language. Piasta, Kim, et al. (2024) conducted a restricted systematic review of whole-class (Tier 1) and small-group (Tier 2) language-focused curricula and interventions designed for preschool through grade 1 classroom use.[4] This review extended the work of Goldfeld et al. (2022) by considering Tier 1 as well as Tier 2 curricula/interventions designed to facilitate children's language learning from 2008 through September 2024. Out of 5,905 journal articles initially identified, 64 articles met all inclusion and exclusion criteria and were reviewed to identify research-tested curricula/interventions that positively affected children's language outcomes. We found 34 unique research-tested language-focused curricula/interventions with positive impacts (see Table 3.2). Importantly, of these, 21 have been research-tested and shown effects when

Key features
Tier 2 intervention for children at risk of reading comprehension difficulties due to low language
Scope and sequence of language-focused learning objectives for G1 (may be expanded)
Lower- and higher-level language targets
Explicit instruction coupled with guided and independent practice opportunities
Incorporation of authentic narrative and expository texts
Language targets
Text structure (narrative, compare-contrast, sequences and cycles, description, cause-effect)
Integration (synthesis, inferencing, prediction, comprehension monitoring)
Word knowledge
Grammar
Research-based language teaching techniques
Focused stimulation (repeated exposure)
Cloze procedures
Rich, extended instruction
Modeling
Dialogic reading
Discussion
Questioning
Think aloud
Key/clue words
Graphic organizers

FIGURE 3.3. Key features of Let's Know!2.

implemented by actual teachers, as opposed to solely research staff, and 13 are available to teachers either commercially or through a public website. Many of these have become available to teachers only within the past few years.

Several recent studies have documented the existing curricula and interventions presently used in early classrooms to support language and literacy. In one statewide study of preschool teachers (n = 497), Schachter et al. (2020) found that all curricula reported by at least five teachers included language and literacy content. Of these popular curricula, however, only two have evidence of potentially

Small-group 20- to 30-minute lessons	
4 topical units (2 narrative, 2 expository)	
Within-unit lesson routine	***Within-lesson routine***
Hook (unit overview to generate interest and set purpose(s) for reading/learning	Set (overview and goal)
Read to Me (exposure to rich text and opportunities to teach/apply learning)	I do (modeling)
Words to Know (vocabulary)	We do (guided practice)
Integration (higher -level language skills)	You do (independent practice)
Close (end -of-unit, hands-on experience to consolidate knowledge and skills)	Close (review)
Enhancements	
Simplification of language input	
Increased scaffolding	
Increased attention to distributed practice	
Revised materials to better support diversity and inclusion	
Enhanced interventionist training	

FIGURE 3.4. Unit and lesson structure of Let's Know!2.

positive effects[5] on children's language learning: High/Scope and Core Knowledge Language Arts. Over half of the teachers (53%) reported using The Creative Curriculum, which does not have documented effects on language learning. In another study, Shea et al. (2024) similarly found that The Creative Curriculum was used in a majority of 98 preschool classrooms, along with evidence that such global curricula may not support language and comprehension to the extent of more focused language and literacy curricula. Shea et al. (2024) also identified two additional curricula used by at least five teachers: Building Language for Literacy (now titled "PreK On My Way") and Opening the World of Learning. Neither of these has documented evidence of impacting children's language and comprehension learning.[6] Beyond preschool, Bridges et al. (2024) noted that no grade 1 teachers participating in the initial Let's Know!2 study (n = 57) reported using language-focused curricula in their classrooms, and none of the literacy curricula reported had evidence of effects on language learning.

TABLE 3.2. Research-Tested Language-Focused Curricula and Interventions as Trialed by and Available to Early Childhood Teachers

	Research conducted with teacher or technology implementing	Research conducted with research staff implementing
Available commercially or via researcher's public website	**Read Aloud Curriculum** (Baker et al., 2013, 2020; Fien et al., 2011; Puhalla, 2011) **Developing Talkers** (Zucker et al., 2013) **Elements of Reading Vocabulary** (Apthorp et al., 2012) **Head Start REDI** (Bierman et al., 2008) **Let's Know!** (Language and Reading Research Consortium et al., 2016a, 2016b, 2017, 2022) **Model of Reading Engagement** (Kim et al., 2021) **Nuffield Early Language Intervention-Preschool** (Fricke et al., 2013, 2017; Haley et al., 2017; West et al., 2021, 2024) **Read It Again! PreK** (Justice et al., 2010) **Story Champs** (Petersen et al., 2022; Spencer et al., 2015a, 2015b; Spencer & Petersen, 2018) **Story Friends and Story Friends plus Classwide Vocabulary Review Strategies** (Goldstein et al., 2016; Kelley et al., 2015, 2020; Madsen et al., 2023; Seven et al., 2020) **Teaching Early Literacy and Language** (Gray et al., 2024) **World of Words** (Neuman et al., 2011, 2021; Neuman & Kaefer, 2018)	
Not (yet?) commercially or publicly available	**Read-Play-Learn** (Dickinson et al., 2019; Hadley et al., 2019) **Early Vocabulary Intervention** (Coyne et al., 2010, 2022a, 2022b) **Evidence-Based Program for Integrated Curricula** (Fantuzzo et al., 2011) **Let's Talk Programme** (Hutchinson & Clegg, 2011) **Reading and Language Intervention** (Duff et al., 2014) **Self-Regulated Strategy Development-Plus** (Kim et al., 2024) *some SRSD but not SRSD Plus materials available online) **Talk Boost** (available in U.K. only; Lee & Pring, 2016) **Words of Oral Reading and Language Development** (Gonzalez et al., 2011; Pollard Durodola et al., 2011) **Unnamed curricula/intervention:** Denton et al. (2010)	**Content-Area Literacy Instruction** (Connor et al., 2017) **Language in Motion** (Phillips et al., 2016, 2021, 2024) **Dialogic Reading-Enhanced** (Lonigan et al., 2013; Phillips et al., 2021, 2024) **Comprehension Monitoring and Providing Awareness of Story Structure** (Phillips et al., 2021, 2024) **Let's Talk!** (Lake & Evangelou, 2019) **Oral Narrative Intervention Programme** (Glisson et al., 2019) **Unnamed curricula/interventions:** Derri et al. (2010) Duncan et al. (2019) Dyson et al. (2017) Goldstein et al. (2017) Lonigan and Phillips (2016) Pullen et al. (2010) Silverman et al. (2013)

Note. The restricted systematic review did not exclude studies with poor designs. Although all of the curricula/interventions listed had evidence of positive effects on at least one

AVAILABILITY AND USE OF LANGUAGE AND COMPREHENSION ASSESSMENTS

A related challenge is that teachers may not know which children in their classrooms are in need of language support. Despite calls for widespread language screening to accompany the literacy screening conducted at schools and early childhood centers, most children are not systematically screened or monitored to identify those who might benefit from extra language support (Adlof & Hogan, 2019; Schachter et al., 2023). Schachter and colleagues (Schachter & Piasta, 2021; Schachter et al., 2023) found that most early childhood teachers informally assessed children's language skills through in-the-moment noticing and documented observations; these teachers reported knowing much less about children's language skills than code-focused literacy skills. Most language assessments are not designed for classroom teacher use, in that they require specialized training, substantial administration and scoring time, and significant cost (Bao et al., 2024).

Several research groups have started to address this gap by creating teacher-friendly assessments to measure lower- and higher-level language skills in early childhood that are reliable and valid. The Narrative Language Measures subtests of CUBED-3 (Petersen & Spencer, 2016) are one such example of screening and progress monitoring assessments. These assess children's listening comprehension and reading comprehension, including narrative, vocabulary, story grammar, and inferencing skills. Another example is the whole-class OWL language screener, which is currently being used to identify children at risk for comprehension difficulties due to low language in Let's Know!2 research (Hogan, Shen, et al., 2024; Piasta, Hogan, et al., 2024). These and additional assessment efforts (Christopulos & Redmond, 2023; Pace et al., 2022) can help teachers identify children who might benefit from extra language and comprehension supports. Of course, completing such assessments is only the first step. Early childhood teachers need to be able to interpret and use such data—along with research-tested language and comprehension instructional resources—to plan and enact effective language and comprehension instruction (Schachter & Piasta, 2021; Schachter et al., 2023).

TEACHERS' UNDERSTANDINGS OF LANGUAGE SKILLS AND PRACTICES

Accumulating research suggests substantial variation in early childhood teachers' understanding of language development and pedagogy. For example, Piasta et al. (2022) measured preservice early childhood teachers' content knowledge of vocabulary, syntax and morphology, narrative, and multilingual development and contextual factors related to language development. Across these dimensions, preservice teachers averaged 69% correct (range of 42–84% correct). On additional measures of vocabulary (Duguay et al., 2015) and morphological (Washburn & Mulcahy, 2019) knowledge, preservice teachers averaged 78% correct (range of 53–100%) and 52% correct (range of 0–83%). Surprisingly, preservice teachers' content knowledge was not related to the amount of credit hours they had completed in their preservice program, either overall or specific to courses with language content or instructional field experiences. Phillips et al. (2020) showed similar variability in in-service preschool teachers' content knowledge of language. They also documented variability in in-service preschool teachers' knowledge and use of key research-based language practices. The National Council on Teacher Quality estimated that 37–45% of elementary teacher preparation programs do not offer sufficient coursework in vocabulary or comprehension (Ellis et al., 2023). These findings suggest a need for further supporting early childhood teachers' language-related knowledge and practice during preservice preparation and professional learning.

Emerging evidence also suggests that teachers and scholars may differ in their understandings of language instruction. Schachter et al. (2021) had preschool teachers and researchers view video clips of classroom language and learning opportunities. They documented that teachers' reported instructional goals were often broader, more contextualized, and less skills-focused than researchers. For instance, in an instructional interaction in which a teacher talks with children about wearing a smock during a messy activity, teachers reported learning goals around behavior management and social-emotional development, whereas researchers noted the vocabulary learning opportunity. Teachers infrequently referenced language-learning goals and often referred to *assessing* skills rather than *teaching* skills (see also Capin et al., 2024). Teachers and researchers also used different terminology when referring to language-related goals and practices. For example, one teacher reported that her intent during a specific learning opportunity was to "teach grammar and proper language," an observing teacher considered the learning opportunity to be about irregular plurals, and researchers discussed the learning opportunity in terms of using a recast to build children's syntactic understanding.

Subsequent studies shed additional light on teachers' understandings of language learning and instruction. As previously noted, Schachter and Piasta (2021) found that preschool teachers commonly used informal noticing to understand children's language needs. Schachter and Piasta's findings further indicated that teachers most frequently used this information in the moment to respond to and support children's language learning (e.g., downward or upward scaffolding during an interaction). This is critical for meeting children's individual learning needs, but it was also notable that only some teachers planned learning opportunities to intentionally build children's language and literacy skills (see also Chen et al., 2024).

More recently, Gabas and colleagues (2024) documented preschool teachers' language practices and pedagogical reasoning.[7] Asked about their goals while viewing videos of language-learning opportunities that took place in their classrooms, teachers frequently discussed wanting children to be able to express themselves (i.e., communicate) and build connections across content, activities, and experiences. Correspondingly, teachers indicated the importance of a rich classroom language environment—including plentiful child talk—and embedded many implicit and in-the-moment language-learning opportunities during classroom instruction. These included research-based practices such as modeling language and new vocabulary to extend children's ideas and support concept development, directly teaching vocabulary words, using open-ended questions, and fostering conversations and discussion (Table 3.1). About half of the teachers planned language-learning opportunities. There was less focus on explicitly teaching language skills. No teachers referenced a scope or sequence for language learning, although some teachers were familiar with language-related state, national, or curricula-specific standards. In fact, policy factors like learning standards were not directly or consistently linked to teachers' classroom practices (Purtell et al., 2024). Altogether, these findings suggest that early childhood teachers understand language as a tool for communication and knowledge building, and their instructional practices and goals reflect this perspective. This may explain why early childhood teachers report teaching language and comprehension skills to a lesser extent (once a month to weekly) than teaching code-focused literacy skills (one to two times per week to daily; Thomas et al., 2023).

Complexity of Effective Language and Comprehension Instruction

Perhaps the most critical challenge to supporting early language and comprehension is inherent in the complexity of learning and teaching these skills. Language and comprehension are among the most complex processes in which we engage as humans. Comprehension, whether oral or reading, draws on and requires integration across multiple modalities and skills (Hogan et al., 2011; Kamhi & Catts, 2017; LARRC, 2015; Pearson et al., 2020). Both depend on children's knowledge and experiences. As a result, children in early childhood classrooms exhibit considerable individual differences in their language and comprehension abilities and needs. Thus, providing effective language and comprehension instruction in early childhood classrooms is likewise complex (Pearson et al., 2020; Snowling et al., 2022).

Many of the evidence-based instructional strategies for supporting language and comprehension (see Table 3.1) are derived from research conducted outside the classroom context. What we have learned from speech-language pathology, psychology, and other fields is essential, and some of these practices have been studied as implemented in authentic early childhood classrooms (Hadley et al., 2022). The classroom-based research, however, is largely descriptive and correlational, based on restricted samples of teachers and children, focused on vocabulary only, and has not clearly established cause and effect. Moreover, this research has often considered specific, individual language practices as these predict children's language and comprehension outcomes rather than holistic classroom practice (Chiang et al., 2017; Hadley et al., 2022) and produced inconsistent results. For example, Barnes et al. (2017) found positive associations between teachers' conceptual talk—but not talk defining or explaining vocabulary words—during shared book reading and children's vocabulary learning in 52 Head Start classrooms. In contrast, Hadley et al. (2023) found that vocabulary talk in 15 publicly funded prekindergarten classrooms—but not conceptual or STEM-related talk—positively predicted children's learning on a comprehensive language measure. Chiang et al. (2017) found that teacher practices to engage grade 1–3 children in defining new words were associated with reading comprehension growth, but not language growth, only when provided after text reading; vocabulary instruction before and during text reading was not associated with learning.

In a recent large-scale study of 100 diverse preschool classrooms and 446 children from across one state, Piasta, Ceviren, et al. (2024) were unable to replicate findings concerning associations of any kind between the amount, complexity, or richness of teachers' classroom talk and children's fall-to-spring learning on a comprehensive language measure. These researchers also did not find evidence that teacher responsivity,[8] including use of communication-facilitating and language-facilitating practices, differentiated classrooms in which children made greater versus less language-learning gains (Zimmermann et al., 2022).

Additional studies conducted within this same project have also been unable to validate other theoretically or research-based language practices. For example, in the full sample of 486 preschool classrooms and 2,004 children, neither the amount nor quality[9] of higher-level, lower-level, or overall language and comprehension learning opportunities in preschool classrooms predicted children's language learning (Cutler et al., 2022; Piasta, 2023; Schachter et al., 2022). The same was true for the amount and quality of shared book reading opportunities and for time spent in other classroom activities (e.g., large group/circle time, play). Quality of teacher-child interactions, as measured via CLASS instructional support, emotional support, and classroom organization domains, did not predict children's language learning nor did the CLASS dimensions of language modeling, concept development, or quality of feedback (Schachter et al., 2022). In fact, of myriad classroom practices considered, only a couple were associated with children's language learning over the preschool year: (1) the amount of time that children spent in small groups without teacher support *negatively* predicted language learning, (2) the amount of time that children spent working individually *negatively* predicted language learning, and (3) the amount of time that children were off-task *negatively* predicted language learning (Piasta, 2023). Notably, policy-related factors, such as class size and composition, curriculum, teacher education and training, and state Quality Rating Improvement System ratings, also did not predict preschool children's language learning (Purtell et al., 2024).

These findings suggest that enacting specific, individual language practices during delineated activities may be too simplistic to realize meaningful change in children's language and comprehension learning. Rather, instruction that supports language and comprehension is likely more complex and involves patterns—or constellations—of practices enacted in early childhood classrooms. Notably, most of the research-tested, language-focused curricula and interventions listed in Table 3.2 use and integrate multiple language and comprehension practices. Researchers have only occasionally explored patterns in teachers' language practices—most notably within the context of shared book reading (Lepola et al., 2023; Zucker et al., 2021; see also Barnes et al., 2020)—as related to children's learning.

Recently, Schachter et al. (in press) followed methods from prior studies on successful teachers' literacy practices and schools that beat the odds (Taylor et al., 2000) and qualitatively analyzed the language-learning opportunities in 30 classrooms where children demonstrated greater-than-typical language gains across the preschool year, as contrasted with 30 classrooms where children demonstrated less gain. Their analyses showed that teachers' instruction in classrooms where children made greater-than-typical language gains was characterized by three sets of practices that were used frequently, concurrently, and consistently throughout activities: (1) children were afforded explicit guidance and opportunities to practice/apply knowledge; (2) teachers cohesively integrated systems of concepts and cognitive challenge across the school day, with shifts to more diverse and challenging content and activities over the school year; and (3) teachers were flexible and adaptive such that instruction and activities were responsive to children's interests and needs.

In enacting these practices, teachers provided rich classroom language environments with substantial opportunities for children to practice and make meaning with language (see Box 3.2). Specific language practices were embedded within these broader constellations of practices (see Table 3.1). Moreover, many practices were closely linked to building children's conceptual knowledge, another critical component of comprehension (Neuman et al., 2021). These same sets of practices could be reliably identified in a larger sample of 100 preschool classrooms in which children exhibited the full range of language-learning gains (Cutler et al., 2024). They exhibited small-to-moderate associations with one another, signaling interconnectivity, and were present across multiple classroom activities (large group, small group, shared book reading, free choice/play). Preliminary analyses suggest that, depending on children's language skills at the start of the preschool year, integrating concepts and challenge and providing guidance and practice were associated with children's language gains (Piasta, Schachter, et al., 2024).

Box 3.2. Annotated Classroom Vignette Showcasing Integrating Concepts and Challenge and Providing Guidance and Practice

Italicized content refers to research-based practices and constellations of practices to facilitate language and comprehension listed in Figure 3.1.

At the start of a science activity, a teacher asks the children to guess what they might find outside living in the ground *[prediction/inference, open-ended question]*. Several children guess "worms." The teacher encourages additional responses, and children name and describe several different insects *[child talk; multi-turn conversation; discussion]*.

On the science table, the teacher places a bucket filled with dirt and worms, along with magnifying glasses. She gives each child a clipboard and pencil. She tells the children to write down everything that they see—they are writing down their "observations" *[abstract language, vocabulary; content teaching]*. She *thinks aloud*, saying "I see long skinny worms," and *models* writing this on her clipboard *[verbal description]*. She guides children's observations using *closed- and open-ended questions*. Children describe what they see *[child talk; verbal description]* and use invented spelling to write words, phrases, and sentences. The teacher encourages new ideas *[responsive language]* and *scaffolds* children's individual writing. She also extends children's verbal descriptions via grammatical *expansions* and adding adjectives, each of which she explains *[responsive language; complex language; vocabulary; differentiation; application and practice]*.

Next, children share aloud some of the descriptions that they wrote *[child talk]*. The teacher then encourages the children to use another "sense"—touch—and share their observations aloud *[repeated exposure, child talk, abstract language, vocabulary; application and practice]*. They use a ruler to measure the worms, compare their length, and determine which are shorter and longer *[complex language; vocabulary]*.

During shared book reading, the teacher selects the book "Diary of a Worm" *[application and practice]*. She introduces the book by stating that it is a fiction book, which means it is a made-up story *[text structure; vocabulary]*. She reads the title and asks what a diary is [*open-ended question*]. After soliciting several answers *[child talk]*, she synthesizes the responses and provides a *child-friendly definition* [*vocabulary]*. She continues to activate children's background knowledge by asking whether they or a brother or sister liked to write in a diary or in their journals *[link to knowledge and experiences]*. She discusses the author and illustrator.

The teacher then reads the book aloud to the children, pausing to ask "what," "how," and "why" questions, check comprehension, and have children share their insights and experiences *[dialogic reading; open-ended questions; cognitively challenging talk and higher-order thinking; model and check for understanding; link to knowledge and experiences]*. At one point, the teacher pauses to have the children turn to their neighbors and discuss what they think will happen next in the story *[peer-to-peer talk; decontextualized language; prediction/inference; discussion]*.

Next, the teacher tells the children that it's time to write in their diaries (i.e., classroom journals) just as the worm did *[repeated exposure; application and practice]*. She instructs them to write about what they had done so far that day including observing the worms *[narrative language]*. She instructs them to write about what they did, how they felt, and whether they liked or disliked the worm activity *[narrative language, decontextualized language]*.

As other children move to tables, she remains on the carpet with two children to scaffold their writing *[differentiation]*. She has the children verbalize what they will write about *[verbal description]*. She offers *recasts* and *expansions* and helps the two children write down their thoughts *[corrective feedback]*. She then circulates among all the children, continuing to *scaffold* their language and writing.

On a subsequent day, the teacher introduces an informational/expository book about worms *[repeated exposure; application and practice]*. She and the children talk about the differences between this book and *Diary of a Worm [text structure; conceptual knowledge]*.

After reading, the teacher demonstrates using a *graphic organizer* to summarize what she knows about worms *[text structure; higher-order thinking]*. As children complete their own graphic organizers *[text structure]*, she encourages them to think about what they learned from their observations and from the book *[repeated exposure; content teaching; conceptual knowledge; application and practice]*.

OPPORTUNITIES TO IMPROVE LANGUAGE AND COMPREHENSION IN EARLY CHILDHOOD

The research that we reviewed in this chapter suggests several opportunities for improving children's language and comprehension skills in early childhood classrooms. We summarize key takeaways for better supporting language and comprehension below.

- Teachers, early childhood learning standards, and education policies should set and emphasize language-learning goals.
- Preservice and in-service professional learning for teachers should incorporate language-related content and pedagogical knowledge, including how language develops, what skills should be targeted, when, and how.
- Teachers can integrate language supports into Tier 1 and Tier 2 instruction within RTI and MTSS frameworks.
- Teachers can use research-based practices and research-tested curricula/ interventions to support language learning.
- Teachers can use both implicit (e.g., rich language environments) and explicit instruction to facilitate children's language.
- Teachers can integrate language-learning opportunities into various classroom contexts and content domains.
- Teachers and other professionals can use validated assessments to identify language needs and differentiate language instruction.
- Teachers can intentionally plan ways to support language learning in their classrooms.

First and foremost, the research is clear that these skills are malleable. In other words, the success of certain language-focused curricula, interventions, and practices signals that teachers and classroom experiences can make a difference in language and comprehension learning. As such, supporting these skills during early childhood education should be a priority. This should be reflected in learning standards and policies, but these may have limited influence on early childhood teachers' classroom instruction. We encourage early childhood teachers to consider language not only as a means for supporting broader communication and conceptual outcomes but as an important learning goal in its own right. Just as teachers target letter-sound correspondences and phonemic awareness as a way of supporting broader reading comprehension, they can also systematically target children's lower- and higher-level language skills while realizing broader communication and conceptual goals and ultimately supporting later reading comprehension.

Learning about language, in terms of development and research-based language practices, should be incorporated and prioritized within early childhood teacher professional learning. As has been noted for literacy, "one cannot be expected to give what one does not possess" (Binks-Cantrell et al., 2012, p. 526). Teachers are well aware that basic language acquisition can occur implicitly through exposure and interactions with others. However, teachers may need more explicit knowledge regarding language development and pedagogy in order to teach language and comprehension skills in their classrooms. Teaching these skills is particularly important for children experiencing language difficulties, those newly learning English, and those who may be less familiar with the sophisticated vocabulary and syntax used in classrooms and texts. This requires explicit knowledge concerning how language is learned and what skills should be targeted, when, and how. As such, early childhood teacher preparation and ongoing professional learning need to emphasize relevant content and pedagogical knowledge and acknowledge that language should be prioritized alongside literacy, STEM, and socioemotional domains.

In addition to knowledge, improving language and comprehension requires that early childhood teachers have tools to help them determine, monitor, and meet children's learning needs. Teachers can think about language learning and instruction within familiar response to intervention (RTI) and multi-tiered systems of support (MTSS; Adlof & Hogan, 2019) frameworks. They can aim for strong Tier 1, whole-class language supports through use of research-based language practices (Table 3.1), providing a rich language environment, and using research-tested, language-focused core and supplemental curricula (Table 3.2). They can use newly developed language screeners and progress monitoring assessments (Table 3.3) to determine those children who may need Tier 2, small-group instruction. For these children, teachers can provide more intensive and targeted language support, perhaps by using a research-based language intervention (Table 3.2). School speech-language pathologists and other qualified individuals may also administer standardized assessments to determine if certain children qualify for additional language supports (e.g., speech-language therapy, English as an additional language services).

TABLE 3.3. Sample Standardized, Screening, and Progress Monitoring Language Assessments

Name	Citation	Domain(s)	Ages	For Teacher Admin.	Available
Standardized summative language assessments					
Clinical Evaluation of Language Fundamentals	(Semel et al., 2003; Wiig et al., 2004)	Comprehension, Syntax, Vocabulary,	Versions for ages 3 through 5 years and ages 5 through 21 years		Publisher
Comprehensive Assessment of Spoken Language	(Carrow-Woolfolk, 2008)	Comprehension, Syntax, Vocabulary, Inference, Pragmatics	Ages 2 through 21 years		Publisher
Expressive One Word Picture Vocabulary Test	(Martin & Brownell, 2011)	Vocabulary	Ages 2 through 18 years		Publisher
Expressive Vocabulary Test	(Williams, 1997–2007)	Vocabulary	Ages 2.5 years through adult		Publisher
Narrative Assessment Protocol-2	(Bowles et al., 2020)	Narrative	Ages 3 through 6 years	P	Email Dr Bowles
Oral and Written Language Scales	(Carrow-Woolfolk, 2011)	Comprehension, Expression, Syntax, Vocabulary, Pragmatics	Ages 3 through 21 years		Publisher
Peabody Picture Vocabulary Test	(Dunn, 2019)	Vocabulary	Ages 2 years through adult		Publisher
Preschool Language Scales	(Zimmerman et al., 2011)	Comprehension, Expression	Ages 2 weeks through 7 years		Publisher
Receptive One-Word Picture Vocabulary Test	(Brownell, 2000)	Vocabulary	Ages 2 through 18 years		Publisher
Test of Oral Language Development	(Newcomer & Hammill, 2008)	Syntax, Vocabulary	Ages 4 through 8 years		Publisher
Test of Narrative Language	(Gillam & Pearson, 2017)	Narrative comprehension	Ages 5 through 11 years		Publisher

Test of Preschool Early Literacy: Definitional Vocabulary subtest	(Lonigan et al., 2007)	Vocabulary	Ages 3 through 5 years		Publisher
Woodcock-Johnson Test of Achievement: Oral Language subtests	(Woodcock et al., 2001)	Comprehension, Vocabulary	Ages 2 years through adult		Publisher
Language screening and progress monitoring measures					
CUBED Narrative Language Measures (Spanish version available)	(Petersen & Spencer, 2016)	Syntax, Vocabulary, Comprehension	Grades prekindergarten through 8	P	Free and paid versions available via *www.languagedynamicsgroup.com/cubed*
Adapted Redmond Sentence Recall Measure	(Christopulos & Redmond, 2023)	Syntax, Verbal Working Memory	Ages 5 through 9 years	P	Freely available at *https://doi.org/10.23641/asha.22044479*
Individual Growth and Development Indicators for Early Literacy: Picture Naming subtest (Spanish version available)	(McConnell et al., 2012)	Vocabulary	Preschool	P	Publisher
OWL Language Screener	(Hogan et al., 2018, 2024)	Comprehension	Grade 1	P	Not publicly available at this time
Preschool Early Literacy Indicators: Vocabulary and Oral Language, Comprehension subtests	(Kaminski et al., 2014)	Vocabulary, Comprehension	Ages 3 through 5 years	P	Publisher
Quick Interactive Language Screener (English–Spanish bilingual version available)	(Golinkoff et al., 2017; Pace et al., 2022)	Syntax, Vocabulary, Language Learning	Ages 3 through 5 years	P	Publisher

Critically, along with providing rich language environments and in-the-moment language instruction, teachers can expand their instruction to include intentionally setting language and comprehension learning goals and aligning their teaching to these goals. These goals and associated research-based practices can be incorporated into lesson planning. For example:

- At the start of a week, a teacher might preview read-aloud books and conceptual learning goals, identify vocabulary words for pre-teaching, and plan a variety of opportunities for children to hear and say these words across classroom contexts and activities (e.g., STEM activities, shared book reading, small-group lessons, dramatic play).
- A teacher may create a routine around shared book reading in which they consistently help children make inferences (e.g., predictions), use think-alouds to demonstrate monitoring understanding, and encourage children to make connections with their existing knowledge and prior experiences.
- A teacher can deliberately introduce different types of books across the year and explicitly teach text structures across the year using graphic organizers.

Teachers can also set specific language and comprehension learning goals for particular children. For example, if a teacher is aware that certain children are challenged by irregular verbs, they may set a related learning goal for those children and, in conjunction with taking advantage of teachable moments, plan specific activities to address that goal. Teachers can also leverage what interests the class or specific children to design language and comprehension learning opportunities that are highly engaging and differentiated for children.

Given early childhood teachers' goals related to conceptual learning and making connections, teachers can integrate many language-learning opportunities into contexts (e.g., shared book reading) and content (e.g., STEM) provided in their classrooms. For instance, math and science provide rich opportunities to model and teach abstract language. Teachers can ask open-ended and inferential questions such that children can engage in multi-turn conversations as the class participates in content-area activities. Integrating language and comprehension instruction across contexts and content provided across the school day also provides ample opportunities for children to practice these skills in meaningful ways. By intentionally targeting language and comprehension across the school day and year, early childhood teachers can engage in constellations of practices that (1) cohesively integrate concepts and provide cognitive challenge; (2) afford children explicit guidance as well as practice opportunities; and (3) are responsive to children's interests and needs.

Last, the complexity of language and comprehension—and classroom instruction to support these skills—needs to be acknowledged. No set of learning standards, state or national policy, or single research-based practice will be an easy fix. Teachers can build their knowledge, better understand the language needs of children in their classrooms, and intentionally use research-tested curricula and intervention programs and constellations of research-based language practices to meet these needs. Teacher educators, researchers, and curriculum/assessment designers can support these teachers by ensuring that they provide the information and effective tools that early childhood teachers need to be able to prioritize language in their classrooms. Starting in early childhood and ensuring that children experience effective learning opportunities as they matriculate through preschool, kindergarten, and grade 1 is our best bet for improving the language and comprehension of all learners.

Reflection Questions

1. What and how do you know about the language-learning needs of children in your classroom and how do these relate to the learning goals that you set?
2. What research-based language practices do you use in your classroom and are these planned or used in the moment?
3. What additional research-based language practices or research-tested curricula/interventions might you use in your classroom and how/when would you use these?

NOTES

1. Standard deviation (*SD*) is a statistical metric to describe variability around average scores. This puts scores from different measures, samples, and studies on the same scale and give an indication as to how scores differ from average or between two groups. For example, the opportunity gap between children from low-income homes and their more advantaged peers in kindergarten literacy has been estimated as 0.47 to 1.06 *SD* (Chatterji, 2006; Reardon & Portilla, 2016).
2. Let's Know! lessons are available on this website, but the website has not been consistently maintained otherwise. Those seeking the most recent findings and publications from LARRC are encouraged to search a database (e.g., Google Scholar) for publications authored by the "Language and Reading Research Consortium."
3. Whether we should aspire or expect to affect standardized measures of language and comprehension is another debate (Clemens et al., 2022; Kamhi & Catts, 2017).
4. The restricted systematic review involved searching PsycInfo and ERIC using search terms adapted from Goldfeld et al. (2022) to identify language-focused curricula and interventions described in peer-reviewed published articles from 2008 to September 2024. Studies had to include at least one language outcome, be conducted in a main-

stream educational setting, designed for preschool to grade 1 teacher/classroom use, and implemented in an English-speaking country with an educational context similar to the United States. We excluded studies of curricula/interventions intended exclusively for use with children with disabilities or those learning English as an additional language.

5. As defined by the What Works Clearinghouse; original search procedures described in Schachter et al. (2020) with these same search procedures repeated in Autumn, 2024 for curricula described in this paragraph.
6. PreK On My Way includes elements of Developing Talkers (Zucker et al., 2019), which does have evidence of effects on language learning, but—to our knowledge—PreK On My Way as a curriculum has not been evaluated.
7. Pedagogical reasoning refers to teachers' thinking and decision making about instructional planning, goals, activities, and implementation.
8. As measured by the Conversational Responsiveness and Assessment and Fidelity Tool (see Cabell et al., 2011).
9. Amount of learning opportunities measured via an adapted version of the Individualizing Student Instruction coding scheme (Connor et al., 2009; Pelatti et al., 2014). Quality of learning opportunities measured via the Teacher Behavior Rating Scale (Assel et al., 2008).

REFERENCES

Adlof, S. M., & Hogan, T. P. (2019). If we don't look, we won't see: Measuring language development to inform literacy instruction. *Policy Insights from the Behavioral and Brain Sciences, 6*(2), 210–217.

Assel, M. A., Landry, S. H., & Swank, P. R. (2008). Are early childhood classrooms preparing children to be school ready?: The CIRCLE Teacher Behavior Rating Scale. In L. M. Justice & C. Vukelich (Eds.), *Achieving excellence in preschool literacy instruction* (pp. 120–135). Guilford Press.

Baker, D. L., Santoro, L., Biancarosa, G., Baker, S. K., Fien, H., & Otterstedt, J. (2020). Effects of a read aloud intervention on first grade student vocabulary, listening comprehension, and language proficiency. *Reading and Writing, 33*(10), 2697–2724.

Bao, X., Komesidou, R., & Hogan, T. P. (2024). A review of screeners to identify risk of developmental language disorder. *American Journal of Speech-Language Pathology, 33*(3), 1548–1571.

Barnes, E. M., Dickinson, D. K., & Grifenhagen, J. F. (2017). The role of teachers' comments during book reading in children's vocabulary growth. *The Journal of Educational Research, 110*(5), 515–527.

Barnes, E. M., Grifenhagen, J. F., & Dickinson, D. K. (2020). Mealtimes in Head Start pre-k classrooms: Examining language-promoting opportunities in a hybrid space. *Journal of Child Language, 47*(2), 337–357.

Binks-Cantrell, E., Washburn, E. K., Joshi, R. M., & Hougen, M. (2012). Peter effect in the preparation of reading teachers. *Scientific Studies of Reading, 16*(6), 526–536.

Bratsch-Hines, M. E., Burchinal, M., Peisner-Feinberg, E., & Franco, X. (2019). Frequency of instructional practices in rural prekindergarten classrooms and associations with child language and literacy skills. *Early Childhood Research Quarterly, 47*, 74–88.

Bridges, M. S., Arslan, Z., Wilson, A., Lightcap, Z., Piasta, S. B., Fleming, K. K., DeSantis, M., & Hogan, T. P. (2024, July 11–13). *Grade 1 teachers' reported literacy curricula and practices to support language* [Poster presentation]. Annual Meeting of the Society for the Scientific Study of Reading, Copenhagen, Denmark.

Bridges, M. S., Curran, M., Neal, C., Piasta, S., Fleming, K., & Hogan, T. (2023). Adapting curricula for children with language comprehension deficits. *Language, Speech, and Hearing Services in Schools, 54*(4), 1066–1079.

Burchinal, M. R., Vandergrift, N., Pianta, R., & Mashburn, A. (2010). Threshold analysis of association between child care quality and child outcomes for low-income children in pre-kindergarten programs. *Early Childhood Research Quarterly, 25*(2), 166–176.

Cabell, S. Q., Justice, L. M., Piasta, S. B., Curenton, S. M., Wiggins, A., Pence Turnbull, K. L., & Petscher, Y. (2011). The impact of teacher responsivity education on preschoolers' language and literacy skills. *American Journal of Speech-Language Pathology, 20*, 315–330.

Capin, P., Dahl-Leonard, K., Hall, C., Yoon, N. Y., Cho, E., Chatzoglou, E., et al. (2024). Reading comprehension instruction: Evaluating our progress since Durkin's seminal study. *Scientific Studies of Reading, 29*, 1–30.

Chatterji, M. (2006). Reading achievement gaps, correlates, and moderators of early reading achievement: Evidence from the Early Childhood Longitudinal Study kindergarten to first grade sample. *Journal of Educational Psychology, 98*(3), 489–507.

Chen, S., Phillips, B. M., & Dong, S. (2024). Unpacking the language teaching belief-practice alignment among preschool teachers serving children from low-SES backgrounds. *Teaching and Teacher Education, 140*, 104465.

Chiang, H., Walsh, E., Shanahan, T., Gentile, C., Maccarone, A., Waits, T., et al. (2017). *An exploration of instructional practices that foster language development and comprehension: Evidence from prekindergarten through grade 3 in Title I schools* (NCEE 2017-4024). *https://eric.ed.gov/?id=ED575194*

Christopulos, T. T., & Redmond, S. M. (2023). Positive predictive values associated with adapting the Redmond Sentence Recall measure into a kindergarten screener for developmental language disorder. *Language, Speech, and Hearing Services in Schools, 54*(2), 636–647.

Clemens, N. H., & Fuchs, D. (2022). Commercially developed tests of reading comprehension: Gold standard or fool's gold? *Reading Research Quarterly, 57*(2), 385–397.

Connor, C. M., Piasta, S. B., Fishman, B., Glasney, S., Schatschneider, C., Crowe, E., et al. (2009). Individualizing student instruction precisely: Effects of child instruction interactions on first graders' literacy development. *Child Development, 80*(1), 77–100.

Cutler, L., Piasta, S. B., Helsabeck, N. P., Purtell, K. M., Schachter, R. E., & Gabas, C. (2022, July). *Language and literacy opportunities and early childhood learning gains: Foundations for reading comprehension.* Annual Meeting of the Society for the Scientific Study of Reading, Newport Beach, CA, USA.

Cutler, L., Schachter, R. E., Gabas, C., Piasta, S. B., Zimmerman, K., Purtell, K. M., et al. (2024). *Generative early language practices in early childhood classrooms* [Manuscript submitted for publication]. Crane Center for Early Childhood Research and Policy, The Ohio State University.

Duguay, A., Kenyon, D., Haynes, E., August, D., & Yanosky, T. (2015). Measuring teachers' knowledge of vocabulary development and instruction. *Reading and Writing, 29*(2), 321–347.

Ellis, C., Holston, S., Drake, G., Putman, H., Swisher, A., & Peske, H. (2023, June). *Teacher prep review: Strengthening elementary reading instruction*. National Council on Teacher Quality. *www.nctq.org/review/standard/Reading-Foundations#findings*

Gabas, C., Schachter, R. E., Wernick, P., Purtell, K. M., & Piasta, S. B. (2024). *What shapes early childhood teachers' practices to support language learning?* [Manuscript in preparation]. University of Nebraska at Lincoln.

Goldfeld, S., Beatson, R., Watts, A., Snow, P., Gold, L., Le, H. N. D., et al. (2022). Tier 2 oral language and early reading interventions for preschool to grade 2 children: A restricted systematic review. *Australian Journal of Learning Difficulties, 27*(1), 65–113.

Hadley, E. B., Barnes, E. M., & Hwang, H. (2022). Purposes, places, and participants: A systematic review of teacher language practices and child oral language outcomes in early childhood classrooms. *Early Education and Development*, 1–23.

Hadley, E. B., Liu, S., McKenna, M., & Hull, K. (2024). *Tracing the impact of COVID-19 school closures on early language and literacy from pre-k through 1st grade* [Manuscript submitted for publication]. University of South Florida.

Hadley, E. B., Newman, K. M., & Kim, E. S. (2023). Identifying levers for improvement: Examining proximal processes and contextual influences on preschool language development. *Early Education and Development, 34*(1), 181–207.

Hanson, R., & Bobrowski, J. (2024). *Early childhood program participation: 2023* (NCES 2024-112). National Center for Education Statistics, Institute of Education Sciences, U.S. Department of Education. *http://nces.ed.gov/pubsearch/pubsinfo.asp?pubid=2024112*

Hentges, R. F., Devereux, C., Graham, S. A., & Madigan, S. (2021). Child language difficulties and internalizing and externalizing symptoms: A meta-analysis. *Child Development, 92*(4), e691–e715.

Hjetland, H. N., Brinchmann, E. I., Scherer, R., Hulme, C., & Melby-Lervåg, M. (2020). Preschool pathways to reading comprehension: A systematic meta-analytic review. *Educational Research Review, 30*, 100323.

Hogan, T. H., Shen, Y., Piasta, S. B., Fleming, K., & Bridges, M. S. (2024). *Characterizing children with low language comprehension via a grade 1 screener* [Manuscript in preparation]. MGH Institute of Health Professions.

Hogan, T. P., Bridges, M. S., Justice, L. M., & Cain, K. (2011). Increasing higher level language skills to improve reading comprehension. *Focus on Exceptional Children, 44*(3), 1–19.

Kamhi, A. G., & Catts, H. W. (2017). Epilogue: Reading comprehension is not a single ability—implications for assessment and instruction. *Language, Speech, and Hearing Services in Schools, 48*(2), 104–107.

Kelley, E. S., Barker, R. M., Peters-Sanders, L., Madsen, K., Seven, Y., Soto, X., et al. (2020). Feasible implementation strategies for improving vocabulary knowledge of high-risk preschoolers: Results from a cluster-randomized trial. *Journal of Speech, Language, and Hearing Research, 63*(12), 4000–4017.

Kent, S. C., & Wanzek, J. (2016). The relationship between component skills and writing quality and production across developmental levels: A meta-analysis of the last 25 years. *Review of Educational Research, 86*(2), 570–601.

Language and Reading Research Consortium. (2015). Dimensionality of language ability in young children. *Child Development, 86*(6), 1948–1965.

Language and Reading Research Consortium. (2016). Use of the curriculum research framework for developing a reading-comprehension curricular supplement for the primary grades. *The Elementary School Journal, 116*(3), 459–486.

Language and Reading Research Consortium, Arthur, A. M., & Davis, D. L. (2016a). A pilot study of the impact of double-dose robust vocabulary instruction on children's vocabulary growth. *Journal of Research on Educational Effectiveness, 9*(2), 173–200.

Language and Reading Research Consortium, Jiang, H., & Davis, D. (2017). Let's know! Proximal impacts on prekindergarten through grade 3 students' comprehension-related skills. *The Elementary School Journal, 118*(2), 177–206.

Language and Reading Research Consortium, Jiang, H., Logan, J. A., & Jia, R. (2018). Modeling the nature of grammar and vocabulary trajectories from prekindergarten to third grade. *Journal of Speech, Language, and Hearing Research, 61*(4), 910–923.

Language and Reading Research Consortium, Johanson, M., & Arthur, A. M. (2016b). Improving the language skills of pre-kindergarten students: Preliminary impacts of the Let's know! experimental curriculum. *Child & Youth Care Forum, 45*(3), 367–392.

Language and Reading Research Consortium, Lo, M.-T., & Xu, M. (2022). Impacts of the Let's know! Curriculum on the language and comprehension-related skills of prekindergarten and kindergarten children. *Journal of Educational Psychology, 114*(6), 1205–1224.

Lepola, J., Kajamies, A., Laakkonen, E., & Collins, M. F. (2023). Opportunities to talk matter in shared reading: The mediating roles of children's engagement and verbal participation in narrative listening comprehension. *Early Education and Development*, 1–23.

Logan, J. A. R., Piasta, S. B., Purtell, K. M., Nichols, R., & Schachter, R. E. (2024). Early childhood language gains, kindergarten readiness, and grade 3 reading achievement. *Child Development, 95*(2), 609–624.

McMaster, K., Kendeou, P., Bresina, B. C., Slater, S., Wagner, K., White, M. J., et al. (2019). Developing an interactive software application to support young children's inference-making. *L1-Educational Studies in Language and Literature*, 1–30.

Neuman, S. B., Samudra, P., & Danielson, K. (2021). Effectiveness of scaling up a vocabulary intervention for low-income children, pre-k through first grade. *The Elementary School Journal, 121*(3), 385–409.

Pace, A., Curran, M., Van Horne, A. O., de Villiers, J., Iglesias, A., Golinkoff, R. M., et al. (2022). Classification accuracy of the quick interactive language screener for preschool children with and without developmental language disorder. *Journal of Communication Disorders, 100*, 106276.-

Pelatti, C. Y., Piasta, S. B., Justice, L. M., & O'Connell, A. (2014). Language- and literacy-learning opportunities in early childhood classrooms: Children's typical experiences and within-classroom variability. *Early Childhood Research Quarterly, 29*(4), 445–456.

Pearson, P. D., Palincsar, A. S., Biancarosa, G., & Berman, A. I. (2020). *Reaping the rewards of the reading for understanding initiative*. National Academy of Education. *https://naeducation.org/reaping-the-rewards-of-reading-for-understanding-initiative/*

Peng, P., Lin, X., Ünal, Z. E., Lee, K., Namkung, J., Chow, J., & Sales, A. (2020). Examining the mutual relations between language and mathematics: A meta-analysis. *Psychological Bulletin, 146*, 595–634.

Petersen, D. B., & Spencer, T. D. (2016). Using narrative intervention to accelerate canonical story grammar and complex language growth in culturally diverse preschoolers. *Topics in Language Disorders, 36*(1), 6–19.

Petersen, D. B., Staskowski, M., Spencer, T. D., Foster, M. E., & Brough, M. P. (2022). The effects of a multitiered system of language support on kindergarten oral and written language: A large-scale randomized controlled trial. *Language, Speech, and Hearing Services in Schools, 53*(1), 44–68.

Phillips, B. M., Lonigan, C. J., Kim, Y.-S. G., Clancy, J., & Connor, C. M. (2024). Impact of supplemental multicomponent early childhood language instruction. *Journal of Educational Psychology, 116*(6), 1034–1051.

Phillips, B. M., Oliver, F., Tabulda, G., Wood, C., & Funari, C. (2020). Preschool teachers' language and vocabulary knowledge: Development and predictive associations for a new measure. *Dyslexia, 26*(2), 153–172.

Pianta, R. C., La Paro, K. M., & Hamre, B. K. (2004). *Classroom assessment scoring system.* Brookes.

Pianta, R. C., La Paro, K. M., & Hamre, B. K. (2006). *Classroom assessment scoring system: Pre-k.* Center for Advanced Study of Teaching and Learning.

Piasta, S. B. (2023, March 28). *Supporting language development in early childhood classrooms: Current efforts and new directions* [Invited presentation]. Research to Practice, Reading and Writing Centre, Department of Education, Queensland, Australia.

Piasta, S. B., Bridges, M. S., Park, S., Nelson-Strouts, K., & Hikida, M. (2022). Teachers' content knowledge about oral language: Measure development and evidence of initial validity. *Reading and Writing, 35*, 2131–2153.

Piasta, S. B., Ceviren, A. B., Schachter, R. E., Purtell, K. M., Logan, J. A. R., Cutler, L., et al. (2024). *Preschool circle time: Linguistic features of teacher and child talk and prediction of language learning* [Manuscript in preparation]. Crane Center for Early Childhood Research and Policy, The Ohio State University.

Piasta, S. B., Hogan, T. P., Bridges, M. S., Fleming, K. K., Shen, Y., Arslan, Z., et al. (2024). Language-focused tier 2 intervention: Proximal effects on first graders' lower- and higher-level language and comprehension skills. *Stage 1 registered report submitted for publication.*

Piasta, S. B., Kim, H., & Liu, Y. (2024). *Tier 1 and tier 2 research-tested language-focused programs for use in preschool through grade 1 classrooms* [Manuscript in preparation]. The Ohio State University.

Piasta, S. B., Language and Reading Research Consortium, & Jiang, H. (2016, July). *Targeting lower- and higher-level language skills to support comprehension: Initial results for Let's Know!* Annual Meeting of the Society for the Scientific Study of Reading, Porto, Portugal.

Piasta, S. B., Schachter, R. E., Purtell, K. M., Logan, J. A. R., Cutler, L., Zimmerman, K., et al. (2024). *Do generative language practices predict preschool children's language learning?* [Manuscript in preparation]. Crane Center for Early Childhood Research and Policy, The Ohio State University.

Purtell, K. M., Helsabeck, N. P., Schachter, R. E., Cutler, L., Piasta, S. B., & Logan, J. A. R. (2024). *Associations between early childhood education policy factors and children's language skills* [Manuscript in preparation]. Crane Center for Early Childhood Research and Policy, The Ohio State University.

Reardon, S. F., & Portilla, X. A. (2016). Recent trends in income, racial, and ethnic school readiness gaps at kindergarten entry. *AERA Open*, *2*(3), 2332858416657343.

Rogde, K., Hagen, Å. M., Melby-Lervåg, M., & Lervåg, A. (2019). The effect of linguistic comprehension instruction on generalized language and reading comprehension skills: A systematic review. *Campbell Systematic Reviews*, *15*(4), e1059.

Rowe, M. L., & Snow, C. E. (2020). Analyzing input quality along three dimensions: Interactive, linguistic, and conceptual. *Journal of Child Language*, *47*(1), 5–21.

Schachter, R. E., Ceviren, A. B., Logan, J. A. R., Piasta, S. B., Purtell, K. M., Justice, L. M., & O'Connell, A. A. (2022). *Instructional quality and children's language gains* [Unpublished analyses]. Department of Child, Youth and Family Studies, University of Nebraska–Lincoln.

Schachter, R. E., Gabas, C., Purtell, K. M., & Piasta, S. B. (in press). Generative versus constrained contexts: Differentiating the language learning opportunities in early childhood classrooms. *Literacy Research and Instruction*.

Schachter, R. E., Matthews, A., & Piasta, S. B. (2021). How do differing stakeholders perceive instances of literacy instruction? *Journal of Early Childhood Literacy*, *21*(1), 104–126.

Schachter, R. E., Piasta, S., & Justice, L. (2020). An investigation into the curricula (and quality) used by early childhood educators. *NHSA Dialog, The Research-to-Practice Journal for the Early Education Field*, *23*(2), 21–50. *https://journals.uncc.edu/dialog/article/view/1021*

Schachter, R. E., & Piasta, S. B. (2021). Doing assessment: A multicase study of preschool teachers' language and literacy data practices. *Reading Research Quarterly*, *57*(2), 515–535.

Schachter, R. E., Yeomans-Maldonado, G., & Piasta, S. B. (2023). Early childhood teachers' emergent literacy data practices. *Journal of Literacy Research*, Advance online publication, *55*(1), 5–27.

Schmitt, M. B., Logan, J. A. R., Tambyraja, S. R., Farquharson, K., & Justice, L. M. (2017). Establishing language benchmarks for children with typically developing language and children with language impairment. *Journal of Speech, Language, and Hearing Research*, *60*(2), 364–378.

Seven, Y., Hull, K., Madsen, K., Ferron, J., Peters-Sanders, L., Soto, X., et al. (2020). Classwide extensions of vocabulary intervention improve learning of academic vocabulary by preschoolers. *Journal of Speech, Language, and Hearing Research*, *63*(1), 173–189.

Shea, Z. M., Piasta, S. B., Shen, Y., Hudson, A. K., Zettler-Greeley, C. M., Lewis, K., & Logan, J. A. R. (2024). *Are associations between use of emergent literacy-focused curricula and children's literacy gains moderated by risk status, receipt of intervention, or preschool setting?* [Manuscript submitted for publication]. The Ohio State University.

Silverman, R. D., Johnson, E., Keane, K., & Khanna, S. (2020). Beyond decoding: A meta-analysis of the effects of language comprehension interventions on k–5 students' language and literacy outcomes. *Reading Research Quarterly*, *55*(S1), S207–S233.

Snowling, M. J., West, G., Fricke, S., Bowyer-Crane, C., Dilnot, J., Cripps, D., et al. (2022). Delivering language intervention at scale: Promises and pitfalls. *Journal of Research in Reading*, *45*(3), 342–366.

Taylor, B. M., Pearson, D., Clark, K., & Walpole, S. (2000). *Beating the odds in teaching all students to read: Lessons from effective schools and accomplished teachers.* Center for the Improvement of Early Reading Achievement.

Thomas, L. J. G., Piasta, S. B., Bailet, L. L., Zettler-Greeley, C. M., & Lewis, K. (2023). Promoting meaning-focused skills: Creating a foundation for comprehension in early childhood classrooms. *The Reading Teacher, 76*(4), 421–428.

Washburn, E. K., & Mulcahy, C. A. (2019). Morphology matters, but what do teacher candidates know about it? *Teacher Education and Special Education, 42*(3), 246–262.

Weiland, C., Moffett, L., Rosada, P. G., Weissman, A., Zhang, K., Maier, M., et al. (2023). Learning experiences vary across young children in the same classroom: Evidence from the individualizing student instruction measure in the Boston public schools. *Early Childhood Research Quarterly, 63*, 313–326.

Zimmermann, K., Cutler, L., Piasta, S. B., Purtell, K. M., Schachter, R. E., & Logan, J. A. R. (2022). *CRAFT: Summary of results* [unpublished analyses]. Crane Center for Early Childhood Research and Policy, The Ohio State University.

Zucker, T. A., Bowles, R., Pentimonti, J., & Tambyraja, S. (2021). Profiles of teacher and child talk during early childhood classroom shared book reading. *Early Childhood Research Quarterly, 56*, 27–40.

Zucker, T. A., Carlo, M. S., Landry, S. H., Masood-Saleem, S. S., Williams, J. M., & Bhavsar, V. (2019). Iterative design and pilot testing of the Developing Talkers tiered academic language curriculum for pre-kindergarten and kindergarten. *Journal of Research on Educational Effectiveness, 12*(2), 274–306.

4

From Ears to Eyes

Supporting Reading Comprehension through Systematic Instruction on Listening Comprehension

Young-Suk Grace Kim and Molly Leachman

Guiding Questions

1. What is the role of listening comprehension in reading comprehension?
2. What skills and knowledge contribute to listening comprehension?
3. What are evidence-based instructional approaches that improve listening comprehension?

THE ROLE OF LISTENING COMPREHENSION IN READING COMPREHENSION

Reading comprehension is the understanding of written texts. Despite appearing simple, this process is highly complex. As we read, we create a mental model based on the text—a representation of its content in our minds, including elements such as characters, setting, time, causation, and objectives (Graesser et al., 1994; Lynch & van den Broek, 2007). This mental model includes both the explicit content of the text and our inferences and interpretations. According to the direct and indirect effects model of reading (DIER, pronounced "dear"; Kim, 2017a, 2020a, 2020b, 2023), constructing this mental model for reading comprehension relies on a number of skills and knowledge areas shown in Figure 4.1. In this chapter, we focus on the role of listening comprehension and associated skills and knowledge in reading comprehension. Details about other skills and their roles can be found in Kim (2020a, 2020b, 2023).

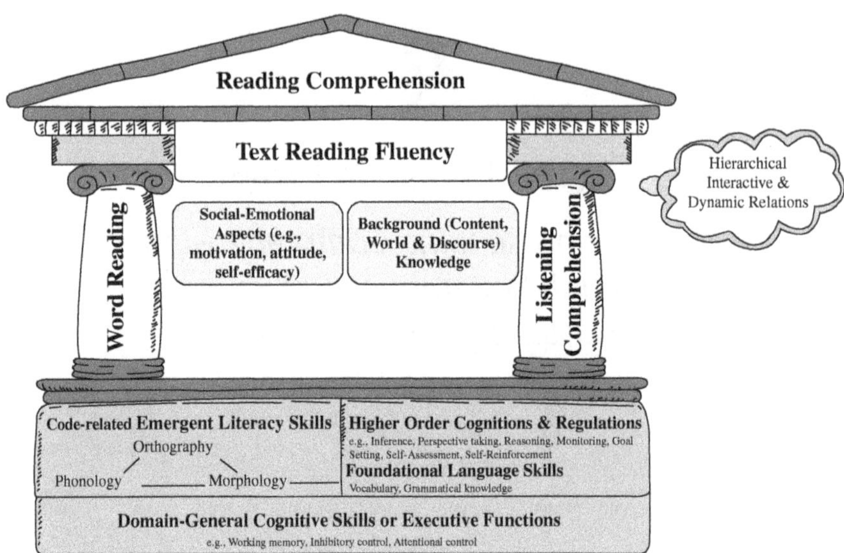

FIGURE 4.1. A heuristic illustration of the DIER model, which shows component skills and their hierarchical relations. Interrelations among these skills are not fully shown. From Kim (2017a, 2020a, 2020b, 2023). Copyright © 2025 Young-Suk Grace Kim. Reprinted by permission.

As shown in Figure 4.1, the two fundamental skills that support reading comprehension and text reading fluency are word reading and listening comprehension, depicted as the two pillars. In other words, individuals with higher word reading and listening comprehension skills achieve higher performance in reading comprehension, whereas those with lower skills in these areas have lower reading comprehension. Numerous studies have demonstrated that word reading and listening comprehension both contribute to reading comprehension for students learning to read in different languages, writing systems, and orthographic depths: English (Adlof et al., 2006; Kim, 2017a, 2020a; Kim & Wagner, 2015; LARRC, 2015; Lonigan et al., 2018), Korean (Kim, 2011, 2015, 2020b), Greek (Kendeou et al., 2013), Malay (L. W. Lee & Wheldall, 2009), other alphabetic languages (Florit & Cain, 2011), Chinese (Joshi et al., 2012; Peng et al., 2021), and second language reading (H. Lee et al., 2022). Furthermore, recent studies that have measured these skills with precision (or with reduced measurement error) have shown that differences in students' word reading and listening comprehension skills essentially explain their differences in reading comprehension performance (Foorman et al., 2018; Kim, 2015, 2017a and b, 2020a and b; Lonigan et al., 2018).

According to DIER, the effects of word reading and listening comprehension on reading comprehension differ and vary depending on the phase of reading development (Kim, 2020a, 2020b, 2023). In the early phases of reading development, such as in kindergarten and grade 1 in the U.S. context, word reading skills largely determine reading comprehension performance, with listening comprehension contributing relatively little. As students progress and develop their word reading skills, the importance of listening comprehension in reading comprehension increases. By around grade 2, listening comprehension begins to play a more significant role than word reading in influencing reading comprehension for English-speaking students in the United States (Kim et al., 2015). The significance of listening comprehension continues to grow over time, such that, by middle school, differences in listening comprehension predominantly explain differences in reading comprehension (e.g., Foorman et al., 2018). Note, however, grade levels are proxies for developmental phases, and therefore, even within the same grade (e.g., grade 2), the extent to which listening comprehension versus word reading contributes to reading comprehension differs as a function of individuals' word reading skills. For example, for second graders who have more advanced word reading skills, listening comprehension would have a greater influence on reading comprehension compared to second graders who have lower word reading skills. Applying this logic of the constraining role of word reading in reading comprehension to languages with shallow or transparent orthographies where letter-sound or grapheme-phoneme correspondences are more consistent (e.g., Italian, Spanish), word reading skills are acquired earlier (Seymour et al., 2003), and, therefore, the role of listening comprehension in reading comprehension becomes prominent sooner (Kim, 2020a, 2023).

In summary, theoretical models and empirical evidence clearly indicate that listening comprehension is essential for reading comprehension, and its role increases as students develop their word reading skills. Therefore, building a strong foundation in listening comprehension, in addition to word reading, is crucial for developing reading comprehension skills.

DEEPER UNDERSTANDING OF LISTENING COMPREHENSION

Despite the wide use of the term *listening comprehension,* surprisingly few studies clearly define it. In our work, we define listening comprehension as "the ability to comprehend spoken language at the discourse level—including conversations, stories (i.e., narratives), and informational oral texts—that involves the processes of extracting, constructing, and [integrating] meaning" ([ ] added; Kim & Pilcher, 2016, p. 160). In other words, listening comprehension is the ability to listen to and understand texts presented in oral language (i.e., oral texts), and concrete examples of oral texts include stories, information on the radio, TV programs, informational texts (e.g., lectures, debates, classroom instruction), and conversations. Listening comprehension is essentially the same as reading comprehension, with the only difference being the nature of the text: reading comprehension involves written texts, whereas listening comprehension involves oral texts (Kim, 2020a, 2023; Kim & Pilcher, 2016). This is a significant point because it indicates that listening comprehension is a complex skill, similar to reading comprehension, although reading comprehension additionally involves word reading processes and associated skills (see the word reading pillar and its foundational skills shown in Figure 4.1).

To delve deeper into comprehension, let us briefly review the process of building a mental model of text—one's thoughts or mental structure of what the text (oral or written) is about (Graesser et al., 1994; Kintsch, 1988). According to the construction-integration model (Kintsch, 1988), readers and listeners construct multiple levels of mental models as they listen to or read texts. The first and lowest level is called the surface code, where readers (in the case of written text) or listeners (in the case of oral text) mentally represent the linguistic input of the text, such as individual words and phrases. Based on the surface code representation, readers build initial propositions or ideas called the textbase representation. These initial propositions are based on local information (e.g., clauses, a sentence) and need to be cross-checked for accuracy in relation to other propositions in the text and content and world knowledge. For example, the beginning of a text might state that John is known for his punctuality and is never late to meetings. However, a later part of the text might state that he is frequently late to meetings. The understanding that John is a punctual person is a textbase representation, as is the understanding that he is usually late to meetings. Although these textbase representations may be correct in the context of their respective parts of the text or at the textbase representation level, the apparent contradiction must be resolved to establish coherence for the entire text. This process of resolving inconsistencies and integrating information using information across the text and one's world and content knowledge is called the integration process, and the highest level of the mental model, called the situation model, is formed after the integration process.

According to the direct and indirect effects model of text comprehension and production (DIET; Kim, 2016; Kim & Pilcher, 2016), the process of constructing the surface code, textbase, and situation model representations relies on specific language and cognitive skills. Figure 4.2 illustrates how different language and cognitive skills are mapped onto the various levels of mental representations according

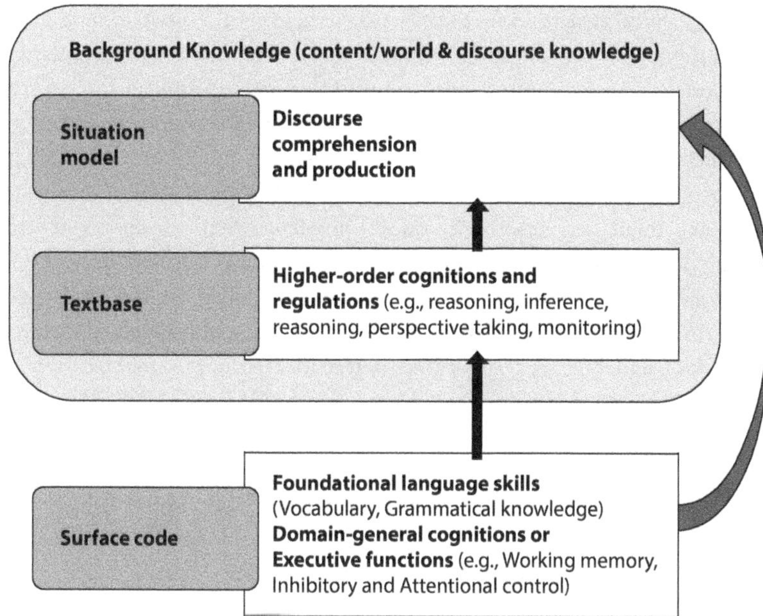

FIGURE 4.2. Direct and indirect effects model of text comprehension and production (adapted from Kim, 2016; Kim & Pilcher, 2016). Copyright © 2025 Young-Suk Grace Kim. Reprinted by permission.

to DIET. Domain-general cognitive skills or executive functions, such as working memory, inhibitory and attentional control, and cognitive flexibility, as well as foundational oral language skills, such as vocabulary and grammatical knowledge, are necessary for constructing surface code and textbase representations. As noted above, textbase representations are prone to inconsistencies, necessitating an integration process. For the integration process, higher-order cognitive skills like monitoring, reasoning, and inferencing are essential, as these allow checking the consistency of propositions across the text, making inferences, and establishing a coherent mental model of the text. Constructing the situation model also requires background knowledge—world and content knowledge and discourse knowledge, which includes text structure knowledge. World and content knowledge play an important role in comprehension (e.g., Hwang et al., 2022), particularly for the integration of information presented in the text with prior knowledge (Kintsch, 1988). Text structure knowledge also plays a crucial role by offering a mental framework for organizing different elements of a text (Kintsch, 2013; see Bogaerds-Hazenberg et al., 2021 for a review of evidence). In the narrative genre, for example, typical structures include the introduction of characters and setting at the beginning, characters engaging in a series of events that create problems and conflicts due to differing motivations, and a resolution at the end.

In summary, DIET states that the construction and integration processes articulated in the construction-integration model (Kintsch, 1988) require a combination of domain-general cognitive skills, foundational oral language skills, higher-order cognition and regulation, and background knowledge (e.g., content knowledge, world knowledge, and discourse knowledge; Kim, 2016, 2020a; Kim & Pilcher, 2016). Studies have shown that these skills and knowledge are indeed related to listening comprehension such that individuals with more advanced language and cognitive skills and knowledge perform better in listening comprehension tasks (e.g., Florit et al., 2009, 2014; Just & Carpenter, 1992; Kim, 2015, 2016, 2017a, 2020a; Lepola et al., 2012) and reading comprehension (e.g., Ahmed et al., 2016; Cain et al., 2004; Cromley & Azevedo, 2007).

DIER specifies several key hypotheses regarding the nature of the relations among these skills and knowledge areas. One hypothesis is that skills build on one another (the hierarchical relations hypothesis; Kim, 2017a, 2020a, 2020b). Looking at the listening comprehension pillar in Figure 4.2, reading comprehension is built on listening comprehension, which is built upon background knowledge and higher-order cognition and regulation, which, in turn, are built on foundational oral language skills. The foundational oral language skills, in turn, are built on domain-general cognitions or executive functions. This series of relations results in chain effects (Kim, 2015, 2016, 2017, 2020a). For example, weak domain-general cognitive skills, such as attentional control, negatively influence vocabulary acquisition and sentence structure understanding, which, in turn, influence higher-order cognitions, such as inference-making and listening comprehension, and, ultimately, reading comprehension. These indicate that listening comprehension mediates and explains the relations of executive functions, foundational oral language skills, and higher-order cognitions to reading comprehension (Kim, 2015, 2017, 2020a, 2020b).

The second hypothesis regarding the relation between skills depicted in Figures 4.1 and 4.2 is that they influence each other interactively during the comprehension process and development (interactive relations hypothesis; Kim, 2020a, 2020b, 2023). During the comprehension process, higher-order processes (such as integration) interact iteratively and bidirectionally with lower-order processes (such as constructing textbase representations). In terms of interactive relations during development, language skills and cognitive skills and knowledge develop bidirectionally. For example, vocabulary knowledge influences listening comprehension, and conversely, listening comprehension influences vocabulary development through listening experiences because listening to texts increases exposure to vocabulary words, thereby enhancing vocabulary knowledge. Similarly, background knowledge influences listening comprehension, and listening comprehension, in turn, supports the development of background knowledge via exposure to oral texts.

In summary, listening comprehension involves constructing meaning from oral texts, and this meaning-making process relies on domain-general cognitive skills, foundational oral language skills, higher-order cognitive skills, and background knowledge. All these components are hierarchically and interactively related.

INSTRUCTIONAL APPROACHES THAT PROMOTE THE DEVELOPMENT OF LISTENING COMPREHENSION AND ORAL LANGUAGE SKILLS

Multicomponent Approach

One apparent implication of the theoretical models DIET and DIER and empirical evidence is that improving listening comprehension requires a *multicomponent* approach, where instruction targets multiple skills and knowledge areas shown in Figure 4.2. Previous oral language interventions often focused primarily on vocabulary (e.g., Coyne et al., 2009; Neuman et al., 2011; see Silverman et al., 2020 meta-analysis), and vocabulary is essential as shown in DIER and DIET. However, the theoretical models and evidence reviewed above also highlight the importance of and a need for addressing a broader range of skills, including problem-solving and reasoning skills and background knowledge, beyond vocabulary to enhance listening comprehension development.

In line with this, efforts have been underway to inform listening comprehension instructional approaches that include multiple component skills. For example, as part of the Reading for Understanding Initiative funded by the Institute of Education Sciences, our team developed a multicomponent language intervention called COMPASS (Comprehension Monitoring and Providing Awareness of Story Structure) for students from prekindergarten to grade 4. COMPASS employs a repeated interactive reading approach, an evidence-based approach (Lonigan & Whitehurst, 1998; Noble et al., 2019) in which students listen to texts (e.g., stories) multiple times and answer comprehension questions of different types to support comprehension. In addition to interactive book reading, COMPASS explicitly teaches text structure for narratives (commonly known as story grammar) and vocabulary, and incorporates oral retell to support text comprehension. COMPASS consists of 10 weeks of lessons, expected to be taught three times a week, for approximately 25 minutes per session. Large-scale empirical studies that employed small group instruction have demonstrated that students who received COMPASS instruction outperformed those who received business-as-usual instruction in several areas. For preschoolers, COMPASS instruction led to better performance in creating grammatically correct sentences using specific words provided and also in comprehending narrative texts (Phillips, Kim et al., 2021). For third graders, COMPASS instruction improved comprehension monitoring compared to those who received business-as-usual instruction for all students across baseline oral language skills and improved vocabulary and listening comprehension for those with weaker oral language skills (Connor et al., 2018). Furthermore, when COMPASS was implemented along with an extended form of Dialogic Reading (i.e., an instructional approach to extend conversation when reading), it substantially improved preschoolers' and kindergartners' vocabulary and comprehension monitoring compared to those in the business-as-usual condition (Phillips et al., 2024).

STORY DETECTIVE

Story Detective is a multicomponent listening comprehension instructional program that is based on theoretical models DIER and DIET and extends our earlier efforts in COMPASS. There are several important features that characterize Story Detective that significantly extend COMPASS. First, Story Detective includes additional critical skills and knowledge areas aligned with the DIET model and empirical evidence, building upon what is already taught in COMPASS. These include explicit and systematic instruction in vocabulary, grammatical knowledge/sentence structures, comprehension monitoring, different types of inferencing, and perspective-taking, using interactive book reading. Importantly, these skills are taught in an integrated and interconnected manner. For example, in Story Detective, we teach the meaning of the word *cause* as a vocabulary term, and also within the context of understanding the causal structure of a story to facilitate text comprehension. We also connect the understanding of causal structures to sentence structure instruction—such as when teaching interrogatives: Who are the characters? What do they do? Why do they take certain actions?—which, in turn, are explicitly linked to text structure instruction (e.g., characters, setting, events, conflict/problem, and resolution).

The second way Story Detective extends COMPASS is through more extensive and explicit teaching of metacognition about comprehension (i.e., being aware of and monitoring one's understanding of stories and using problem-solving skills when needed). Students are taught throughout Story Detective that listening comprehension is akin to detective work (hence the name Story Detective), where they solve a problem or mystery. Students need to monitor whether stories make sense to them, and if they do not, they need to take actions such as asking questions. Students are explicitly taught that comprehension requires thinking, such as connecting different parts of the story, connecting the story with what they know, connecting it to their lives and experiences, and understanding viewpoints of different characters. They are guided to look for clues in the story, prompted by teacher questions in relevant sections of stories, for deep comprehension of stories.

Lastly, Story Detective is more intensive, with 22 weeks of instruction, compared to the 10 weeks offered by COMPASS. The increase in intensity reflects the understanding that listening comprehension, as a higher-order complex construct, requires substantial instruction and takes an extended time for development and improvement. Story Detective currently offers fully developed materials specifically designed for kindergartners, although it can also be extended down to transitional kindergarten or extended up to first grade. Transitional kindergarten is a bridge between preschool and kindergarten to help prepare children for kindergarten. Activities aimed at target skills (e.g., vocabulary, grammatical knowledge, and sentence proficiency) are developed around and integrated with the anchor story. The anchor text also enhances children's background knowledge, which is essential for comprehension (Bransford et al., 1981; Miller & Keenan, 2009). For example, texts in the first two units are built on the theme "community people" and include content about various occupations and their associated responsibilities. Target skills are systematically and gradually introduced, with each week's lesson building on the previous week's lesson and units cumulatively. Target skills in the lessons are also taught in a systematic and explicit manner using the gradual release of responsibility framework (e.g., I-do, We-do, You-do; Fisher & Frey, 2008), which includes clearly defined strategies for scaffolding and feedback. Instructional materials include lesson plans, stories with accompanying professional illustrations printed in a big-book format, vocabulary cards (full-color pictures that present the words), grammar cards, illustrations for inference-making and comprehension monitoring, graphic organizers, videos of story reading, and optional home extension activities. Lesson plans include detailed outlines, clearly specify the sequence of the lesson and comprehension questions, and provide specific wordings, such as asking, "Does the story make sense to you?" when teaching comprehension monitoring. Additionally, materials are available electronically, using platforms like Google Slides, to facilitate easy access and presentation.

Box 4.1. Key Features of Story Detective

- A multicomponent listening comprehension program that explicitly and systematically targets the following skills and knowledge: vocabulary, sentence structure (grammatical knowledge), inference, perspective-taking, comprehension monitoring, text structure, and oral retell
- Can be taught either as teacher-led whole group or small group instruction. Has 22 weeks with four 5-week units plus additional reviews
- Has three instructional sessions per week
- Uses repeated interactive book reading
- Each week has an anchor narrative text featuring five to six professional illustrations
- Anchor stories are read in each session with different types of questions
- During the first reading of the story, questions focus on target vocabulary words and literal comprehension, and referential inference
- During the second reading, further literal comprehension questions are asked, and higher-order inferential questions (beyond the referential ones) are introduced

The final reading (Session 3 of each week) includes further inferential and perspective-taking questions, as well as extension questions (e.g., text to children's life and experiences; lessons, theme, and moral of the story).

Target vocabulary words were carefully selected for their generative functions, including high-utility words across contexts such as *nervous* and *peek*. These words were chosen not only for their high utility but also for their roles in comprehending given texts and understanding key text structural components (e.g., character, setting, problem, solution). Target grammatical features and sentence structures were selected by consulting literature on children's language development and the Common Core State Standards (National Governors Association Center for Best Practices & Council of Chief State School Officers, 2010). Examples include conjunctions (e.g., accurate use of *because*), interrogative structures (e.g., who, what, why, how), and irregular plurals. As illustrated in Figure 4.2, grammatical knowledge, along with vocabulary knowledge, enables students to understand propositions and individual ideas within a story. This understanding serves as a necessary foundation for achieving a deep comprehension of the story by connecting propositions throughout the narrative. Comprehension monitoring was taught using a "silly story" framework where the student listens to a short scenario that may include inconsistencies within the story or that contradicts the student's background knowledge (e.g., "Shelly loves purple. She hates purple"; "Jenny loves writing letters. She uses gum to write."). Not all stories included inconsistencies, but students were asked to identify whether the story made sense, and if not, to explain why. This brief instruction on comprehension monitoring in each session has been successfully used in previous work with young children (see Kim & Phillips, 2016).

Text structure focuses on characters, problems, attempts to solve the problem, and resolutions in Units 1 and 2. In Units 3 and 4, we introduce initiating events and the characters' attempts to solve the problem. With regard to inference, three types of inferences are explicitly taught: referential inferences, causal chains, and character thoughts and emotional reactions (perspective-taking). For referential inferences, we focused on identifying referents for pronouns, such as *it, she, he, they, them, his,* and *her.* Causal inferences identify causal chains between actions and events, and this was aligned with sentence structures (e.g., interrogatives). Perspective-taking focused on understanding the thoughts and emotions of characters in response to events or actions. The general concept of inference was introduced using a simple illustration, such as a picture of a birthday party, where students learned to notice clues in the illustration and connect them to their inferences. Subsequently, referential inferences, causal chain inferences, and perspective-taking were taught within the context of the anchor stories, with the teacher asking targeted questions at appropriate points in the story.

Implementation Study of Story Detective

To examine feasibility and usability, Story Detective was implemented in a small-scale implementation study with a transitional kindergarten teacher and a kindergarten teacher at a charter school that provided English–Mandarin bilingual education in the southwestern part of the United States. This study was focused on implementation and not on whether the program is effective. Thus, it did not include a comparison condition (i.e., a condition in which teachers conduct business as usual or use another program to compare results for Story Detective).

A total of 73 children (38 girls; 58 kindergartners and 15 transitional kindergartners) participated in the study. The majority of the participants were of Asian heritage ($n = 60$), with seven White children, one Hispanic child, and five children of multiracial backgrounds. Additionally, 11 students were classified as English learners, and 3 students were eligible for the free and reduced lunch program, an indicator of poverty in the United States. Story Detective was implemented with the entire class during their English instruction period.

Both participating teachers were novice teachers in their first year of teaching, one having just graduated with a master of teaching, and the other in their last year of their credential program. Teachers participated in two days of practice-based professional development sessions, where they were introduced to the theoretical and empirical background of Story Detective, reviewed the materials, and practiced teaching the program (see Kim et al., 2025 for a similar approach). Subsequently, teachers implemented Story Detective for 12 weeks from winter to spring. Although the original intent was to implement the entire 22 weeks of Story Detective, it was feasible to implement only the first three units (Units 1, 2, and 3 without review weeks) due to the impact of COVID-19. Ongoing support was provided to teachers through weekly classroom visits as well as communication via emails and phone calls. To investigate changes in student performance, assessments were conducted immediately before and after the intervention on the following skills: vocabulary, comprehension monitoring, inference, theory of mind (as a measure of perspective-taking), and narrative comprehension. Due to time constraints, a measure of grammatical knowledge was not included.

In the vocabulary task, children heard target words (e.g., *sob*) and were asked to define them; their responses were scored 0, 1, and 2 for incorrect, partially correct, and precise answers, respectively. For example, when asked the meaning of *sob,* a score of 0 was given if the child answered with an incorrect answer, such as "it means when you saw something" or used the word without sufficient context, such as "it means to sob." Partial credit (1) was given if a partial definition was given, like "when you cry." Full credit (2) was given for responses with proximal meanings to the target definition, as in "sob means to cry so hard you can't breathe." In the comprehension monitoring task, children heard short scenarios and were asked to identify whether they made sense, and, if not, explain why. Inference-making was measured using a nationally normed task, specifically the inference subtask of the Comprehensive Assessment of Spoken Language—Second Edition (CASL-2; Carrow-Woolfolk, 2017). Perspective-taking was measured by using the Theory of Mind Inventory–2 (TOMI-2; Hutchins et al., 2012) and narrative comprehension was measured using the Test of Narrative Language—Second Edition (TNL-2; Gillam & Pearson, 2017).

Table 4.1 presents the reliability estimates, means, standard deviations (*SDs*), minimum, maximum, and effect sizes (Cohen's *d*) for the tasks. Cohen's *d* is the standardized difference between two means (or means of two groups) and indicates how much they differ from each other in terms of standard deviations. Effect sizes are typically interpreted as follows: values equal to or smaller than 0.20 are considered small, around 0.50 are considered moderate, and greater than 0.50 are considered large (Cohen, 1988). However, different criteria may be applied based

TABLE 4.1. Reliabilities, Means, Standard Deviations, Minimum, Maximum, and Effect Sizes

Task	Reliability	Mean	*SD*	Min–Max	ES (*d*)
Pre Vocabulary	.70	4.54	3.48	0–15	—
Post Vocabulary	.82	9.6	5.71	0–24	1.10
Pre Comprehension Monitoring	.87	15.53	8.33	0–31	—
Post Comprehension Monitoring	.85	19.89	7.85	0–35	0.54
Pre Theory of Mind (TOMI-2)	.88	20.47	6.70	1–31	—
Post Theory of Mind (TOMI-2)	.86	22.71	6.29	4–36	0.35
Pre Inference (CASL-2)	.87	14.88	5.13	0–23	—
Pre Inference (CASL-2) SS	NA	100.73	12.99	58–123	—
Post Inference (CASL-2)	.87	16.99	4.92	0–25	0.42
Post Inference (CASL-2) SS	NA	101.86	11.78	57–120	0.09
Pre Narrative Comprehension (TNL-2)	.90	16.87	6.38	0–29	—
Pre Narrative Comprehension (TNL-2) SS	NA	7.65	2.46	2–14	—
Post Narrative Comprehension (TNL-2)	.89	18.28	6.09	0–28	0.23
Post Narrative Comprehension (TNL-2) SS	NA	7.69	2.25	2–12	0.02

Note. SD = standard deviation; Min = minimum; Max = maximum; ES = effect size (Cohen's *d*); Pre = pretest; Post = posttest; SS = Standard Score; TOMI-2 = Theory of Mind Inventory–2; CASL-2 = Comprehensive Assessment of Spoken Language—Second Edition; TNL-2 = Test of Narrative Language—Second Edition. Unless otherwise noted with SS, raw scores are reported. Standard scorse for CASL-2 have a mean of 100 with *SD* of 15, whereas standard scores for TNL-2 have a mean of 10 with *SD* of 3. Reliability estimates are Cronbach's alpha.

on historical information from educational studies, such as those by Kraft (2020). Cohen's guidelines are derived from experimental studies in social psychology that often focus on a single or a few manipulations in tightly controlled lab settings. In contrast, our work was conducted in authentic real-world classroom contexts and targeted the complex skill of listening comprehension, where making a noticeable impact requires an intensive effort and is challenging. After reviewing 1,942 intervention studies in PreK–12 settings, Kraft (2020) proposed alternative benchmarks for effect sizes: small effects are less than 0.05, medium effects range from 0.05 to less than 0.20, and large effects are 0.20 or greater. As noted earlier, the implementation study did not include a comparison condition; therefore, the observed improvements or changes in performance cannot be conclusively attributed to Story Detective alone.

The performance data presented in Table 4.1 indicates that students learned the taught words well, as evidenced by a large effect size of 1.10. Additionally, the effect sizes for comprehension monitoring (0.54), theory of mind (0.35), and inference-making (0.42) were moderate when using Cohen's (1988) guidelines and large when using Krafts' (2020) guidelines. The effect size for narrative comprehension when using raw scores was smaller but meaningful (0.23). However, when using standard scores derived from normative information, the effect sizes for inference-making and narrative comprehension were negligible. These results suggest that although children showed development in their inference-making and narrative comprehension skills from pretest to posttest, these changes are not significantly different from normative development.

We visited teachers weekly to provide support and to observe lesson fidelity and quality in order to evaluate the extent to which teachers implemented Story Detective as intended. Regarding the adherence aspect of fidelity, which involves teaching the various components of the lessons, the participating teachers demonstrated high fidelity, which means they delivered Story Detective as intended to a high degree. They achieved an average score of 4.2 on a scale of 1 to 5, where 1 indicates that few elements of the lessons were taught and 5 indicates that all elements were taught. Regarding overall lesson quality, the average score was 3.6 out of 5, where 1 indicates few children were engaged in the lessons and the teacher was not familiar with the lesson routine, and 5 indicates the vast majority of students were engaged in the instruction and the teacher was prepared for the lesson. Toward the beginning of the curriculum, quality scores were slightly lower as teachers and students were getting used to the routine. By the third unit, lesson quality was high (4 out of 5). The average instruction time was 30 minutes in kindergarten, whereas in the transitional kindergarten class it was approximately 38 minutes. This suggests that more time may be required when using Story Detective with transitional kindergarten students. Overall, our observations indicated that teachers were able to implement Story Detective in transitional kindergarten and kindergarten classroom contexts.

Furthermore, teachers provided positive feedback about the program, noting several key points: the materials were teacher-friendly, children enjoyed the anchor stories, students learned almost all the target vocabulary words, children effectively detected inconsistencies, and students learned story structure elements. However, teachers also noted a challenge: the 30-minute lesson sessions were too long for the children to sit through, especially at the beginning of the academic year. These observations suggest that while the program shows promise in terms of engagement and educational outcomes, adjustments to the lesson duration might enhance its overall effectiveness and suitability for young learners (e.g., breaking the 30-minute session into two sessions in a single day, especially in the fall).

Overall, these results suggest that the multiple skills targeted in Story Detective can be effectively taught to a whole class in real-world classroom settings and that direct instruction can improve these skills. Therefore, Story Detective is usable and feasible and holds potential promise as an educational tool. However, to establish true causal evidence of Story Detective's efficacy—that is, the observed improvement is due to Story Detective, not other factors—further studies with robust experimental designs (e.g., randomized controlled trial), including control conditions, are necessary. Future studies should also investigate the effect of Story Detective when implemented in a small group setting as previous studies have shown that small group instruction is more effective than whole-class instruction (Sørensen & Hallinan, 1986).

CONCLUSION

The theoretical and empirical evidence highlights the critical role of a variety of language and cognitive skills in developing both reading and listening comprehension. DIER and DIET show that successful comprehension, whether of written or oral texts, depends on a hierarchical and interactive network of skills. These include domain-general cognitive skills, foundational oral language skills, higher-order cognitive skills, and background knowledge, which includes world, content, and discourse knowledge. Recent approaches that systematically and explicitly teach multicomponent skills, grounded in theory and evidence, have demonstrated feasibility in real-world classroom settings and show promise in enhancing language and cognitive skills. Although these studies consistently impact target component skills or proximal skills, their effects on the distal outcome of listening comprehension, as measured by standardized and normed tasks, tend to be small or limited (e.g., Connor et al., 2018; LARRC et al., 2017a, 2017b; Phillips, Kim et al., 2021; Phillips et al., 2024). These findings call for future rigorous studies to investigate instructional approaches that support the development of listening comprehension.

In terms of practical takeaways, we encourage readers to reflect on and evaluate reading curricula and materials in light of theories and empirical evidence presented here. We invite teachers and educators to analyze their curricula and consider whether the necessary skills and knowledge for effective comprehension instruction are adequately addressed across all grade levels, including young pre-readers, keeping in mind that listening comprehension serves as the foundation for reading comprehension.

In conclusion, the integration of theoretical frameworks like DIER and DIET with empirical evidence underscores the importance of a multifaceted approach to comprehension instruction. By recognizing the interplay of various language and cognitive skills, educators can better address the complexities of both reading and listening comprehension. While current research highlights the challenges of significantly improving a complex skill like listening comprehension, it also points to the potential of comprehensive, evidence-based instructional methods in enhancing language and literacy acquisition. As educators reflect on their curricula, it is essential to ensure that all necessary skills and knowledge are adequately addressed. By doing so, we can work toward more effective literacy education that supports students' overall comprehension development.

Reflection Questions

1. Are there any elements, skills, or knowledge that are not represented or missing in the curriculum?
2. Are there any skills or knowledge that need to be emphasized more?
3. Is there a systematic and integrated approach in place? If not, what are some strategies to enhance and use the existing curriculum with additional resources to support students from diverse backgrounds and needs?

ACKNOWLEDGMENTS

This research was supported by Grants R305A130131 and R305A200312 from the Institute of Education Sciences (IES), U.S. Department of Education to the first author. The content is solely the responsibility of the authors and does not necessarily represent the official views of the funding agencies.

REFERENCES

Adlof, S. M., Catts, H. W., & Little, T. D. (2006). Should the simple view of reading include a fluency component? *Reading and Writing: An Interdisciplinary Journal, 19*, 933–958.

Ahmed, Y., Francis, D. J., York, M., Fletcher, J. M., Barnes, M., & Kulesz, P. (2016). Validation of the direct and inferential mediation (DIME) model of reading comprehension in grades 7 through 12. *Contemporary Educational Psychology, 44–45*, 68–82.

Bogaerds-Hazenberg, S. T. M., Evers-Vermeul, J., & Bergh, H. (2021). A meta-analysis on the effects of text structure instruction on reading comprehension in the upper elementary grades. *Reading Research Quarterly, 56*(3), 435–462.

Bransford, J. D., Stein, B. S., Shelton, T. S. & Owings, R. A. (1981). Cognition and adaptation: The importance of learning to learn. In J. Harvey (Ed.), *Cognition, social behavior and the environment* (pp. 93–110). Hillsdale, NJ: Lawrence Erlbaum Associates.

Cain, K., Oakhill, J., & Bryant, P. (2004). Children's reading comprehension ability: Concurrent prediction by working memory, verbal ability, and component skills. *Journal of Educational Psychology, 96*, 31–42.

Carrow-Woolfolk, E. (2017). *Comprehensive Assessment of Spoken Language (CASL-2) 2nd Edition*. Western Psychological Services.

Cohen, J. (1988). *Statistical power analysis for the behavioral sciences* (2nd ed.). Erlbaum.

Connor, C. M., Phillips, B., Kim, Y.-S. G., Lonigan, C. J., Kaschak, M. P., Crowe, E., Dombek, J., & Al Otaiba, S. (2018). Examining the efficacy of targeted component interventions on language and literacy for third and fourth graders who are at risk of comprehension difficulties. *Scientific Studies of Reading, 22*(6), 462–484.

Coyne, M. D., McCoach, D. B., Loftus, S., Zipoli, R., Jr., & Kapp, S. (2009). Direct vocabulary instruction in kindergarten: Teaching for breadth versus depth. *Elementary School Journal, 110*, 1–18.

Cromley, J. G., & Azevedo, R. (2007). Testing and refining the direct and inferential mediation model of reading comprehension. *Journal of Educational Psychology, 99*, 311–325.

Fisher, D., & Frey, N. (2008). *Better learning through structured teaching: A framework for the gradual release of responsibility* (p. 4). Alexandria, VA: ASCD.

Florit, E., & Cain, K. (2011). The simple view of reading: Is it valid for different types of alphabetic orthographies? *Educational Psychology Review, 23*, 553–576.

Florit, E., Roch, M., Altoè, G., & Levorato, M. C. (2009). Listening comprehension in preschoolers: The role of memory. *British Journal of Developmental Psychology, 27*, 935–951.

Florit, E., Roch, M., & Levorato, M. C. (2014). Listening text comprehension in preschoolers: A longitudinal study on the role of semantic components. *Reading and Writing: An Interdisciplinary Journal, 27*, 793–817.

Foorman, B. R., Koon, S., Petscher, Y., Mitchell, A., & Truckenmiller, A. (2015). Examining general and specific factors in the dimensionality of oral language and reading in 4th and 10th grades. *Journal of Educational Psychology, 107*, 884–899.

Foorman, B. R., Petscher, Y., & Herrera, S. (2018). Unique and common effects of decoding and language factors in predicting reading comprehension in grades 1–10. *Learning and Individual Differences, 63*, 12–23.

Gillam, R. B., & Pearson, N. A. (2017). *Test of narrative language: Second edition*. Pro-Ed.

Graesser, A. C., Singer, M., & Trabasso, T. (1994). Constructing inferences during narrative text comprehension. *Psychological Review, 101*(3), 371–395.

Hutchins, T. L., Prelock, P. A., & Bonazinga, L. (2012). Psychometric evaluation of the Theory of Mind Inventory (ToMI): A study of typically developing children and children with autism spectrum disorder. *Journal of Autism and Developmental Disorders, 42*(3), 327–341.

Hwang, H., Cabell, S. Q., & Joyner, R. E. (2022). Effects of integrated literacy and content-area instruction on vocabulary and comprehension in the elementary years: A meta-analysis. *Scientific Studies of Reading, 26*(3), 223–249.

Joshi, R. M., Tao, S., Aaron, P. G., & Quiroz, B. (2012). Cognitive component of componential model of reading applied to different orthographies. *Journal of Learning Disabilities, 45*, 480–486.

Just, M. A., & Carpenter, P. A. (1992). A capacity theory of comprehension: Individual differences in working memory. *Psychological Review, 99*(1), 122–149.

Kendeou, P., Papadopoulos, T. C., & Kotzapoulou, M. (2013). Evidence for the early emergence of the simple view of reading in a transparent orthography. *Reading and Writing: An Interdisciplinary Journal, 26*, 189–204.

Kim, Y.-S. (2011). Proximal and distal predictors of reading comprehension: Evidence from young Korean readers. *Scientific Studies of Reading, 15*(2), 167–190.

Kim, Y.-S. (2015). Language and cognitive predictors of text comprehension: Evidence from multivariate analysis. *Child Development, 86*, 128–144.

Kim, Y.-S. G. (2016). Direct and mediated effects of language and cognitive skills on comprehension or oral narrative texts (listening comprehension) for children. *Journal of Experimental Child Psychology, 141*, 101–120.

Kim, Y.-S. G. (2017a). Why the simple view of reading is not simplistic: Unpacking the simple view of reading using a direct and indirect effect model of reading (DIER). *Scientific Studies of Reading, 21*(4), 310–333.

Kim, Y.-S. G. (2020a). Hierarchical and dynamic relations of language and cognitive skills to reading comprehension: Testing the direct and indirect effects model of reading (DIER). *Journal of Educational Psychology, 112*(4), 667–684.

Kim, Y.-S. G. (2020b). Toward integrative reading science: The direct and indirect effects model of reading (DIER). *Journal of Learning Disabilities, 53*(6), 469–491.

Kim, Y.-S. G. (2023). Simplicity meets complexity: Expanding the simple view of reading with the direct and indirect effects model of reading. In S. Cabell, S. Neuman, & N. Patton-Terry (Eds.), *Handbook on the science of early literacy* (pp. 9–22). Guilford Press.

Kim, Y.-S. G., Harris, K., Goldstone, R., Camping, A., & Graham, S. (2025). The science of teaching reading is incomplete without the science of writing: A randomized control trial of integrated teaching of reading and writing. *Scientific Studies of Reading, 29*, 32–54.

Kim, Y.-S. G., & Phillips, B. (2016). Five minutes a day to improve comprehension monitoring in oral language contexts: An exploratory intervention study with prekindergartners from low-income families. *Topics in Language Disorders, 36*(4), 356–367.

Kim, Y.-S. G., & Pilcher, H. (2016). What is listening comprehension and what does it take to improve listening comprehension? In R. Schiff & M. Joshi (Eds.), *Handbook of interventions in learning disabilities* (pp. 159–174). Springer.

Kim, Y.-S. G., & Wagner, R. K. (2015). Text (Oral) reading fluency as a construct in reading development: An investigation of its mediating role for children from Grades 1 to 4. *Scientific Studies of Reading, 19*, 224–242.

Kintsch, W. (1988). The use of knowledge in discourse processing: A construction-integration model. *Psychological Review, 95*, 163–182.

Kintsch, W. (2013). Revisiting the construction–integration model of text comprehension and its implications for instruction. In D. E. Alvermann, N. J. Unrau, & R. B. Ruddell (Eds.), *Theoretical models and processes of reading* (6th ed., pp. 807–839). International Reading Association.

Kraft, M. A. (2020). Interpreting effect sizes of education interventions. *Educational Researcher, 49*(4), 241–253.

Language and Reading Research Consortium. (2015). The dimensionality of language ability in young children. *Child Development, 86*, 1948–1965.

Language and Reading Research Consortium, Jiang, H., & Davis, D. (2017a). Let's Know! Proximal impacts on prekindergarten through Grade 3 students' comprehension-related skills. *The Elementary School Journal, 188*(2), 177–206.

Language and Reading Research Consortium, Lo, M., & Xu, M. (2017b). Impacts of the Let's Know! Curriculum on the language and comprehension-related skills of prekindergarten and kindergarten children. *Journal of Educational Psychology, 114*(6), 1205–1224.

Lee, L. W., & Wheldall, K. (2009). An examination of the simple view of reading among beginning readers in Malay. *Reading Psychology, 30*, 250–264.

Lee, H., Jung, G., & Lee, J. H. (2022). Simple view of second language reading: A meta-analytic structural equation modeling approach. *Scientific Studies of Reading, 26*(6), 585–603.

Lepola, J., Lynch, J., Laakkonen, E., Silvén, M., & Niemi, P. (2012). The role of inference making and other language skills in the development of narrative listening comprehension in 4- to 6-year old children. *Reading Research Quarterly, 47*, 259–282.

Lonigan, C. J., Burgess, S. R., & Schatschneider, C. (2018). Examining the simple view of reading with elementary school children: Still simple after all these years. *Remedial and Special Education, 39*, 260–273.

Lynch, J. S., & van den Broek, P. (2007). Understanding the glue of narrative structure: Children's on- and off-line inferences about characters' goals. *Cognitive Development, 22*(3), 323–340.

Miller A. C., Keenan J. M. (2009). How word reading skill impacts text memory: The centrality deficit and how domain knowledge can compensate. *Annals of Dyslexia, 59*, 99–113.

National Governors Association Center for Best Practices, Council of Chief State School Officers. (2010). *Common core state standards for English language arts and literacy in history/social studies, science, and technical subjects.* National Governors Association Center for Best Practices, Council of Chief State School Officers. *www.corestandards.org/assets/CCSSI_ELA%20Standards.pdf*

Neuman, S. B., Newman, E. H., & Dwyer, J. (2011). Educational effects of a vocabulary intervention on preschoolers' word knowledge and conceptual development: A cluster-randomized trial. *Reading Research Quarterly, 46*, 249–272.

Noble, C., Sala, G., Peter, M., Lingwood, J., Rowland, C., Gober, F., & Pine, J. (2019). The impact of shared book reading on children's language skills: A meta-analysis. *Educational Research Review, 28*, 100290.

Peng, P., Lee, K., Luo, J., Li, S., Joshi, R. M., & Tao, S. (2021). Simple view of reading in Chinese: A one-stage meta-analytic structural equation modeling. *Review of Educational Research, 91*(1), 3–33.

Phillips, B., Kim, Y.-S. G., Lonigan, C. J., Connor, C. M., Clancy, J., & Al Otaiba, S. (2021). Supporting language and literacy development with intensive small-group interventions: An early childhood efficacy study. *Early Childhood Research Quarterly, 57*, 75–88.

Phillips, B. M., Lonigan, C. J., Kim, Y.-S. G., Clancy, J., & Connor, C. M. (2024). Impact of supplemental multicomponent early childhood language instruction. *Journal of Educational Psychology, 116*(6), 1034–1051.

Seymour, P. H. K., Aro, M., & Erskine, J. M. (2003). Foundation literacy acquisition in European orthographies. *British Journal of Psychology, 94*, 143–174.

Silverman, R. D., Johnson, E., Keane, K., & Khana, S. (2020). Beyond decoding: A meta-analysis of the effect of language comprehension interventions on K–5 students' language and literacy outcomes. *Reading Research Quarterly, 55*(S1), S207–S233.

Sørensen, A. B., & Hallinan, M. T. (1986). Effects of ability grouping on growth in academic achievement. *American Educational Research Journal, 23*(4), 519–542.

Whitehurst, G. J., & Lonigan, C. J. (1998). Child development and emergent literacy. *Child Development, 69*(3), 848–872.

5

Improving Elementary Students' Reading Comprehension through Structured and Systematic Translation of Research to Practice

Kausalai Kay Wijekumar, Kacee Lambright, Ashley Stack, Javier Garza, and Pilar Sierra

Guiding Questions

1. What does the research say about how students can use text structure to help them comprehend?
2. What are evidence-based practices teachers can use to support students in learning about how to use text structure to help them comprehend?

Reading comprehension is an essential skill that requires active engagement with text guided by intentional and automatized application of strategies and underlying skills. Reading comprehension depends on many prerequisites such as decoding, vocabulary knowledge, and background about text and topic (Perfetti & Stafura, 2014; Scarborough, 2001). These prerequisites are necessary ingredients but do not ensure comprehension success. Teaching children to read fluently does not automatically result in text comprehension. Theoretical models and empirical findings suggest that comprehension requires readers to intentionally process text, select important ideas, generate a gist, summarize the text, and fill in any gaps with inferences, resulting in a logically associated memory of the text (Kintsch, 2005; Wijekumar et al., 2024).

The comprehension journey begins at birth and continues throughout one's lifetime, supported initially by families, teachers, and communities (e.g., book clubs). As a critical foundation for all human activities, comprehension is a major focus of instruction in English language arts (ELA) classrooms at all grade levels. Forty years of tracking student performance on the National Assessment of Educational Progress comprehension measures show very little change in student outcomes over decades (NAEP, 2022). Even more troubling are the results that showcase opportunity gaps for students from minoritized, socioeconomically disadvantaged, and linguistically diverse communities. Results from the recent NAEP assessments show that two-thirds of all middle-grade students (69%) scored below the Proficient level in reading (NAEP, 2022). The problem is worse for African American and Hispanic middle school students, with 84 and 89%, respectively, reading below the Proficient level. The situation has been persistently dire for many years, with researchers and policymakers describing illiteracy in the United States as a national health crisis with long-term negative impacts that result from inequities in reading competencies (Lyon, 2001; Reardon, 2011, 2013). The lack of student reading proficiency at the national level can be humanized at the individual level by a sixth-grade student from an urban high-poverty school immediately after the COVID-19 pandemic who said, "I hate reading. I have failed English language arts every year in school, and this year will be the same, so you might as well give up on me now."

Researchers and practitioners have sought to solve this comprehension problem by developing and deploying hundreds of solutions. Whole organizations have been formed and dedicated to studying the problem, refining theoretical models of reading, understanding reading difficulties, and conducting strong research to promote evidence-based instruction in classrooms.

One of the interventions developed to improve reading comprehension and featured in the What Works Clearinghouse and other sites is the Intelligent Tutoring System for the Structure Strategy (ITSS). Multiple randomized controlled studies conducted with over 120 classrooms and 32 schools show statistically significant and positive effects favoring elementary and middle-grade classrooms or schools that used the ITSS software as a partial substitute for ELA class time (Wijekumar et al., 2012; 2014, 2017, 2024). In this chapter, we present the journey from the first-generation ITSS to the Knowledge Acquisition and Transformation (KAT) framework, which has produced much-improved results for learners through the dedicated, timely support afforded to teachers implementing ITSS and KAT in their classrooms. We begin with a description of ITSS followed by implementation barriers systematically addressed throughout implementation. Our four solutions focus on: (1) aligning curricula scope and sequence to focus on main ideas, summaries, and inferences; (2) ensuring students are familiarized with assessments; (3) improving teacher and school leader knowledge factors; and (4) developing methods for the sustainability of solutions. The resulting KAT Framework combines ITSS with teacher-led instruction to achieve much stronger impacts on comprehension for K–12 students (Wijekumar et al., in press), while creating long-term solutions for teachers and schools.

DESCRIPTION OF ITSS AND REVIEW OF THE RESEARCH

Comprehension requires readers to read text fluently, select important ideas, connect information logically (e.g., the cause and the effect), and create a gist (i.e., main idea) of longer text to store in long-term memory. Consequently, students who comprehend well use text structures to organize information in memory, create a gist, and integrate this new information with their prior knowledge (Wijekumar, 2019). Compared to successful comprehenders, striving readers engage in knowledge-telling, trying to memorize everything and recall the text verbatim (Meyer, Brandt, & Bluth, 1980). *Memorizing does not work for most texts in ELA and content areas, as it is ineffective and inefficient. In contrast, selecting the most important ideas to save into long-term memory saves fewer ideas and is hierarchically organized, making the memory structure efficient and effective.* Storing the entire document in memory is not possible in longer and more complex texts. Additionally, retrieving the information read becomes problematic when readers have to sift through the entire text to find information for problem-solving or answering questions on a test. In summary, storing the key idea units into a gist or main idea allows for a more efficient and effective organization of memory.

ITSS was designed to present web-based instruction to students in grades 4–8 about using text structures to select important ideas, generate logically connected gists or main ideas, extend main ideas to summaries, and extrapolate inferences to promote coherent representations of text in memory. The first generation of ITSS software (2001 to 2012) focused primarily on a pedagogical agent modeling the identification of signal words, classification of text structures, and writing a main idea statement using text structure sentence stems. Approximately seven to ten lessons focused on comparison, cause and effect, problem and solution, sequence, and description text structures. For example, in a text comparing Presidents Lincoln and Washington, the words *in contrast, similarly,* and *differences* signaled that someone or something is being compared. In cause-and-effect text structure passages, the author may use *led to, because, due to,* and *consequently* to signal the causal relationships between ideas.

Students interacting with ITSS read passages appropriate for their grade level with narrations available for students with decoding challenges. After the passage is read, students are shown how to identify the text structure by finding signaling words or imposing structures when no signals are present in the text. Once the text structure is identified, students learn how to use sentence stems shown in Figure 5.1 to select ideas from the text and generate a main idea statement. Figure 5.1 presents the sentence stems used in the most recent version of ITSS, focusing primarily on higher-order text structures. We now acknowledge that sequence and description text structures are nested inside all texts. However, most of the critical thinking or inference questions rely on students' ability to compare and contrast, solve problems, and see the causal relationships between ideas. This process is the externalized version of the memory structures required for comprehension. Students also learn how to extend the main idea statement to a summary by adding supporting evidence from the text. For example, within the ITSS lessons, the presence of the words *different, in contrast,* and *compared* signaled a comparison text structure; therefore, students were guided to use the main idea sentence stem in Figure 5.1 to summarize the comparison. When applied to the passage about presidents, the following is a sample main idea applying the sentence stem: *Lincoln and Washington were compared on order of presidency, jobs, and children.* The external representation of the main idea was designed to promote the encoding of memory that was hierarchically organized, as shown in Figure 5.2. In Figure 5.2, the more important ideas

CAUSE, PROBLEM, SOLUTION: The cause of the problem is __________. The problem is _____ and the solution is _____.

PROBLEM AND SOLUTION: The problem is _____ and the solution is ______.

CAUSE AND EFFECT: The cause is _____ and the effect is _____.

COMPARISON: ______ and ______ were compared on ______, ______, and ______.

FIGURE 5.1. Main idea sentence stems presented in ITSS and KAT.

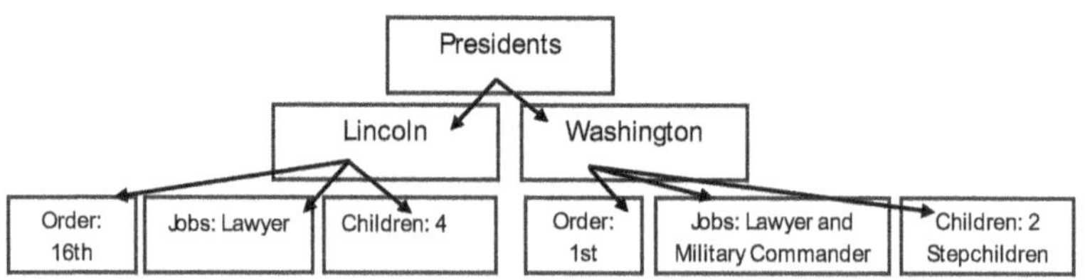

FIGURE 5.2. Externally represented main idea and corollary logically organized memory structure.

are at the top of the memory tree, with details or supporting evidence associated as secondary nodes. This allows readers to have a more efficient, hierarchically, and logically organized memory of text with important information taking precedence over details.

ITSS is student-managed web-based software. Students log in with a username and password and work at their own pace. The system is typically used to supplement ELA classroom instruction for about 40 minutes each week. Teachers allocate approximately 40 minutes weekly within their ELA block of class time. Typically, ELA time is about 70 to 90 minutes daily, and ITSS time is only a small fraction of the time during the week. Students log in to the computer with their username and password under the supervision of the teacher. ITSS is not a full curriculum, and students complete lessons at their own pace. The system provides assistance in Spanish at the word, sentence, and passage levels for English learners. ITSS interactions with students include modeling, practice tasks, assessments, scaffolding, and feedback. In addition, the ITSS program includes instruction about vocabulary and inference to support students' comprehension. The system adjusts subsequent lessons based on student mastery of concepts. The first-generation ITSS was delivered to students with only two hours of professional development for teachers. Teachers can run reports on key indicators of mastering main ideas, signaling words, and summaries to monitor student progress.

The theoretical foundation for ITSS was derived from multiple theoretical models, including the construction–integration (C-I) model (Kintsch, 2005) and the text structure model (Meyer, 1975), with the latter being a more transparent approach to supporting the generation of a coherent mental representation through selecting important ideas and logically connecting them. In the C-I model, comprehension happens through top-down and bottom-up processing of text promoted through summarization and inferencing. In the text structure model, important ideas are selected and encoded using logical text structure connections to form a coherent mental representation of the text. In the applied text structure strategy instructional approach, students encode information as they read, scaffolded by sentence stems that guide the selection of important ideas in the text, connecting the ideas using the sentence stems for writing the main idea statement, and integrating long-term memory as the author intended and signaled. That main idea is then extended to form a summary by associating text evidence to support the important information. Finally, inferences are used to fill in the gaps and unstated information.

Meta-analyses of text structure instruction by Hebert et al. (2016) and Boegards-Hazenberg et al. (2021) present evidence that instructing students at all grade levels about text structures improves comprehension with strong effect sizes on summarization (g = 0.57) and recall (g = 0.37). Studies have shown that the method is useful to young learners (Williams et al., 2014) and older students (Ji et al., 2018; Wijekumar et al., 2017). According to the ITSS WWC Intervention report (2020), ITSS research evidence Meets WWC Group Design Standards without reservations and reports positive and statistically significant effect sizes (ES) and improvement indices (IP) at the upper elementary and middle school grades (i.e., grade 4 (ES = 0.19, IP = +9, and $p < .01$), grade 5 (ES = 0.20, IP = +9, $p < .01$), and grade 7 (ES = 0.18, IP = +9, $p < .01$)). This review focused on whether the research comparison groups were randomly assigned, attrition of participants was within approved numbers, measures were reliable and valid, and the data analyses techniques were appropriate to draw causal conclusions about the research. When these conditions are met and results show positive effects, the WWC reports on the findings in the intervention report. Based on a synthesis of findings from 23 randomized controlled trials that met WWC Group Design Standards, the WWC Practice Guide, "Providing Reading Interventions for Students in Grades 4–9," recommended that teachers, "Routinely use a set of comprehension-building practices to help students make sense of the text" (p. 11) and use text structures to help students learn how to get the gist of text (Vaughn et al., 2022).

These promising results are a good starting point for improving comprehension. However, not all teachers teach students about how to use text structure to understand text. For example, a fourth-grade student participating in the 2012 studies noted that they used a different method to write their main idea statement because their teacher told them to do so. When we inquired about this, we found that the teacher was teaching students to use the first and last sentence of a text to formulate a main idea instead of using text structures to do so. We were told by the teacher that the textbook used that technique and took precedence over the ITSS instruction we had shared with them. Recognizing that teachers are often constrained by the curricula in place, we started a plan to provide stronger professional development to teachers in subsequent studies to support them in integrating ITSS regardless of the program or materials available in their schools.

EVOLUTION FROM ITSS TO THE KAT FRAMEWORK BY OVERCOMING BARRIERS

During the efficacy studies of ITSS in economically challenged schools, the urgency to help all the children comprehend was central to our work. In collaboration with the principal and teachers from one participating school, we uncovered contextual factors that may limit the success of any intervention being deployed in schools. Four critical challenges are described here, along with the techniques we developed to solve them.

IMPLEMENTATION CHALLENGE 1: MISALIGNMENT OF CURRICULA SCOPE AND SEQUENCE

During the 2016 ITSS efficacy study, the team presented a 1-day professional development to teachers and administered pretests to students after the random assignment was completed. Teachers were asked to start implementing the ITSS software once a week for 45 minutes immediately after pretests. The research team monitored student logins to the system and noted that none of the classrooms in one school were using the software. We scheduled a meeting with the principal and teachers to inquire about the lack of login activity on ITSS.

Vignette 1

> During the meeting, teachers and the principal noted that the textbook scope and sequence did not address main ideas until the eighth week of the school year. Teachers stated, "we plan to use ITSS during week 8 when we teach main ideas. We do not see a need to use ITSS when our skill of the week is author's purpose or character traits." Additionally, teachers noted that, "our textbook recommended using text structures for expository texts only and, therefore, ITSS would only be relevant for those texts." Further complicating the situation, teachers reported that, "we use different techniques for summarizing based on the genre of text. For narrative texts, we use an approach called Who, What, When, Where, but, for biographies, we complete a timeline graphic organizer, and, for poetry, we never write a summary or main idea." Teachers referred to the textbook and state standards to justify their rationale.

Our team immediately began a careful review of the entire curriculum, state standards, and professional development content from the five years prior to this study. We also gathered high-stakes assessment data from different states to study patterns of mastery of reading comprehension constructs such as main ideas, summaries, inferences, author's purpose, vocabulary, and so on. Each state has reading standards for elementary grades and presents specific constructs that students must master as part of the grade-level standards. For example, in Texas, fifth-grade students must be able to generate a main idea, summarize a text, and generate inferences. The end-of-year high-stakes assessments measure how well students have mastered these constructs and present data by standard. The teachers and administrators noted that students typically perform poorly on main ideas, summaries, and inferences. We studied the data to corroborate these statements.

As we indicated in a curricular review we conducted that was published in Beerwinkle et al. (2018), high-stakes assessment patterns reveal valuable insights into why children were failing to master comprehension and, more importantly, showcased that the textbooks presented arbitrary spiraling of skills in isolation and the wrong dosage for essential comprehension skills such as main ideas, summaries, and inferences. Being able to determine the main idea is important for generating efficient and effective long-term memory of text and should receive more attention than author's purpose. A reader must attend to the main idea of the passage after reading. This main idea provides a stable foundation and can be leveraged by the reader to extend to inferences, author's purpose, and character traits. This pattern was replicated in reviews of textbooks across the world in a special issue published in 2021 (Peti-Stantić et al., 2021; Wijekumar et al., 2021; Zhang et al., 2021). Problematically, the reviewed textbooks presented each state standard as a skill of the week, and that week was dedicated to one skill. For example, students spent a whole week on author's purpose followed by one week on some other skill. Throughout the year, main ideas were taught twice and author's purpose was taught three times, resulting in not enough time in the instructional approach to master deriving main ideas, resulting in the wrong dosage of addressing essential main idea skills for students.

This "skills-in-isolation" approach also poses another challenge for readers. Each week, students receive changing reasons for reading the text. When the skill of the week was author's purpose, students just read for author's purpose—not for main ideas and summaries leveraged for author's purpose. During the subsequent week, students read for character traits—again, not leveraging the main idea to generate character traits. As teachers had pointed out, the textbooks covered skill after skill and never engaged students in integrating multiple skills, such as determining the author's purpose, identifying character traits, and deriving the main idea or summarizing. Teachers agreed that this revolving door for the purpose of reading likely confuses students and does not allow students the time and opportunity to master essential skills. This skills deficit is highly correlated to failing the high-stakes assessment (Stevens et al., 2022).

We shared our review of curricula, assessments, and standards with practitioners. The team agreed that presenting main ideas, summaries, and inferences for all texts read was likely to improve comprehension, and we needed a solution that would help facilitate instruction because the textbook did not provide any strategies or time to teach main ideas prior to week eight. Our solution was to create an instructional guide for teachers for each textbook passage to assist in delivering instruction with fidelity. It was also agreed that this instruction must be efficient and concise so as not to interfere with the skill of the week in the textbook. The KAT Comprehension Lesson Guide shown in Figure 5.3 was developed in collaboration with the teachers, and instructional delivery was practiced and timed to ensure a 15–20-minute segment.

The KAT instructional routine helps teachers overcome the challenge of using the textbook, which focuses on one skill at a time, by proposing a six-step, teacher-led KAT lesson on vocabulary, main idea, summary, and inference in every English, science, and social studies classroom reading for 15–20 minutes each day. The method is meant to be applied in every genre of text (e.g., poetry, biography, narrative, expository). After the main idea and summary foundation are established, the students continue with the textbook's skills of the week. Often, the main idea is leveraged to understand or infer author's purpose, character traits, and genre study. Completing a main idea for all texts supports students in creating strong memories of texts across genres. We created a searchable library of online resources called the KAT-MOOV-Library and stored these KAT guides for teacher use on the *literacy.io* website. The library has over 5,000 KAT guides, videos, and activities in English and Spanish. There are KAT guides for every lesson from 12 textbook series used in partner schools (e.g., HMH, Journeys, CKLA, Wit and Wisdom). Teachers using any of these textbooks can download the KAT guide to accompany all their lessons for each week to deliver instruction with fidelity.

For this intervention, KAT provided teacher-led instruction that aligned the curricula and scope and sequence of the state ELA standards and ITSS software was used to provide individualized instruction to students. The instructional guides used in the intervention frame the implementation of the six steps: (1) introducing vocabulary; (2) identifying or imposing the top-level structure of the text as cause and effect, problem and solution, or comparison; (3) selecting important ideas using the text structure as a guide (e.g., Effect—What happened? Cause—Why did it happen?); (4) writing the main idea; (5) extending the main idea to a summary by adding supporting text evidence; and (6) extrapolating inferences (e.g., how did the character feel about what happened?). The rationale for each step is presented in Figure 5.4. Once a week, teachers continued to use the ITSS software to deliver additional individualized instruction to each learner. The integration of the KAT guide with the ITSS delivery promoted the regular use of the software and allowed teachers to regularly review progress of student mastery of main idea and summarization skills. Furthermore, the teachers learned how to teach main ideas, summaries, and inferences with all texts regardless of genre and skill of the week prescribed by the textbook.

KAT + READING COMPREHENSION INSTRUCTIONAL GUIDE This page must be completed for every text students read.
Story/Article/Chapter: NewsELA Article—Armyworms threaten Africa's fragile food supply. *https://newsela.com/view/ck9noof6303mt0iqjh7t0b6e7*
Text Structure(s): (*Identify if cause and effect, problem and solution, or comparison text structures organize the text.*) Cause, Problem, Solution
Introduction Make sure to introduce text structure as you introduce the reading without explicitly stating text structure.
Food is necessary for survival, but today we will read about a serious problem with the food supply in Africa caused by an invasive species: the armyworm. Listen to see if you can identify any possible solutions to the armyworm's destructive presence as we read.
Vocabulary Identify important, useful, or difficult words that are essential to comprehension.
Vocabulary words: (***Bold*** *the words you plan to teach BEFORE the lesson.*) **Coordinate, agriculture, pesticide, trench**
Signaling words: (*Identify words or phrases that clue the reader to the text structure and key ideas.*) danger, destroying, to lose, cause, damaged, affected, threat, defeat
Main Idea Use the higher-order sentence stems to generate a main idea statement.
Overall main idea for the whole passage: (*Use sentence stems: For example, for cause and effect, use: The cause is ____ and the effect is ____.*) The cause is that the fall armyworm from the Americas is in Africa. The problem is the fall armyworms eat important food sources for people in Africa and are spreading quickly. The first solution is pesticides, but the worms have some resistance to them. Other solutions are to dig a ditch around farms, bring in birds, or burn crops.

(continued)

FIGURE 5.3. Sample KAT Lesson Guide.

Multiple-choice question practice: (*Create a multiple-choice question asking students to select the best main idea. Put the answer in italics.*) What is the best main idea of the selection? A. *Armyworms are eating food crops in parts of Africa and experts are trying to stop the insects from destroying farms.* B. Armyworms came to Africa on plants sent from South America and are quickly spreading. C. Farmers are digging ditches to prevent the armyworms from getting to their farms. D. Armyworms do not like cold weather and, as a result, move to Africa.
Summary Make sure to extend the main idea by including details supporting each part. For example, for cause, problem, and solution write your added details in blue.
Summary for the whole section: The cause is that the fall or armyworm came from the Americas on either flights or plants to Africa. The problem is the fall armyworms eat important food sources for people in Africa, such as corn, soybeans, and potatoes, and are spreading quickly. The first solution is pesticides, but the worms developed resistance to the poisons when they lived in the Americas. Other solutions are to dig a ditch around farms, bring in birds, or burn crops.
Multiple-choice question practice: (*Create a multiple-choice question asking students to select the best main idea. Put the answer in italics.*) What is the best summary of the selection? A. *Armyworms came to southern Africa and are eating important food crops. People in southern Africa have limited food, and the armyworms are making it worse. Experts are trying to figure out how to stop the worms.* B. An emergency United Nations meeting was held to discuss the fall army-worm problem. The insect has caused damage to crops in Zambia, Zimbabwe, and Ghana. These countries have lost all of their food. Pesticides do not always work on these insects. C. The fall armyworm is a caterpillar that becomes the armyworm moth after the caterpillar stage. During the fall, the army worm moves to warmer climates. It is from the Americas. The armyworm eats corn, rice, soybeans, and other crops as a caterpillar. D. Armyworms are eating crops in western Africa. The bugs have developed a resistance to pesticides, so experts need their need other ideas. Digging trenches around farms and bringing birds to eat the worms are both possibilities. Governments in Africa are working with farmers to get rid of the worms.

(continued)

FIGURE 5.3. *(continued)*

Inference Create inference questions that ask the students to infer by examining the evidence to support their reasoning
Inference questions: (*Include both open-ended and multiple choice questions.*) **Open-ended:** (*What is the most likely reason the author included ____? The author wrote the article mainly to ____. Why did the author include ____ in the passage?*) What can the reader infer about when the fall armyworm is a threat? **Multiple-choice:** (*For example, the reader can conclude from paragraph X that____. What is the most likely reason that ?* ***Based on the selection, how do*** *most likely feel about____?*) Which sentence best shows that the armyworms present a problem to the people in Africa? A. *On Tuesday, experts from around the world met for emergency United Nations talks in Harare, the capital of Zimbabwe.* B. The armyworm is destroying that food that Africans cannot afford to lose. C. Reports say Malawi, Mozambique, and Namibia are also affected. D. The first armyworms were seen in Nigeria and Togo last year. **Multiple-choice vocabulary inference:** (*For example, which words in paragraph X help the reader understand the meaning of X? Which meaning of X is used in paragraph X?*) Which definition best fits how security is used in the last?

FIGURE 5.3. *(continued)*

IMPLEMENTATION CHALLENGE 2: HIGH- AND LOW-STAKES ASSESSMENTS POSE CHALLENGES FOR MOST CHILDREN

After the teams agreed to use the KAT guides daily and the implementation was proceeding as intended, we hit another snag. The first benchmark administered by the school, at the 12th week of school, showed that most students continued to underperform on the main idea and summary questions on the test. Teachers were noticeably upset that many students who could write the main idea independently could not showcase their knowledge on the test.

KAT Steps	Example	Rationale	Practical Application
1. Preteach important vocabulary	Meaning and morphology for word DECLINE	Explicit vocabulary instruction yields gains in comprehension	Essential for Special Ed, English Learners, and Striving Readers
2. Read the text (Silent or Aloud)	Silent reading or read aloud	Processing text-based information helps develop a coherent mental representation	Read aloud for students with decoding problems like dyslexia (or young students)
3. Identify the top-level text structure of a passage	Clue words and decision tree to identify text structure	Situation model and top-down processing of text to find important ideas	Most children are unable to find important ideas when reading. This focuses attention
4. Generate a main idea using cause/effect, problem/solution, or text structure comparison	Use text structure sentence stems: "The cause is ____ and the effect is_____."	Create a node in long-term memory using the gist with logical connections and associations between the important ideas.	Text structure sentence stems provide a logical approach to selecting important ideas and connecting them in memory
5. Extend the main idea to form a summary	The cause is ___ [add text evidence for cause]. The effect is___ [add text evidence for effect].	Associate added evidence from the text to expand on the gist node and imprint in long-term memory.	Showing children how the main idea and summary are closely related
6. Extrapolate inferences & extend knowledge	Identify why the author wrote passage (*i.e., author's purpose*)	Fill gaps in knowledge by inferring beyond the stated information in the text	Engage students with locally and culturally relevant inferences to promote utility value

FIGURE 5.4. KAT Framework and ITSS steps and rationale.

Vignette 2

Another meeting was arranged to review the benchmark test and the questions to identify possible causes for this new problem. As each question was reviewed, teachers started explaining that the academic language on the test was causing the students to misunderstand the questions. Teacher A noted, "in class, I just ask them to write a main idea. On the test, there is all this fancy academic language that confuses the kids. For example, the test is written

> as, 'Based on the selection you just read, what are likely the key ideas?' My students get really confused when they use the word selection and key ideas in the test." Furthermore, they noted that for the main idea and summary questions, all the multiple-choice answer choices were plausible and accurate, but one was the more correct answer. Teacher A again, "all the answer choices have correct information from the passage. Most of my kids pick the first answer they come across because it has information from the passage." Students chose the answer without attending to whether the answer choice was the main idea or not.

To solve the testing problems that students faced, the teams agreed to add multiple-choice versions of each main idea and summary question to the KAT guide so that teachers could regularly model how test questions are posed and answered. Additionally, the research team reviewed hundreds of sample test questions to compile a list of possible academic vocabulary used to present the questions to familiarize students with the language. Consequently, we requested that teachers model main idea and summary writing with text structure followed by answering multiple-choice questions with text structure-based explanations for how the correct answer was selected. The research team populated each KAT guide with multiple-choice questions that used a variety of academic language stems to help students understand the many different variations on the main idea and summary questions. See samples we created in video format at the following link: *https://it.literacy.io/TeacherLibrary/Files/ViewPublicFile/ae0b314a-d576-4843-b4c0-d4f6768ce7bc*. During the second benchmark, students improved from a mean of 17% on the main idea and summary scores to over 65%. By the third and all subsequent benchmarks, students were all at 90% on the main idea and summary questions.

IMPLEMENTATION CHALLENGE 3: NOT ALL TEACHERS AND ADMINISTRATORS HAVE THE REQUIRED BACKGROUND KNOWLEDGE ABOUT COMPREHENSION

During the 2016 study, we conducted biweekly classroom observations to document adherence fidelity and met with teachers in grade-level professional learning communities (PLCs) facilitated by the principal. Two important results emerged from the classroom observations and were verified during the PLC meetings. First, teachers implemented the KAT guide and used the text structure sentence stems to generate main ideas in the classroom. However, they also followed that instruction with whatever strategy and resources were presented in the textbook. Consequently, students were receiving contradicting instructions on how to generate main ideas. They used the text structure sentence stems during the first 15–20 minutes. During the last segment of the ELA time, they were instructed to use strategies such as reading the text again, using beginning-middle-end to write a summary, and reviewing details to find a main idea. During some observations, we noted that additional strategies, such as hashtagging the main idea, were used to generate main ideas. The team knew it was critical that we meet and discuss our observations with the teachers.

Vignette 3

> Teachers felt pressured by the administrators to follow the curriculum purchased. Teacher B said, "my principal stopped by for an observation and asked me why I was teaching main idea and summary when the scope and sequence of the textbook showed the skill of the week to be character traits." Discussions with the principals showed that they did not understand the KAT Framework deeply enough to jettison previous or textbook strategies from their instructional routines. Another teacher said, "well, I teach the main idea using the KAT Framework, but summaries are different, and I use the beginning-middle-end strategy for that." Teachers and administrators were misled by the curriculum that separated the main idea and summaries as separate skills of the week and also presented different strategies for each text by genre (e.g., expository, narrative, poetry). Teacher B noted that narratives were summarized using who, what, when, where. When the genre was poetry, students were asked to focus on author's purpose, but it was not tied to a main idea. Biographies were taught by memorizing dates as a sequence of events, not why the biography was written.

After thoroughly examining the instructional resources, our team discovered that for teachers who faithfully followed the textbook, there were many contradictions to the KAT Framework (i.e., main idea and summary) in the variety of graphic organizers available to teach main idea and a lack of information about how to teach students to accurately and concisely summarize texts. We discovered through professional learning community (PLC) meetings that many teachers were reluctant to veer too far from the district-adopted textbook because district mandates required that teachers use the resources provided. It became apparent to the team that building a professional development experience for teachers, unlike any they had attended previously, was an essential next step. To change teacher practice, we knew this constituted compiling evidence and examples to demonstrate why it was so important that they release the ineffective practices they had used in the past to ensure future success for their students.

We also noted that teacher adoption of the KAT Framework varied. The data showed that teachers' years of experience, degrees, and preferences did not predict their enthusiasm for adopting the framework. The team agreed that teachers' variations in content and pedagogical knowledge appeared to influence their implementation. In recent research studies, we administered a survey of content and pedagogical knowledge to all practitioners. Recent studies by Hudson et al. (2023), Rice et al. (2024), and Stack et al. (2024) present evidence about teacher and administrator content and pedagogical knowledge, along with results from teacher practice-based professional development (PBPD; Ball & Cohen, 1999; Desimone, 2009). Teachers in all three studies had limited background knowledge about comprehension and strategies prior to the professional development.

Consequently, we reformulated our plans for PBPD, revised activities for future PLC meetings, and reviewed our fidelity observation instrument. We customized the PBPD with local materials and resources to promote implementation fidelity, eliminate contradictions, and encourage teacher autonomy in instruction. The KAT PBPD is rooted in social cognitive theories that stress the importance of meaningful learning in situated contexts (Grossman et al., 2009). This revised PBPD focused on lots of practice for the teachers and administrators, used the local curricula materials, and specifically discussed eliminating unproven and contradicting strategies. Previous PBPD sessions only presented the KAT Framework guidelines without noting the contradictions and their role in diminishing the positive impacts. We also required the principals to attend the PBPD so that they were able to support the KAT Framework implementation. Finally, we opted to measure teacher knowledge about comprehension strategies and pedagogy to inform and frame PBPD session content. The revised PBPD for KAT was two days with a focus on the following:

- Reviewing the causes for reading comprehension problems with data from the local schools
- Modeling planning and lesson delivery using the KAT Framework
- Reflections and reviews of teachers comparing this method to their previous instructional routines
- Planning and delivering locally relevant KAT lessons using the school's textbook passages, guided by expert teacher ambassadors. Teacher ambassadors were identified from previous research studies. Teachers using the text structures with fidelity were invited to serve as ambassadors

- Practicing using KAT with poetry, biography, narrative, and expository texts
- Reviewing and contrasting the KAT Framework with the textbook and other non-evidence-based strategies. Reminders to eliminate contradictions to main idea and summary instruction. We shared the results from previous research studies and videotaped observations of classrooms where students follow the KAT Framework with fidelity. We then showed a video of what happens when contradictions are introduced, causing confusion for the students.
- Studying student benchmark scores and ITSS progress monitoring to provide small-group or one-on-one instruction for students who need additional practice.

The KAT PBPD focuses on promoting equity in teacher access to requisite content and pedagogical knowledge so that teachers know how to promote students' prerequisite skills, stay consistent with the KAT Framework, review benchmark scores, and utilize technologies effectively to achieve the best results. Via the KAT PBPD, teachers learn why it is important to maintain fidelity to the KAT Framework and reduce contradictions that likely overburden students with too many different strategies.

We conducted research to study this new model. In recent randomized controlled studies on the effectiveness of this revised PBPD, we found impressive positive results favoring the intervention teachers who completed it (Hudson et al., 2023). Students in classrooms led by more knowledgeable teachers performed better on standardized and researcher-designed measures of comprehension. Further analysis of data after one year of implementation showed even stronger content and pedagogical knowledge for teachers (Rice et al., 2024).

IMPLEMENTATION CHALLENGE 4: LONG-TERM SUSTAINABILITY OF CHANGE WITH KAT AND ITSS

For long-term sustainability, there needs to be a system for supporting teachers, monitoring progress, and maintaining new practices. It was important to consider how KAT with ITSS enables sustainability. First, the KAT PBPD promotes implementation with the two-day PBPD, which utilizes large and small group instruction supported by expert trainers and teacher ambassadors. PBPD embodies six essential characteristics of quality professional development: (1) collective participation of teachers from the same school or school district; (2) grounding

PBPD around the characteristics, strengths, and needs of students in the teachers' current classrooms; (3) devoting attention to the content and pedagogical content knowledge of teachers; (4) providing opportunities for active learning and practice (e.g., teachers view modeling videos, practice delivering instruction, reflect on their teaching, and receive scaffolded feedback from expert group leaders); (5) using the same materials during PBPD that will be used in the classrooms (e.g., curricula and textbook review to align instructional practices to KAT); and (6) offering feedback on performance while learning so that understandings and skills critical for implementation are developed in the classroom. Second, we schedule bimonthly meetings with teachers and support staff at all schools involved in the research study to answer questions about implementation and gauge progress. Third, we provide as-needed virtual (e.g., using SWIVL webcams) and face-to-face co-teaching opportunities throughout the school year (Ball & Cohen, 1999; Garet et al., 2001). Fourth, we offer a crowd-sourced teacher resource library, which contains over 5,500 resources for teachers to search and find easily. The KAT-MOOV 360 platform continuously facilitates and curates an online practitioner learning community with evidence-based resources shared with a national and international audience. The resource library also contains videos of the PBPD to support teachers who may want to review the materials and view model instructional routines. These resources are available in English and Spanish. Monthly newsletters are mailed through the system to share updates and support for teachers.

Finally, we created an observation tool that can be used to measure specific elements of comprehension and vocabulary instruction, including main idea (using text structure or not), summarization, and inferencing. The administrators involved in the implementation are trained to use the tool in classroom observations, which provides opportunities to share glows and grows with the teachers they observe. As an example, the KAT Framework is built on identifying and using the text structure to determine the main idea of the text. During PD, teachers are shown how to hint at the text structure when introducing a text instead of explicitly stating the text structure prior to reading the text. The goal is for students to listen for discourse markers while reading in order to determine the text structure so they have the skills to transfer this process to independent reading. When a teacher hints at the text structure in the introduction of the lesson, we would give them a glow on the feedback form. If a teacher explicitly states the text structure of the text before students have had an opportunity to formulate their own ideas, we encourage teachers through feedback around the reason for this introduction of the text. The intention is that this feedback will help the teacher grow in their practice.

Vignette 4

> Prior to a scheduled meeting with a group of principals, we requested that they spend time in the ELA teachers' classrooms and take note of the instructional practices they observed in observations. Mr. Jameson, principal at a school in their first year of KAT implementation, was eager to share, "I have never had a great tool to help me when visiting classrooms during reading instruction. I figured that if the students were reading and could answer a few questions I asked, they were doing just fine. When I learned how to use the KAT Observation Fidelity Tool, I realized how I could give specific feedback to teachers about areas where their instruction was glowing, as well as suggestions regarding areas where growth was needed. I also never knew how many non-evidence-based comprehension strategies that were being used in the textbook could actually cause more confusion for students than help them to make logical connections between events in the texts they were reading."

Additionally, our KAT Observation Fidelity Tool is also used to parse out potential contradictions to this evidence-based practice and offer opportunities for intentional conversations with teachers. These conversations may take place with an instructional coach, colleague, or administrator. The KAT PLC meeting agendas were updated with goals to reflect on implementation, student outcomes, and practice for the upcoming week. School district leadership has proven critical to the implementation success and long-term sustainability of the KAT Framework and ITSS.

CONCLUSION

The KAT Framework and associated supports were carefully designed and refined to solve the long-standing and vexing problem of reading comprehension challenges for elementary students. Four of the key strategies that have proven successful include the approach to data gathering and onboarding, reviewing data to inform implementation, and aligning curricula, assessments, and teacher and school leader knowledge factors. The curricula alignment using our KAT guide focusing on essential main idea, summarization, and inferencing skills helps provide consistent and transparent scaffolding for students. Ensuring students understand the assessments helped them with their academic vocabulary surrounding testing. Addressing teacher and school leader knowledge and practices round out supports for achieving high adherence fidelity to the intervention in the classroom. Using the KAT Framework and associated supports can be useful for building reading comprehension in other domains and grade levels as well.

Reflection Questions

1. What evidence-based practices can teachers use to support students in learning how to use text structure to help them comprehend?
2. What challenges might teachers face in trying to implement text structure instruction and how can they overcome these challenges?
3. How do you use text structures, main ideas, summaries, and inferences in your classroom?

REFERENCES

Ball, D., & Cohen, D. (1999). Developing practice, developing practitioners: Toward a practice-based theory of professional education. In L. Darling-Hammond & G. Sykes (Eds.), *Teaching as the learning profession* (pp. 3–32). Wiley.

Beerwinkle, A., Wijekumar, K., Walpole, S., & Aguis, R. (2018). An analysis of the ecological components within a text structure intervention. *Reading and Writing: An Interdisciplinary Journal, 31*(9), 2041–2064.

Boegards-Hazenberg, S. T. M., Evers-Vermeul, J., & van den Bergh, H. (2021). A meta-analysis on the effects of text structure instruction on reading comprehension in the upper elementary grades. *Reading Research Quarterly, 56*(3), 435–462..

Bonnie J. F. Meyer, Brandt, D. M., & Bluth, G. J. (1980). Use of top-level structure in text: Key for reading comprehension of ninth-grade students. *Reading Research Quarterly, 16*(1), 72–103.

Desimone, L. M. (2009). Improving impact studies of teachers' professional development: Toward better conceptualizations and measures. *Educational Researcher, 38*(3), 181–199.

Garet, M. S., Porter, A. C., Desimone, L., Birman, B. F., & Yoon, K. S. (2001). What makes professional development effective? Results from a national sample of teachers. *American Educational Research Journal, 38*(4), 915–945.

Grossman, P., Hammerness, K., & McDonald, M. (2009). Redefining teaching, re-imagining teacher education. *Teachers and Teaching: Theory and Practice, 15*(2), 273–289.

Hebert, M., Bohaty, J. J., Nelson, J. R., & Brown, J. (2016). The effects of text structure instruction on expository reading comprehension: A meta-analysis. *Journal of Educational Psychology, 108*(5), 609–629.

Hudson, A. K., Lambright, K., Zhang, S., Wijekumar, K., Owens, J., & McKeown, D. (2023). Professional development in a pandemic: Transforming teacher knowledge of reading comprehension instruction. *Educational Technology Research and Development, 71*(4), 1–27.

Ji, X. R., Beerwinkle, A., & Wijekumar, K. (2018). Using latent transition analysis to identify effects of an intelligent tutoring system on reading comprehension of seventh-grade students. *Reading and Writing, 31*, 2095–2113.

Kintsch, W. (2005). An overview of top-down and bottom-up effects in comprehension: The construction-integration perspective. *Discourse Processes, 39*(3), 125–126.

Lyon, G. R. (2001). *Measuring success: Using assessments and accountability to raise student achievement.* Hearing before House Committee on Education and the workforce, subcommittee on Education Reform, 107th Congress. *www.nrrf.org/learning/statement-of-dr-g-reid-lyon-before-the-u-s-house-subcommittee-on-education-and-the-workforce-hearing*

Meyer, B. J. F. (1975). *The organization of prose and its effects on memory.* North-Holland.

National Assessment of Educational Progress. (2022). *www.nationsreportcard.gov/highlights/reading/2022/*

Perfetti, C., & Stafura, J. (2014). Word knowledge in a theory of reading comprehension. *Scientific Studies of Reading, 18*(1), 22–37.

Peti-Stantić, A., Keresteš, G., & Gnjidić, V. (2021). Can textbook analysis help us understand why Croatian students seldom read their textbooks?. *Technology, Knowledge and Learning, 26*(2), 293–310.

Reardon, S. F. (2011). The widening academic achievement gap between the rich and the poor: New evidence and possible explanations. In G. J. Duncan & R. J. Murnane (Eds.), *Whither opportunity? Rising inequality, schools, and children's life chances* (pp. 91–116). Russell Sage Foundation and Spencer Foundation.

Reardon, S. F. (2013). The widening income achievement gap. *Educational Leadership, 70,* 10–16.

Rice, M., Lambright, K., & Wijekumar, K. (kay). (2024). Professional development in reading comprehension: A meta-analysis of the effects on teachers and students. *Reading Research Quarterly, 59*(3), 424–447.

Scarborough, H. S. (2001). Connection early language and literacy to later reading (dis) abilities: Evidence, theory, and practice. In S. B. Neuman & D. K. Dickinson (Eds.), *Handbook of early literacy research* (pp. 97–110). Guilford Press.

Stack, A., Wijekumar, K., & Rice, M. (2024). School leader knowledge and practices: Results from a randomized controlled trial. Manuscript Submitted for Review.

Stevens, E. A., Murray, C. S., Scammacca, N., Haager, D., & Vaughn, S. (2022). Middle school matters: Examining the effects of a schoolwide professional development model to improve reading comprehension. *Reading and Writing, 35*(8), 1839–1864.

Vaughn, S., Gersten, R., Dimino, J., Taylor, M. J., Newman-Gonchar, R., Krowka, S., et al. (2022). Providing reading interventions for students in grades 4–9 (WWC 2022007). National Center for Education Evaluation and Regional Assistance (NCEE), Institute of Education Sciences, U.S. Department of Education. *https://whatworks.ed.gov*

Wijekumar, K., Beerwinkle, A., Harris, K. R., & Graham, S. (2019). Etiology of teacher knowledge and instructional skills for literacy at the upper elementary grades. *Annals of Dyslexia, 69*(1), 5–20.

Wijekumar, K. K., Lei, P., Rice, M., Beerwinkle, A., Zhang, S., & Meyer, B. J. (2024). A web-based intelligent tutoring system for reading comprehension delivered to fifth-grade students attending high-poverty schools: Results from a replication efficacy study. *Journal of Educational Psychology, 116*(8), 1333–1351.

Wijekumar, K., Meyer, B. J. F., & Lei, P. (2012). Large-scale randomized controlled trial with 4th graders using intelligent tutoring of the structure strategy to improve nonfiction reading comprehension. *Journal of Educational Technology Research and Development, 60,* 987–1013.

Wijekumar, K., Meyer, B. J., Lei, P. W., Lin, Y. C., Johnson, L. A., Spielvogel, J. A., et al. (2014). Multisite randomized controlled trial examining intelligent tutoring of structure strategy for fifth-grade readers. *Journal of Research on Educational Effectiveness, 7*(4), 331–357.

Wijekumar, K. (K.), Meyer, B. J. F., & Lei, P. (2017). Web-based text structure strategy instruction improves seventh graders' content area reading comprehension. *Journal of Educational Psychology, 109*(6), 741–760.

Wijekumar, K., Zhang, S., Peti-Stantic, A., Joshi, R.M. (2021). Why textbooks matter: A global review of reading textbooks. *Technology, Knowledge and Learning.*

Williams, J. P., Pollini, S., Nubla-Kung, A. M., Snyder, A. E., Garcia, A., Ordynans, J. G., & Atkins, J. G. (2014). An intervention to improve comprehension of cause/effect through expository text structure instruction. *Journal of Educational Psychology, 106*(1), 1–17.

Zhang, S., Wijekumar, K. (kay), & Han, B. (2021). An analysis of grade 4 reading textbooks used in mainland China: Do the texts and activities support higher order reading comprehension skills? *Technology Knowledge and Learning,* 26(2), 251–291.

6

Best Practices for Supporting Motivation during Reading Comprehension Instruction

Eunsoo Cho, Sarah Reiley, and Philip Capin

Guiding Questions

1. What is reading motivation? What are the key factors that contribute to intrinsic motivation in reading?
2. Why is it essential for teachers to consider motivation when designing reading comprehension instruction?
3. How can teachers integrate motivational practices to enhance students' engagement and reading comprehension?

Mrs. Davis has dedicated herself to enhancing reading comprehension of her fifth-grade students. Over the past two years, she read a book focused on supporting reading comprehension, listened to podcasts, and carefully reviewed a practice guide published by the What Works Clearinghouse on the topic. This learning journey transformed her teaching. Rather than simply asking literal questions to check for student understanding of the text, she now teaches comprehension strategies and poses deeper, thought-provoking questions. As a result, she sees her students are more engaged in her classroom. Despite these improvements, Mrs. Davis observes that some students continue to remain disengaged during reading instruction. Some still complain that reading is "too boring" or "too hard" or dismiss it with "I'm not a reading person," avoiding eye contact, staring out the window, or giggling with their classmates. Others seem overly focused on racing through texts, getting the "right" answers, or trying to dominate the peer discussion without truly engaging with the material or seeking deeper meaning. While some colleagues attribute this challenge to a lack of student motivation, Mrs. Davis feels uncomfortable with this sentiment. She firmly believes that every child wants to succeed and is convinced that she can play a role in motivating her students. However, she is unsure of the next steps to take to engage every student in the reading process more fully.

This challenge is all too familiar to many teachers, as research highlights that student disengagement is a pervasive issue, exacerbated by the impact of the pandemic (National Association of State Boards of Education, 2021). While teachers recognize the critical role of reading motivation in developing comprehension skills, their beliefs about motivation—what it is and whether it is malleable—directly influence their willingness to invest effort in fostering it (Hardre & Hennessey, 2013). Also, many teachers often feel uncertain about how to cultivate a love of reading in their students (Gambrell, 1996). Motivating disengaged students is one of the most challenging tasks teachers face.

We begin this chapter by emphasizing that motivation is not a fixed trait but a dynamic construct that can be cultivated through intentional, research-based instructional practices. Numerous factors influence students' motivation to read, including their interest in and background knowledge of the topic, their purpose for reading, and their sense of competence. Moreover, motivation does not develop in isolation; it is shaped by contextual influences such as familial support, a classroom environment that fosters autonomy and belongingness, and the degree to which reading materials reflect a child's culture and experiences. These factors collectively determine the energy a student brings to a reading task (Eccles & Wigfield, 2020; Cartwright & Duke, 2019). Shifting this perspective is an essential first step toward creating a classroom that fosters motivation. To do so effectively, teachers need a framework for understanding the complexities of motivation and the practical tools to address the diverse motivational needs of their students. Unfortunately, teacher preparation programs and professional development opportunities often overlook the psychological foundations of motivation and the importance of integrating motivational practices into reading comprehension instruction (Pressley, 2006). This chapter aims to bridge that gap by presenting a research-based framework for understanding reading motivation, describing research-based strategies that support intrinsic reading motivation, and highlighting studies that apply motivational principles to reading comprehension instruction. Finally, we illustrate how teachers can enact the principles of motivational reading comprehension instruction.

FRAMEWORK FOR UNDERSTANDING READING MOTIVATION

What Is Reading Motivation?

Reading motivation refers to the desire to engage in reading (Deci & Ryan, 2001; Guthrie & Humenick, 2004; Eccles & Wigfield, 2002). To further elaborate on the definition of reading motivation, we draw on an analogy from Cartwright and Duke (2019), who compare reading to driving. In this model, texts represent the roads, while readers act as drivers, driving the car and navigating their journey. Motivation serves as both the ignition and the fuel for driving—essential for starting the reading process and sustaining engagement for comprehension.

Students enter the classroom with varying levels of fuel. Some arrive with a full tank, ready to sustain their motivation, while others may be running on empty from the start. Even when students have sufficient motivation to read, their reasons for doing so can differ. Some are intrinsically motivated, driven by curiosity and a love of reading, while others are more influenced by extrinsic factors, such as grades, recognition, or tangible rewards like screen time or extra recess. These varying motivations shape students' cognitive engagement, persistence, and emotional experiences with reading, ultimately leading them down different paths (Cho et al., 2023). Thus, motivation is the driving force that initiates, sustains, and supports students' engagement and comprehension in the reading process.

Motivation isn't something students have or do not have. Instead, motivation exists on a continuum, reflecting varying degrees of autonomy in the reasons students engage in reading (Deci & Ryan, 2001). As illustrated in Figure 6.1,

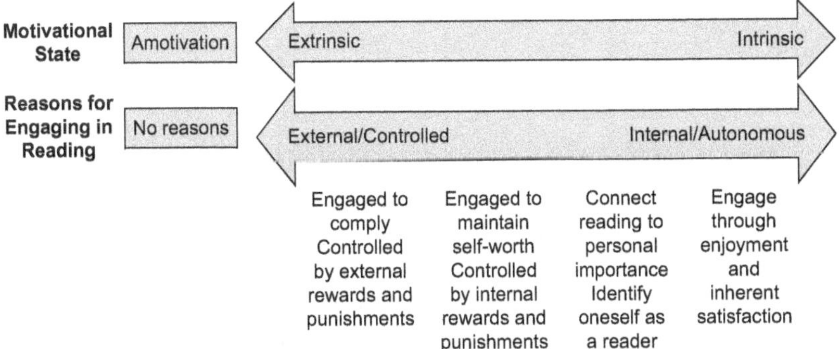

FIGURE 6.1. Continuum of motivation.

students' motivation can range from amotivation to externally regulated states (extrinsic motivation) and, ultimately, to highly internalized, self-regulated motivation (intrinsic motivation). At one end of the continuum is amotivation, where students do not engage in reading at all. This often occurs when students feel incompetent, disengaged, or do not see value in the reading activities presented in class. In response, teachers may rely on consequence-based strategies, such as rewards (e.g., extra recess) or punishments (e.g., reprimanding), to promote compliance. While these approaches can improve on-task behavior, they rarely foster genuine interest or sustained reading engagement because they stem from external pressures and restrict students' sense of autonomy. Extrinsic motivation, however, is not limited to external rewards and punishments. Students may also read to achieve good grades, complete homework, outperform peers, or gain approval from teachers, parents, or peers. In these cases, motivation is primarily driven by feelings of pride, guilt, or anxiety rather than genuine enjoyment of reading. As a result, this form of motivation emphasizes performance and seeking recognition from others over authentic engagement, making it less likely to cultivate a lasting love of reading.

As students progress along the continuum, they may begin to internalize the value of reading, developing a positive self-concept as readers and becoming more autonomous in their reasons for engaging with texts. This autonomy can lead to the most intrinsic forms of motivation, where students read for the joy of reading itself or out of personal interest in a topic. When students develop intrinsic motivation, they become engaged readers. Engaged readers are strategic and purposeful, actively seeking to understand and connect with texts (cognitive engagement), on-task, and have the stamina to persist (behavioral engagement). They also derive enjoyment and satisfaction from reading (emotional engagement), which ultimately supports their reading comprehension (Wigfield & Guthrie, 2000; see Figure 6.2).

WHY IS INTRINSIC READING MOTIVATION IMPORTANT?

Reading comprehension requires students to construct a mental model of the situation described in the text. This process begins with engagement at the word and phrase levels, where students develop a text-based understanding that is then integrated with their existing knowledge to form a coherent mental representation (Kintsch, 1994; van den Broek et al., 1999). Rather than passively receiving information, students actively draw on memory, make inferences, and continuously update their mental models as they read. This goal-directed process demands not

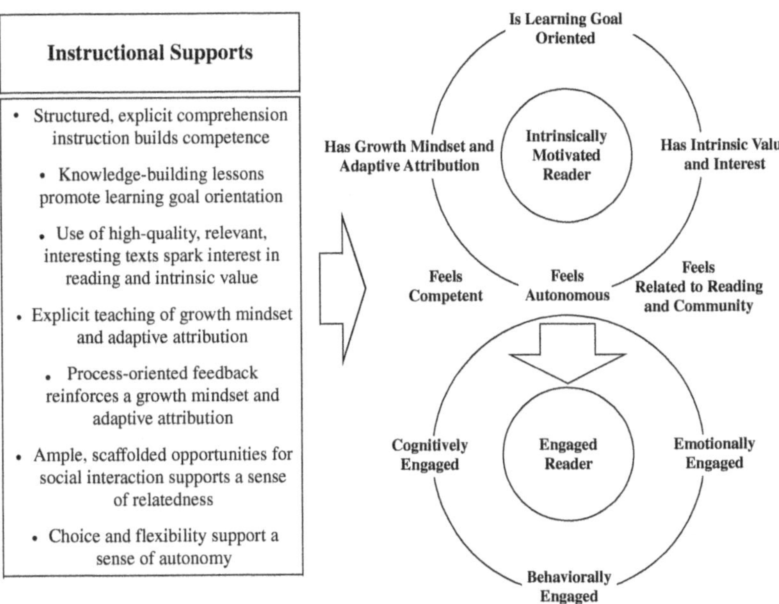

FIGURE 6.2. Intrinsically motivated and engaged reader and instructional practices that support intrinsic motivation.

only cognitive effort but also a willingness to engage deeply with the text (Wigfield et al., 2016).

Several prominent models of reading, such as the Simple View of Reading (Gough & Tunmer, 1986) and the reading rope model (Scarborough, 2001), identify the skills essential for comprehension in two broad domains: word reading and linguistic comprehension. More recent frameworks explicitly integrate motivation as a foundational component. For instance, the active view of reading (Duke & Cartwright, 2021) highlights reading as an active, multifaceted process in which motivation interacts with cognitive and linguistic factors to support comprehension.

Motivation plays a crucial role in shaping students' reading engagement, influencing the depth of their cognitive involvement, their persistence with reading tasks, and their emotional experiences with reading (see Figure 6.2). By definition, intrinsically motivated readers derive greater joy and enjoyment from reading, which, in turn, enhances their cognitive engagement with texts. When students are interested in a topic—whether due to personal curiosity or because of situational interest sparked by text content or instructional features—and are oriented toward learning, their intrinsic motivation supports better recall of ideas and overall comprehension (Hidi, 2001). This occurs because intrinsically motivated students are more likely to invest the cognitive effort needed to make meaningful connections with the text. On the other hand, motivation driven by external goals, such as earning high grades or gaining recognition, can increase anxiety and lead to distractions. These task-irrelevant concerns divert cognitive resources from comprehension, making it harder for students to engage deeply with the material (Cho et al., 2023). At the behavioral level, different types of motivation shape the level of effort and persistence with reading tasks. Motivation also influences how much and how broadly students read, contributing to reading development over time (Wigfield & Guthrie, 1997; Troyer et al., 2019). When students are motivated to read, they spend more time on reading, interact more deeply with texts, and persist through challenging text materials. These positive experiences with comprehension build confidence and reinforce ongoing motivation to read, creating a self-sustaining cycle. Thus, the relationship between intrinsic motivation and comprehension is both developmental and reciprocal.

KEY FACTORS OF INTRINSIC READING MOTIVATION AND RELATED INSTRUCTIONAL PRACTICES

According to the self-determination theory (Deci & Ryan, 2001), three core psychological needs—*autonomy, relatedness* (or belongingness), and *competence*—are essential for fostering intrinsic motivation (Box 6.1). When these needs are met within the reading environment, students are more likely to engage with texts for personal enjoyment and meaning rather than for external rewards or pressures. Additionally, motivation theories emphasize that students' *beliefs, goals,* and *values* are deeply interconnected with their motivation to read (Boxes 6.2 and 6.3), shaping both their engagement and persistence with texts (Schiefele et al., 2012; Wigfield & Guthrie, 2000).

Box 6.1. Three Psychological Needs for Intrinsic Motivation

Autonomy—A sense of initiative and ownership over one's actions and decisions.

Relatedness—A sense of belongingness and connection.

Competence belief and self-efficacy—Feeling of mastery and confidence in one's ability to succeed.

Box 6.2. Beliefs

Mindset—Beliefs about the nature of personal intellectual abilities. A growth mindset views abilities as developable, while a fixed mindset sees them as unchangeable.

Attribution—Beliefs about the cause of success or failure. Attribution to controllable factors, such as effort, is considered adaptive.

Box 6.3. Goals and Values

Achievement goal orientation—Reasons why students engage in achievement-related behaviors. Performance goal orientation focuses on demonstrating ability or avoiding failure. Mastery goal orientation emphasizes learning and improvement.

Value—Subjective importance of a task. Intrinsic value is the enjoyment of satisfaction gained from the task itself.

Interest—A predisposition to engage with a certain topic (personal or topic interest) or a psychological state of engaging that encompasses affective and cognitive components (situational interest).

AUTONOMY

Autonomy refers to the psychological need to feel self-directed and in control of one's actions (Deci & Ryan, 2001). Research shows that autonomy-supportive instruction, which nurtures students' sense of choice, can significantly enhance intrinsic motivation (Reeve & Cheon, 2021). In the context of reading, this means allowing students to select texts that align with their interests, choose how they engage with reading assignments, and providing flexibility in responding to texts—such as offering creative alternatives to traditional book reports. Also, offering explanatory rationales for academic expectations can further support autonomy (Guthrie et al., 2007; Meece & Miller, 1999). When students feel a sense of control over their reading experiences, they are more likely to develop intrinsic motivation, leading to greater engagement, persistence, and ownership of their learning.

RELATEDNESS

Relatedness—also referred to as belongingness—is the psychological need to feel connected to others, experience meaningful relationships, and be valued within a community (Deci & Ryan, 2001). When students perceive that they are part of a supportive learning environment where their thoughts, identities, and contributions are valued, they are more likely to engage in academic activities with intrinsic motivation. When students feel a sense of belonging in their reading community, they are more likely to engage with texts authentically, persist through reading challenges, and develop a deeper appreciation for literacy. Conversely, a lack of belonging—such as feeling isolated in reading tasks or encountering texts that do not reflect their experiences—can lead to disengagement and reduced motivation. Instructional strategies such as collaborative strategic reading (CSR; Klingner & Vaughn, 1998), paired reading, writing group summaries, and small group text-based projects can position students as team members with shared goals. It is essential for students to receive explicit instruction on how to participate constructively in collaborative groups, ensuring that every voice is heard and each member can contribute meaningfully. For example, in CSR, students work in teams to develop a shared understanding of the text, identify the gist, and engage in question-and-answer discussions. They are taught specific expert roles (e.g., gist expert) and provided with sentence stems to help lead the discussion. These structured scaffolds with collaboration ensure students engage in meaningful dialogue and collective learning. These cooperative activities can be naturally enjoyable, allowing students to engage with peers, share ideas, and deepen their understanding.

COMPETENCE BELIEFS

Fostering a sense of competence and control over reading ability and outcomes is essential for promoting students' autonomy in their reading behaviors. Perceived competence, or self-efficacy, is critical in initiating and sustaining engagement with the text (Chapman & Turner, 1995; Deci & Ryan, 2001; Schunk, 2003). When students doubt their reading ability or perceive a text as too difficult, they are more likely to feel discouraged and disengaged. In contrast, students who believe in their reading capabilities approach texts with confidence and persist even when faced with challenges. Research indicates that struggling readers who are minimally responsive to intervention often exhibit lower perceived competence than their typically developing peers. In contrast, students who respond well tend to have similar levels of perceived competence (Cho et al., 2015). This finding suggests that fostering a strong sense of reading competence is particularly important for students who experience persistent reading difficulties.

One of the strongest sources of perceived competence is the mastery experience (Usher & Pajares, 2008). Research shows that explicit instruction in reading comprehension strategies—such as previewing, monitoring comprehension, summarizing, and questioning—not only improves comprehension but also strengthens students' confidence in their reading abilities (Unrau et al., 2018). To support students in successfully applying these strategies, teachers can provide direct instruction and modeling, followed by guided and independent practice with meaningful feedback. This approach is especially important when working with complex texts, as students may initially struggle to access them independently. Setting achievable goals that emphasize content mastery and build on prior knowledge can help sustain engagement and create a pathway to success. Each small success in reading activities reinforces perceived competence, ultimately enhancing students' intrinsic motivation to read.

MINDSET AND ATTRIBUTION BELIEFS

Beyond competence beliefs, two other key beliefs—mindset and attribution—are critical for sustaining students' intrinsic motivation for reading, particularly in the face of setbacks. Mindset, or beliefs about whether their intelligence and reading ability are malleable, is closely tied to motivation, engagement, and achievement (Dweck, 2000; Yeager & Dweck, 2012; Cho et al., 2019). Students with a growth mindset, who believe their reading ability can improve through effort and effective strategies, are more likely to be intrinsically motivated and persist through challenges. They view difficulties as opportunities for growth rather than signs of failure. In contrast, students who see reading ability as a fixed trait may interpret slow progress or extra effort as evidence of incompetence.

Closely related to mindset is attribution, or how students explain their successes and failures (Weiner, 1985). Students who attribute reading outcomes to uncontrollable factors, such as a perceived lack of ability, are less likely to be intrinsically motivated and more prone to disengagement. In contrast, those who link their performance to controllable factors like effort or strategy use are more likely to exert effort in improving their comprehension. When students adopt a growth mindset and attribute success to effort and strategy rather than innate talent, they develop a stronger sense of autonomy, moving closer to an intrinsic motivational state. These adaptive beliefs provide the fuel students need to continue reading despite obstacles.

Several instructional practices can help cultivate a growth mindset and adaptive attribution beliefs. One effective approach is process-oriented feedback that emphasizes progress and effort rather than fixed ability (Haimovitz & Dweck, 2017). When students encounter setbacks, teachers can provide timely, specific feedback that includes constructive suggestions for improvement. This type of feedback shifts students' focus away from external comparisons and toward viewing mistakes as learning opportunities. Conversely, praising intelligence or natural ability (e.g., "You are a smart kid!") can inadvertently reinforce fixed-mindset beliefs and discourage effort.

Another powerful approach is explicit instruction on brain malleability and attribution training. Research shows that when students understand that abilities develop through effort and effective strategies, they adopt more positive attitudes toward learning and show stronger academic growth (Blackwell et al., 2007; Cho et al., 2025). Attribution training, which helps students reinterpret setbacks as opportunities to refine their approach, has been particularly effective for struggling readers when combined with strategy instruction, including those with learning disabilities (Berkeley et al., 2011). For example, explicitly teaching students to recognize how their positive or negative thoughts impact their reading can be beneficial. Providing prompts and guided practice in using self-talk that attributes reading outcomes to strategy use (e.g., "You made a mistake on that one. Think of a different strategy that could help.") can reinforce adaptive thinking and improve reading persistence. By consistently reinforcing the connection between effort, strategy use, and progress, teachers foster intrinsic motivation essential for long-term academic success.

LEARNING GOAL ORIENTATION, INTRINSIC VALUES, AND INTEREST

The goals and values that students hold regarding reading also shape their motivation and engagement. According to achievement goal orientation theory (Dweck & Leggett, 1988), students who adopt a learning goal orientation—striving to develop competence, deepen understanding, and master new skills—are more likely to experience intrinsic motivation. In contrast, those with a performance goal orientation tend to focus on external validation, such as earning high grades or outperforming peers, which can undermine sustained engagement in reading. Ideally, reading instruction should foster a mastery goal orientation, in which students read not simply to complete tasks but to derive meaning, enjoyment, and personal growth from the process (Cho et al., 2019, 2023).

To cultivate learning goal orientation, teachers should design instruction emphasizing rich, meaningful content rather than focusing on performance-based incentives like test scores or letter grades. One effective approach is integrating interdisciplinary themes—drawing from science, history, and current events—to help students see the real-world relevance of reading. For instance, a unit on climate change that incorporates scientific articles, historical accounts, and opinion pieces can encourage students to read for understanding rather than merely completing an assignment. Additionally, instructional practices should support self-reflection and growth, rather than external comparisons (Meece et al., 2006).

Relatedly, intrinsic motivation is closely linked to intrinsic value, or the personal importance students place on reading. Research suggests that students who genuinely value reading and find it interesting are more likely to engage in voluntary reading, leading to stronger comprehension and literacy outcomes (Durik et al., 2006). This intrinsic value is linked to personal or topic interest—what students bring to the classroom. However, interest can also be nurtured by enhancing situational interest in a text or reading context (e.g., through personal relevance, novelty, or unexpected elements). Situational interest—a temporary curiosity sparked by external factors—can serve as an entry point to individual interest, a deeper, self-sustained engagement with reading (Hidi & Renninger, 2011). Teachers can strategically design instruction to leverage situational interest and transition it into a lasting passion for reading.

One effective method for supporting intrinsic value and interest is selecting high-interest, culturally relevant texts that connect to students' experiences (Wei et al., 2021). For example, a science text about urban ecosystems might resonate more deeply with students if it includes local environmental concerns they recognize in their community. Similarly, literature featuring characters who share students' backgrounds and experiences can make reading feel more personally relevant and engaging. Over time, when students repeatedly encounter personally relevant, intellectually stimulating, and interactive reading experiences, their situational interest can evolve into enduring individual interest.

RESEARCH ON READING COMPREHENSION INSTRUCTION WITH MOTIVATIONAL SUPPORTS

Research shows that intrinsic motivation can be supported in various ways. Designing content and instruction that focuses on building competence, providing opportunities to develop positive belief systems, offering mastery experiences, ensuring relevance, and promoting social collaboration all play a crucial role in fostering intrinsic motivation (Guthrie & Cox, 2001). Each of these components aims to shift the "destination" for reading, moving from reading because they are told to do so toward reading because they choose to. Purposefully designed instructional activities with these goals in mind can fuel intrinsic motivation and set the direction toward greater engagement and autonomy.

CONCEPT-ORIENTED READING INSTRUCTION

Description

Concept-oriented reading instruction (CORI) is a comprehensive program for grades 3–5 that integrates science and reading by building units around conceptual themes (Guthrie, 2007; Wigfield et al., 2004). CORI was developed on the premise that reading engagement is a product of motivation and cognitive activity (Guthrie et al., 1996, 2007). The program includes explicit instruction on cognitive strategies, such as activating background knowledge, questioning, summarizing, using graphic organizers, and text structure. However, it also incorporates purposeful motivational supports related to several components of intrinsic motivation (for a video example of a CORI lesson, see *www.readingrockets.org/topics/comprehension/articles/concept-oriented-reading-instruction-cori*). A typical 65-minute CORI lesson includes oral reading fluency practice, where oral reading fluency practice is replaced with students participating in hands-on activities related to the science concepts approximately two days per week, a mini-lesson on comprehension, and small group work in guided reading, independent reading, and writing.

Researchers have studied the implementation of CORI in a number of settings. A synthesis of the outcomes of 11 different implementation programs found that CORI had, on average, a moderate positive impact on students' intrinsic reading motivation and a high positive impact on students' standardized reading comprehension scores, as well as on researcher-developed measures of reading outcomes (Guthrie et al., 2007). Compared to students in control groups who received instruction in cognitive reading strategies without purposeful motivational support, students in the CORI groups made significantly greater gains in reading outcomes (Wigfield et al., 2004).

Key Practices

The CORI framework leverages targeted instructional practices to address the key motivational constructs it seeks to support—learning goals, competence, relevance, choice, and collaboration (Guthrie et al., 2007; Wigfield et al., 2004). A key feature of CORI is its use of conceptually and thematically related units. These units enable students to connect text content to their background knowledge, personal experiences, and other texts. Purposefully curated text sets allow students to build cumulative knowledge and deepen their understanding of topics. Unlike traditional basal readers or instructional programs that jump between unrelated topics, CORI's concept-oriented thematic units encourage students to pursue mastery, fostering a sense of expertise while supporting both content learning and reading skill development. To further enhance comprehension, explicit instruction in reading strategies is provided. Strategies like summarizing, questioning, and using text features are introduced gradually and practiced repeatedly to ensure mastery. By successfully applying these strategies, students gain confidence, motivating them to tackle new and more challenging texts. Throughout instruction, students are guided to set short-term, achievable goals, such as completing specific text sections, summarizing ideas, or identifying key vocabulary. These goals help students focus on their progress and experience success in manageable steps. Each mastery experience contributes to their sense of competence and builds motivation for continued learning. Fluency practice is another critical element in CORI, with students engaging in repeated reading of texts such as poems or short passages related to the thematic unit. This practice strengthens their reading fluency and builds their confidence in their abilities, reinforcing their motivation.

CORI connects text content to hands-on activities that bring learning to life. For example, students studying ecosystems might construct food webs or investigate plant life cycles, engaging with the topic in ways that make the text relevant and meaningful. These experiential activities increase students' intrinsic motivation to learn more and foster a desire to explore the topic further through reading.

Another essential aspect of CORI is student autonomy. Throughout instruction, students are offered meaningful choices, such as selecting texts that align with their interests or subtopics they want to investigate within a thematic unit. They may also choose reading partners or decide how to share their learning. This emphasis on autonomy supports students' intrinsic motivation and helps them develop independence as readers. Collaborative activities also play a central role in CORI. Students engage in paired reading, summary exchanges, and group projects like creating posters or presentations. These activities foster a sense of belonging and shared purpose, supporting students' social motivation and strengthening their connection to the classroom community.

MODEL OF READING ENGAGEMENT

Description

Similar to CORI, the model of reading engagement (MORE) intervention is rooted in content literacy instruction built on thematic units. However, whereas CORI is targeted at upper elementary, MORE was developed for students in grades 1–3. MORE is predicated on research that suggests that literacy skills can be improved by building domain knowledge via repeated exposure to related topics (Duke et al., 2021; Hirsch, 2016; Kim et al., 2024). Moreover, research suggests that students with high levels of domain-specific knowledge are more likely to engage with, comprehend, and recall challenging texts than students with little domain-specific knowledge (Cervetti et al., 2016). The importance of domain-specific knowledge extends to struggling readers (Schneider et al., 1989), underscoring the importance of a knowledge-building curriculum. MORE seeks to deliberately build domain-specific knowledge to support reading comprehension using spiraled content literacy instruction. Science content gradually increases in complexity across grade levels. For example, grade 1 materials focus on animal survival, grade 2 focuses on scientific inquiry of past events (e.g., dinosaur extinction), and grade 3 focuses on scientific research about living systems. The intervention also includes related nonfiction reading over the summer. The units are purposefully designed to draw on related themes, concepts, and scientific vocabulary, allowing children to build schemas and content knowledge through literacy activities (Kim et al., 2021). In a randomized control trial across 30 elementary schools, students receiving the MORE intervention in grades 1–3 outperformed their peers on measures of science vocabulary, science reading comprehension, and general reading comprehension. These gains were sustained in a 14-month follow-up assessment in grade 4 (Kim et al., 2023; Kim et al., 2024).

Key Practices

MORE leverages a variety of elements of curriculum design and instructional strategy to foster various elements of student engagement in reading, including interest, mastery goals, perceived competence, and autonomy. For resources on MORE, see *https://engagewithmore.org/home*.

Spiraled thematic units provide students with recurrent exposure to topics, concepts, and vocabulary, fostering the development of domain-specific schema and enabling them to connect new knowledge to prior understanding. This repeated engagement emphasizes mastery of science content and vocabulary, supporting both a mastery orientation to science and reading (Guthrie et al., 2009). Within these units, teacher-led interactive read-aloud about high-interest content helps spark situational interest. For instance, a first-grade unit on animal survival might begin with a captivating text exploring a hypothetical question: Who would win in a fight—a grizzly bear or a polar bear?

Concept mapping further supports schema development by making connections explicit and visual. Through this strategy, students can see and build on the relationships between ideas, helping them perceive their progress and boosting their sense of competence. Collaborative research, writing, and discussion activities centered on thematic topics provide opportunities for students to work together as teammates, fostering a sense of belonging and enhancing their engagement in learning (Lepola et al., 2016).

A key component of this approach is fostering a sense of autonomy by offering students choices in activities and texts. Students can select specific topics to study in more depth, such as focusing on a particular Arctic animal, and are encouraged to engage in wide reading about thematically related texts. This autonomy extends to summer reading opportunities, allowing students to explore additional texts of their choice within the thematic framework. By combining these practices, the approach nurtures intrinsic motivation, supports skill development, and enhances students' connection to the material (Deci & Ryan, 2001; Guthrie et al., 2007).

INTERVENTION TO SUPPORT MINDSET AND READING TOGETHER

Description

Intervention to support mindset and reading together (i-SMART) aims to enhance reading comprehension and foster positive motivation through explicit instruction in reading comprehension strategies. These strategies are embedded within thematically related text sets carefully curated to build students' science knowledge that supports a growth mindset, particularly the concept of neuroplasticity. Central to i-SMART is the promotion of a growth mindset, which emphasizes that the brain can grow and adapt through effort and learning. The intervention explicitly positions a growth mindset as the foundation for supporting motivation, ensuring that students see themselves as capable of improvement with sustained effort. This emphasis seemed particularly critical for students who struggle with reading, as these challenges often impact their confidence and willingness to engage.

Although i-SMART was originally developed as a small group intervention for Tier 2 instruction, its principles have resonated with classroom teachers, who observed that challenges with motivation and engagement with reading in upper elementary English/Language Arts classes extend beyond struggling readers. Recognizing this broader applicability, three classroom teachers implemented the i-SMART lessons with their entire classes over the course of a spring semester. Initial findings show that the thematic integration of growth mindset and reading strategies proved beneficial for all learners, including students with reading difficulties. After participating in i-SMART lessons, students showed more positive reading motivation. For example, in posttest mindset assessments, they attributed their reading challenges to effort more than ability and had lower fixed-mindset beliefs. In addition, they improved their knowledge about growth mindset and showed greater growth in reading comprehension at posttest than peers who did not receive the intervention. Moreover, students with reading difficulties who received i-SMART in classrooms demonstrated less maladaptive motivational and emotional responses to reading (lower anxiety, ability attribution, performance goal orientation) and improved reading comprehension compared to those who did not receive i-SMART. These preliminary results from the classwide implementation of i-SMART were promising, indicating that i-SMART has the potential to support diverse learners in various educational contexts.

Key Practices

The i-SMART curriculum strengthens students' reading comprehension and mindset knowledge through structured, evidence-based instruction. The lessons unfold in two phases, each emphasizing specific instructional practices that promote reading comprehension, strategic thinking, and applying a growth mindset to learning. These practices include explicit teaching of reading comprehension strategies, building mindset knowledge, collaborative practice, and applying a growth mindset to reading through quizzes, assessments, and reflection.

The first phase of i-SMART introduces students to essential reading comprehension strategies through CSR (Klingner & Vaughn, 1998). CSR teaches students to preview a text by activating prior knowledge and predicting content, monitoring comprehension using fix-up strategies such as rereading and analyzing word structure, summarizing key ideas using the "get the gist" strategy, and consolidating understanding through asking and answering questions. These strategies help students develop the skills expert readers use before, during, and after reading. Phase I lessons focus on reading texts about the brain, building foundational knowledge to support comprehension of the growth mindset texts introduced in Phase II.

In the second phase, students deepen their learning by applying comprehension strategies to texts that build knowledge about the growth mindset. These texts are organized into four units that sequentially develop students' understanding of how the brain grows, how the reading brain functions and changes with practice, how cognitive learning strategies enhance reading skills, and how emotional regulation supports persistence in reading challenges. By integrating reading comprehension with neuroscience and mindset knowledge, students develop a deeper awareness of how effort, strategy use, and perseverance contribute to reading success.

To reinforce comprehension and mindset knowledge, i-SMART incorporates collaborative learning through a gradual release of responsibility, shifting from teacher-led instruction to peer-supported practice. Early lessons focus on teacher modeling and scaffolded practice, while later lessons encourage students to work in small groups, where each student takes on the role of an "expert reader." These structured discussions provide opportunities for students to support one another, engage in meaningful conversations about their reading, and build confidence in their ability to comprehend complex texts.

Throughout Phase II, students apply a growth mindset to their reading through quizzes, assessments, and structured reflection activities. Pre- and post-unit assessments track their progress in comprehension and strategy use, while reflection activities help them recognize the link between effort, persistence, and success. At the end of each unit, Growth Mindset Booster Lessons provide additional opportunities to review key concepts, reflect on learning, and demonstrate an understanding of mindset principles. By monitoring their progress and engaging in structured self-reflection, students develop a stronger belief in their ability to grow as readers.

MRS. DAVIS'S PLAN FOR IMPLEMENTING BEST PRACTICES FOR SUPPORTING READING MOTIVATION

After gaining a deeper understanding of the various motivational constructs related to intrinsic motivation and their associated research-based practices, Mrs.

TABLE 6.1. Factors Related to Intrinsic Motivation and Their Associated Research-Based Practices

Motivation construct	Definition	Research-based practice examples
Autonomy	Psychological need for control over one's experience	• Provide student choice in text selection and/or grouping. Scaffold these choices by providing explicit instruction related to appropriate text selection and effective group work. • Provide students with flexibility in the ways in which they may demonstrate learning outcomes. • Offer a rationale for expectations and the reading activities.
Relatedness	Basic psychological need for connectedness and belongingness	• Foster social engagement through paired reading, collaborative strategic reading, group summaries, and group projects. • Model and scaffold effective group interactions to ensure all members actively and meaningfully contribute.
Perceived competence or self-efficacy	Belief in one's own ability to complete a task successfully or do well in a given domain	• Scaffold new content and skills with explicit instruction, modeling, and guided practice to build confidence for independent work. • Build background knowledge about text topics and position students as emerging experts on the content learned. • Provide frequent practice opportunities, such as daily fluency exercises or applying reading strategies across texts. • Provide varied text choices and scaffolds to support reading at and beyond students' comfort levels. Teach them to select texts that balance challenge and confidence. • Set achievable goals and visualize progress.
Growth mindset and adaptive attribution	The belief that abilities are malleable and shaped by effort and learning outcomes is attributed to controllable factors like effort and persistence rather than fixed ability.	• Give specific, process-focused feedback with scaffolded guidance for improvement. • Explicitly teach neuroplasticity, linking it to reading growth, and challenge fixed-mindset beliefs. • Teach students to use growth mindset self-talk and adaptive attribution. • Explicitly link progress to their effort and strategy use.
Learning goal orientation	Aims to improve on or master the content or skill	• Select text sets that deepen knowledge and promote wide reading on a topic. • Center reading instruction around knowledge building with guiding questions. • Prioritize content mastery over competition and grades. • Provide meaningful opportunities for students to share and apply their learning.
Intrinsic value and interest	Being driven by internal desire, including personal and situational interest.	• Connect texts to real-life experiences and hands-on learning. • Choose high-interest, high-quality, and relevant texts.

Davis is ready to transform her approach to reading instruction. By applying the motivational strategies she has learned, she feels equipped to ignite her students' intrinsic motivation and set them on a path to become lifelong readers and learners.

FILLING THE TANK: BUILDING COMPETENCE

To fuel her students' motivation, Mrs. Davis focuses on building competence by systematically developing knowledge through a content-rich curriculum. Before diving into a textbook chapter on ecosystems, she reviews key concepts like biodiversity, food chains, and habitats to activate students' schema. She encourages students to share what they already know, helping them connect existing knowledge to the new content. Mrs. Davis then introduces the unit theme—ecosystems—and provides an overview of the topics, such as rainforest ecosystems, desert habitats, and ocean environments.

To support comprehension, particularly for those who struggle with it, Mrs. Davis incorporates explicit strategy instruction. She introduces one reading strategy at a time, beginning with how to summarize a text. She scaffolds this strategy through guided practice, offering students multiple opportunities to apply it with her support. As the unit progresses, she introduces additional strategies, such as using context clues or morphology to determine word meanings and developing text-based and inferential questions. With each strategy, Mrs. Davis ensures students have ample practice and feedback, mastering the techniques before applying them independently. This gradual, step-by-step approach not only helps students internalize these strategies but also builds their competence, fostering a sense of accomplishment and motivation to engage with new material.

STARTING THE ENGINE: SPARKING SITUATIONAL INTEREST

To spark situational interest, Mrs. Davis selects texts and other materials that connect to students' lives and cultures. For example, when reading about ecosystems, she might show a video about local environmental issues or a virtual tour of a rainforest, making the topic feel more relevant. By tying the reading to real-world experiences and current events, she helps students see the value in what they are learning and sparks curiosity. These activities build situational interest, making students eager to engage with the material.

SETTING THE RIGHT DESTINATION: LEARNING GOAL ORIENTATION AND INTRINSIC VALUE

Understanding the importance of learning goal orientation, Mrs. Davis shifts the focus from competition and grades to knowledge building and meaningful engagement with texts. She selects text sets that deepen students' understanding of key topics and encourages wide reading to expand their knowledge base. Rather than relying on worksheets with isolated comprehension questions, she structures reading instruction around guiding questions that promote inquiry and critical thinking. For example, when exploring a challenging chapter on ecosystems, she encourages students to connect the reading to broader scientific concepts and discuss their insights with peers. Instead of focusing solely on correctness, she praises students' efforts to summarize complex ideas and apply their learning in discussions. By prioritizing content mastery and providing meaningful opportunities for students to share their understanding, Mrs. Davis fosters intrinsic motivation and positions reading as a pathway to deeper learning and intellectual growth.

PREPARING FOR ROADBLOCKS: SUPPORT GROWTH MINDSET AND ADAPTIVE ATTRIBUTION

Mrs. Davis is intentional with her feedback, ensuring it is specific, process-focused, and provides scaffolded guidance for improvement. Instead of offering general praise for being "smart," she highlights students' effort and strategy use, reinforcing the connection between persistence and progress. She explicitly teaches students about neuroplasticity, explaining how their brains grow and strengthen with practice, which helps challenge fixed-mindset beliefs about reading ability.

When students encounter difficulties, she encourages them to use growth mindset self-talk and adaptive attribution, viewing setbacks as opportunities to develop their skills. For example, if a student struggles with a complex text, she might say, "Your effort shows—you're working hard to understand this. Let's try breaking it into smaller sections or making notes to clarify key ideas." After a student faces challenges with comprehension, she guides them to reflect on their reading strategies, such as slowing down, rereading, or summarizing, and links their progress to these efforts. By centering her feedback on effort, strategy use, and the brain's capacity to grow, Mrs. Davis nurtures resilience and persistence. She helps students understand that reading proficiency is not a fixed trait but a skill that improves through targeted strategies and sustained effort.

ENJOYING THE JOURNEY: CREATE A SENSE OF BELONGING AND SUPPORT AUTONOMY

Mrs. Davis understands that motivation is deeply influenced by social connections, so she fosters a classroom environment where students feel a sense of belonging and support. For instance, during a unit on ecosystems, she organizes group activities where students collaboratively read and discuss a chapter about local ecosystems. Afterward, each group creates a visual summary of the chapter's key concepts, which they present to the class. This collaborative work not only strengthens students' social bonds but also reinforces the idea that reading is a shared, meaningful activity. In addition to building relatedness, Mrs. Davis also promotes student autonomy by offering choices in their reading. For the ecosystem unit, she curates a selection of texts about different ecosystems, such as rainforests, deserts, and oceans. Students are free to choose which ecosystem they'd like to explore in more detail. This choice encourages intrinsic motivation, as students feel a sense of ownership over their learning and are more engaged in the content they select.

TIERED APPROACH TO SUPPORTING STUDENT MOTIVATION

Research has shown that the practices Mrs. Davis uses to support intrinsic motivation help most students find joy and purpose in reading, making them less dependent on external incentives. By fostering students' internal desire to read through meaningful learning experiences, these strategies minimize the necessity for using extrinsic motivators that may only produce short-term compliance rather than a lasting appreciation for reading. However, Mrs. Davis recognizes that students are at different stages of motivation and, therefore, she adjusts her practices accordingly. For students needing additional motivational support, she implements targeted strategies to address specific barriers to engagement. For example, she uses extrinsic methods, such as token systems or rewards for milestones, but only as a supplement to practices that support intrinsic motivation, to help students transition from external rewards to internalizing the value of reading. Mrs. Davis also provides direct instruction on growth mindset and helps students identify more adaptive attributions for their reading outcomes. For example, she has students sort fixed and growth mindset statements, and she incorporates progress monitoring activities—like those used in i-SMART—that allow students to visualize growth. This instruction is especially important for students who may have ingrained beliefs about their lack of ability or who face personal or emotional barriers that make reading feel irrelevant or difficult. Through this comprehensive, tiered approach, Mrs. Davis ensures that every student receives the appropriate level of support, fostering intrinsic motivation and empowering them to develop as self-directed readers.

CONCLUSION

By incorporating research-based practices into daily instruction, teachers can create classroom environments that nurture students' intrinsic motivation and foster a lifelong love of reading. Whether through autonomy-supportive teaching, collaborative learning experiences, or the strategic use of high-interest and culturally relevant texts, educators have powerful tools to engage even the most reluctant readers. As you reflect on the motivational needs of your students, consider experimenting with these evidence-based strategies to support all learners in becoming confident, self-directed readers. Small, intentional changes in instructional practices can make a meaningful difference in shaping students' reading motivation and overall literacy development.

Reflection Questions

1. How can understanding the psychological foundations of reading motivation help you address the diverse motivational needs of students in your classroom?
2. Reflect on where students in your class fall on the motivation continuum and consider how their current motivational states may influence their reading behaviors and comprehension.
3. How do you currently engage students in reading? Based on their motivational characteristics, which research-based strategies could you use to foster intrinsic motivation, and what additional supports could help you engage readers who rely on extrinsic rewards?

REFERENCES

Berkeley, S., Mastropieri, M. A., & Scruggs, T. E. (2011). Reading comprehension strategy instruction and attribution retraining for secondary students with learning and other mild disabilities. *Journal of Learning Disabilities, 44*(1), 18–32.

Blackwell, L., Trzesniewski, K., & Dweck, C. (2007). Implicit theories of intelligence predict achievement across an adolescent transition: A longitudinal study and an intervention. *Child Development, 78*, 246–263.

Cartwright, K. B., & Duke, N. K. (2019). The DRIVE model of reading: Making the complexity of reading accessible. *The Reading Teacher, 73*(1), 7–15.

Cervetti, G. N., Wright, T. S., & Hwang, J. (2016). Conceptual coherence, comprehension, and vocabulary acquisition: A knowledge effect? *Reading and Writing: An Interdisciplinary Journal, 29,* 761–779.

Chapman, J. W., & Turner, W. E. (1995). Development of young children's reading self-concepts: An examination of emerging subcomponents and their relationship with reading achievement. *Journal of Educational Psychology, 87,* 154–167.

Cho, E., Ju, U., Kim, E. H., Lee, M., Lee, G., & Compton, D. L. (2023). Relations among motivation, executive functions, and reading comprehension: Do they differ for students with and without reading difficulties?. *Scientific Studies of Reading, 27*(4), 289–310.

Cho, E., Ju, U., Kim, E. H., & Compton, D. L. (2025). Achievement goal profiles and reading-related outcomes in elementary students with and without reading difficulties. *Learning and Individual Differences, 119*(102661), 102661.

Cho, E., Roberts, G. J., Capin, P., Roberts, G., Miciak, J., & Vaughn, S. (2015). Cognitive attributes, attention, and self–efficacy of adequate and inadequate responders in a fourth grade reading intervention. *Learning Disabilities Research & Practice, 30*(4), 159–170.

Cho, E., Toste, J. R., Lee, M., & Ju, U. (2019). Motivational predictors of struggling readers' reading comprehension: The effects of mindset, achievement goals, and engagement. *Reading and Writing, 32,* 1219–1242.

Deci, E. L., & Ryan, R. M. (2001). Self-determination theory: An approach to human motivation and personality. *American Psychologist, 55*(1), 68–78.

Duke, N. K., & Cartwright, K. B. (2021). The science of reading progresses: Communicating advances beyond the simple view of reading. *Reading Research Quarterly, 56,* S25–S44.

Durik, A. M., Vida, M., & Eccles, J. S. (2006). Task values and ability beliefs as predictors of high school literacy choices: A developmental analysis. *Journal of Educational Psychology, 98,* 382–393.

Dweck, C. S., & Leggett, E. L. (1988). A social-cognitive approach to motivation and personality. *Psychological Review, 95*(2), 256–273.

Dweck, C. (2000). *Self-theories: Their role in motivation, personality and development.* Taylor & Francis.

Eccles, J. S., & Wigfield, A. (2020). From expectancy-value theory to situated expectancy-value theory: A developmental, social cognitive, and sociocultural perspective on motivation. *Contemporary Educational Psychology, 61,* 101859.

Eccles, J., & Wigfield, A. (2002). Motivational beliefs, values, and goals. *Annual Review of Psychology, 53,* 109–132.

Gambrell, L. B. (1996). Creating classroom cultures that foster reading motivation. *Reading Teacher, 50,* 14–25.

Gough, P. B., & Tunmer, W. E. (1986). Decoding, reading, and reading disability. *Remedial and Special Education,* 7(1), 6–10.

Guthrie, J. T., & Coddington, C. S. (2009). Reading motivation. In K. R. Wentzel & D. B. Miele (Eds.), *Handbook of motivation at school* (pp. 517–540). Routledge.

Guthrie, J. T., & Cox, K. E. (2001). Classroom conditions for motivation and engagement in reading. *Educational Psychology Review, 13,* 283–302.

Guthrie, J. T., & Humenick, N. M. (2004). Motivating students to read: Evidence for classroom practices that increase reading motivation and achievement. In P. McCardle & V. Chhabra (Eds.), *The voice of evidence in reading research* (pp. 329–354). Brookes.

Guthrie, J. T., McRae, A., & Lutz Klauda, S. (2007). Contributions of concept-oriented reading instruction to knowledge about interventions for motivations in reading. *Educational Psychologist, 42*(4), 237–250.

Haimovitz, K., & Dweck, C. S. (2017). The origins of children's growth and fixed mindsets: New research and a new proposal. *Child Development, 88*(6), 1849–1859.

Hardré, P. L., & Hennessey, M. N. (2013). What they think, what they know, what they do: Rural secondary teachers' motivational beliefs and strategies. *Learning Environments Research, 16*, 411–436.

Hidi, S. (2001). Interest, reading, and learning: Theoretical and practical considerations. *Educational Psychology Review, 13,* 191–209.

Hirsch, E. D. (2016). *Why knowledge matters: Rescuing our children from failed educational theories.* Harvard Education Press.

Kim, J. S., Burkhauser, M. A., Mesite, L. M., Asher, C. A., Relyea, J. E., Fitzgerald, J., & Elmore, J. (2021). Improving reading comprehension, science domain knowledge, and reading engagement through a first-grade content literacy intervention. *Journal of Educational Psychology, 113*(1), 3–26.

Kim, J. S., Burkhauser, M. A., Relyea, J. E., Gilbert, J. B., Scherer, E., Fitzgerald, J., et al. (2023). Longitudinal randomized trial of a sustained content literacy intervention from first to second grade: Transfer effects on students' reading comprehension. *Journal of Educational Psychology, 115*(1), 73–98.

Kim, J. S., Gilbert, J. B., Relyea, J. E., Rich, P., Scherer, E., Burkhauser, M. A., & Tvedt, J. N. (2024). Time to transfer: Long-term effects of a sustained and spiraled content literacy intervention in the elementary grades. *Developmental Psychology, 60*(7), 1279–1297.

Kintsch, W. (1994). Text comprehension, memory, and learning. *American Psychologist, 49*(4), 294.

Klingner, J. K., & Vaughn, S. (1998). Using collaborative strategic reading. *Teaching Exceptional Children, 30*(6), 32–37.

Lepola, J., Lynch, J., Kiuru, N., Laakkonen, E., & Niemi, P. (2016). Early oral language comprehension, task orientation, and foundational reading skills as predictors of Grade 3 reading comprehension. *Reading Research Quarterly, 51*, 373–390.

Meece, J. L., & Miller, S. D. (1999). Changes in elementary school children's achievement goals for reading and writing: Results of a longitudinal and an intervention study. *Scientific Studies of Reading, 3*(3), 207–229.

Meece, J. L., Anderman, E. M., & Anderman, L. H. (2006). Classroom goal structure, student motivation, and academic achievement. *Annual Review of Psychology, 57*(1), 487–503.

National Association of State Boards of Education (NASBE). (2021). Getting students engaged in learning. *www.nasbe.org/getting-students-engaged-in-learning*

Pressley, M. (2006). *Reading instruction that works: The case for balanced teaching* (3rd ed.). Guilford Press.

Reeve, J., & Cheon, S. H. (2021). Autonomy-supportive teaching: Its malleability, benefits, and potential to improve educational practice. *Educational Psychologist, 56*(1), 54–77.

Renninger, K. A., & Hidi, S. (2011). Revisiting the conceptualization, measurement, and generation of interest. *Educational Psychologist, 46*(3), 168–184.

Scarborough, H. (2001). Connecting early language and literacy to later reading (dis) abilities: Evidence, theory and practice. In S. B. Neuman & D. K. Dickinson (Eds.), *Handbook of early literacy research* (Vol. 1, pp. 97–110). Guilford Press.

Schiefele, U., Schaffner, E., Möller, J., & Wigfield, A. (2012). Dimensions of reading motivation and their relation to reading behavior and competence. *Reading Research Quarterly, 47*(4), 427–463.

Schneider, W., Körkel, J., & Weinert, F. E. (1989). Domain-specific knowledge and memory performance: A comparison of high- and low aptitude children. *Journal of Educational Psychology, 81*, 306–312.

Schunk, D. H. (2003). Self-efficacy for reading and writing: Influence of modeling, goal setting, and self-evaluation. *Reading & Writing Quarterly, 19*, 159–172.

Troyer, M., Kim, J. S., Hale, E., Wantchekon, K. A., & Armstrong, C. (2019). Relations among intrinsic and extrinsic reading motivation, reading amount, and comprehension: A conceptual replication. *Reading and Writing, 32*, 1197–1218.

Unrau, N. J., Rueda, R., Son, E., Polanin, J. R., Lundeen, R. J., & Muraszewski, A. K. (2018). Can reading self-efficacy be modified? A meta-analysis of the impact of interventions on reading self-efficacy. *Review of Educational Research, 88*(2), 167–204.

Usher, E. L., & Pajares, F. (2008). Sources of self-efficacy in school: Critical review of the literature and future directions. *Review of Educational Research, 78*(4), 751–796.

van den Broek, P., Young, M., Tzeng, Y., & Linderholm, T. (1999). The landscape model of reading: Inferences and the online construction of a memory representation. In H. van Oostendorp & S. R. Goldman (Eds.), *The construction of mental representations during reading* (pp. 71–98). Erlbaum.

Wei, Y., Spear-Swerling, L., & Mercurio, M. (2021). Motivating students with learning disabilities to read. *Intervention in School and Clinic, 56*(3), 155–162.

Weiner, B. (1985). An attributional theory of achievement motivation and emotion. *Psychological Review, 92*(4), 548–573.

Wigfield, A., & Guthrie, J. T. (1997). Rdeelations of children's motivation for reading to the amount and breadth or their reading. *Journal of Educational Psychology, 89*(3), 420.

Wigfield, A., & Guthrie, J. T. (2000). Engagement and motivation in reading. In M. L. Kamil, P. B. Mosenthal, P. D. Pearson, & R. Barr (Eds.), *Handbook of reading research* (Vol. 3, pp. 403–422). Erlbaum.

Wigfield, A., Gladstone, J. R., & Turci, L. (2016). Beyond cognition: Reading motivation and reading comprehension. *Child Development Perspectives, 10*(3), 190–195.

Wigfield, A., Guthrie, J. T., Tonks, S., & Perencevich, K. C. (2004). Children's motivation for reading: Domain specificity and instrumental influences. *The Journal of Educational Research, 97*(6), 299–209.

Yeager, D. S., & Dweck, C. S. (2012). Mindsets that promote resilience: When students believe that personal characteristics can be developed. *Educational Psychologist, 47*(4), 302–314.

7

Inferencing and Reading Comprehension

Gina Biancarosa

Guiding Questions

1. What is an inference?
2. Why is inferencing so important to reading comprehension?
3. How can we assess inferencing?

Reading is a gateway skill to education and lifelong success, serving as a bottleneck for students who struggle with reading comprehension. Because students' academic and career progress is greatly determined by their ability to understand what they read, those who fail to comprehend when reading often fail to acquire the skills and knowledge needed for participation in the 21st-century workforce (Murnane et al., 2012). The need to address reading comprehension is dire due to the continued lack of progress in student reading comprehension over the last two decades (U.S. Department of Education, 2022), despite increasing demands for high-level comprehension in the Common Core State Standards (CCSS; National Governors Association Center for Best Practices and Council of Chief State School Officers [NGA & CCSSO], 2010). Moreover, any reading gains observed have been relatively small and primarily seen among average and above-average grade 4 and 8 readers; the lowest quartile of students have seen very little change. States introduced the CCSS to foster education that prepares students to meet expectations in postsecondary education and the career place (NGA & CCSSO, 2010). Yet, state accountability reading assessments suggest that many students are no closer to meeting expectations for college and career readiness and successful postsecondary life (e.g., Lee & Wu, 2017), with 55% of incoming college students lacking sufficient reading skills for a successful first year of study (ACT, 2019).

One reason reading outcomes have not improved is that the field has excelled at helping students who struggle with reading words accurately and quickly but has struggled to address poor reading comprehension when reading words is not the problem (Pearson et al., 2020). Part of the challenge is that traditional reading comprehension assessments provide limited insight into why a student who can read fluently comprehends poorly and, thus, offers no guidance on how to improve the situation (Pearson et al., 2020). Most reading comprehension assessments focus almost exclusively on comprehension as a product (i.e., what is remembered after reading) and provide little information about how a reader arrived at that product: the comprehension process, which, among other things, depends heavily on generating inferences during reading. When reading comprehension measures only report the extent to which readers demonstrate comprehension relative to a criterion or a normative sample, they leave schools and interventionists uninformed of the underlying reasons for poorer comprehension (Klingner, 2004; Snyder et al., 2005; Wixson et al., 1994). As a result, educators and researchers have repeatedly called for measures that reflect individual differences in the comprehension process to better support targeted intervention with students who struggle specifically with comprehension (Klingner, 2004; Pearson & Hamm, 2005; Pearson et al., 2014, 2020; RAND Reading Study Group, 2002; Snyder et al., 2005; Wixson et al., 1994).

Inference-making is a key component of the reading comprehension process. Most reading teachers and researchers can agree on this fact. Yet, a lot of confusion exists around what constitutes an inference, what are different types of inferences and how they differ, how does inferencing contribute to reading comprehension, and how can inferencing ability be assessed. This chapter aims to bring clarity to these issues with an eye toward practical applications in instruction and assessment.

WHAT IS AN INFERENCE?

What is an inference? An inference is the conclusion that a reader draws from explicit information in a text and sometimes from implicit information in the reader's background knowledge. People make inferences all the time in their daily lives because oral and written language rarely provides all the information needed to understand what is said or read. Making inferences often requires background knowledge relevant to the situation at hand, and it requires the active use of that information to flesh out a more complete understanding of the situation (Elbro & Buch-Iverson, 2013; Kendeou, 2015). This fleshed-out understanding is often called a mental model (Johnson-Laird, 1983) or situation model (Kintsch, 1988), and proficient readers prioritize building a coherent one (see Box 7.1).

Box 7.1. Definition of a Situation or Mental Model

A *situation model* or *mental model* is the conceptual understanding that a reader builds from a text.

To understand better what inferences are and how they operate, imagine a classroom in which Ms. Lin asks 2 fourth-grade students to read the following very short story.

> Toby wanted to get Chris a present for his birthday. He went to his piggy bank. He shook it. There was no sound. (Thurlow & van den Broek, 1997, p. 165)

When Ms. Lin asks what they understood about the story, the students give very different answers. Pablo simply repeats the story back: Toby wanted to get Chris a gift and shook his piggy bank, and it didn't make any noise. When pressed for more, Pablo does not have anything more to say. The second student, Sherisa, says that Toby and Chris were friends, so Toby wanted to buy Chris a birthday gift. Toby shook his piggy bank to see if he had any money to buy the gift with, but the bank was empty. Toby was broke. Both students comprehended the story to a certain extent, but Sherisa understood it much more fully than Pablo did.

The story above, like any good story, is not fully explicit. It does not spell out explicitly that Toby wanted to *buy* Chris a gift, nor that he kept his *money* in a piggy bank. It's also not explicit that he didn't have money. Most likely, you, like Sherisa, understood these things at a glance. That is, you made the same inferences about how the events of the story related to Toby's goal of getting a gift for Chris, likely without even being aware you were making them. You mentally supplied missing information that was only implied by the text of the story, but that was required for the story to be coherent. This type of inferencing does not always come automatically to young readers, as was the case for Pablo.

Indeed, without those inferences, the story reads as a string of non sequiturs. That is how Pablo experienced the story: as a series of disconnected facts. Pablo likely does not understand that readers need to interact with the text to make meaning, that the reader's role is one of coherence-building. (It's also possible that the student lacks the requisite background knowledge to make the inferences.) In contrast, the second student clearly understands that they need to interact with the text. They inferred missing details like that Toby was aiming to buy a gift for Chris, that people keep money in piggy banks, and that no sound meant an empty piggy bank with no money in it.

Of course, there are other inferences a student might make as well. For example, Sherisa also inferred that Toby and Chris were friends, but this inference is not strictly true nor necessary for the text to make sense. That is, they might be cousins, siblings, or simply classmates. Imagine a third student, Ellie, who infers that Toby and Chris were the same age and classmates, that Chris was a boy and not a girl, that the piggy bank was ceramic or metal but certainly not transparent, and even that Toby kept his piggy bank on top of a tall dresser. Each of these inferences, like Sherisa's one about Toby and Chris being friends, could also enrich one's understanding of the story, but they are not required for the heart of the story to make sense. What distinguishes these inferences from those made by Sherisa is that they are not *necessary* in the way Sherisa's other inferences *were* necessary to the logic of the story (i.e., for the story to make sense).

In fact, depending on the resource consulted, there are as many as 9 (Rice et al., 2023; see Table 7.1) or even 13 (Graesser et al., 1994) types of inferences or as few as 1 (Gauche & Pfeiffer Flores, 2022). For example, researchers disagree as to whether anaphor, or pronoun, resolution (e.g., determining that "he" in the second and third sentences of the Toby story refers to Toby) constitutes a true inference (e.g., Rice et al., 2023) or not (Gauche & Pfeiffer Flores, 2022). Similarly, there is some disagreement about whether the distinction between *local* and *global* inferences is a meaningful one. For instance, some define local inferences as involving adjacent areas of text (i.e., within a few sentences of each other), whereas global inferences involve connecting information from more distant areas of the text and often relate to text-level concepts, like goals, themes, and so on (Albrecht & O'Brien, 1993; Graesser et al., 1994; Kendeou, 2015; LARRC & Muijselaar, 2018). But others have adhered to a definition that is more related to the distance between ideas to be connected within a text; that is, they have distinguished between inferences that bridge textual information that is close versus distant within a text (Barth et al., 2015; Carlson et al., 2014).

For the purposes of this chapter, we will concern ourselves with necessary inferences, also called coherence inferences (Cain et al., 2001), which imbue coherence to a text, just like Sherisa's inferences did. We will pay less attention to the concepts of local versus global and other types of inferences except so far as the assessments reviewed make these distinctions and include more than coherence inferences. We will focus on coherence inferences because of their pivotal role in poor reading comprehension.

TABLE 7.1. Types of Inferences and Definitions according to Rice (2023)

Superordinate type	Type	Definition
Word meaning	Lexical	Using word parts to guess the meaning of a new word
	Context clues	Using surrounding text to guess the meaning of a new word
	Anaphor resolution	Linking an anaphor (e.g., pronoun) with its antecedent
Coherence	Bridging	Linking current text information with prior text information
	Causal	Identifying causes or causal relationships
	Gap-filling	Linking current text information with necessary background knowledge
Elaborative	Knowledge-based	Linking current text information with background knowledge to draw conclusions or make predictions that are not necessary
	Text-connecting inference	Linking information across different texts
	Schema-based inference	Connecting prior experience or knowledge with the text

INFERENCING AND POOR COMPREHENSION

Reading, it turns out, relies heavily on the reader's ability to make inferences in pursuit of a coherent understanding of text (Graesser et al., 1994; Kintsch, 1988). Moreover, difficulty in inferencing is one reason why some students struggle specifically with reading comprehension, even when they can decode text well (Cain & Oakhill, 1999, 2006; Oakhill & Cain, 2018). That is, there is a group of struggling readers, called students with specific reading comprehension difficulties (SRCD), who struggle not with reading the words on a page but with the comprehension process. These readers, just like the first student who read the Toby passage, have difficulty making the inferences necessary to build a coherent mental model of what they read. That is, readers with SRCD, like the first student, can read and understand at a basic level but fail to make inferences as they read. Research suggests that this difficulty in making inferences is not due to a lack of background knowledge either, but rather to the process of activating and integrating that background knowledge into one's understanding of a text (e.g., Barth et al., 2021; Cain et al., 2001; Elbro & Buch-Iversen, 2013).

Furthermore, readers who struggle with inference-making seem to struggle specifically with the gap-filling ones that the second student in the vignette excelled at making rather than with the elaborative but unnecessary ones that the third student made. To understand why the type of inference readers make can make a difference in their comprehension, consider the fundamental differences in the roles they fill. While the second student's inferences serve to fill gaps in the story and lend it coherence, the third student's inferences serve to flesh out, or elaborate, nonessential ideas presented in the story. Suffice it to say that the coherence inferences, such as those made by the second student, are the ones most necessary to reading comprehension and the ones that best differentiate good and poor comprehenders (Cain & Oakhill, 1999; Cain et al., 2001). That is, while more skilled comprehenders make more inferences in general than do less skilled comprehenders, the difference in the number of coherence inferences they make is greater than for other kinds of inferences.

One question that often arises about poor comprehenders who struggle with making coherence inferences is whether their difficulty is generalized or specific to reading. Reading is not the only context in which inference-making is of utility. For example, movies, television shows, podcasts, audiobooks, and so on often require viewers and listeners to make inferences to understand content. Currently, it is unclear whether the difficulty in making inferences is context-general or context-specific. Some evidence suggests that inferencing skill generalizes to some extent, with research demonstrating moderate correlations between different modalities (e.g., viewing shows and reading; Kendeou et al., 2008; Magliano et al., 2013). However, other research suggests that inference-making is context-specific in that children make fewer inferences when listening to aural narratives (e.g., narratives read aloud) than when reading written ones (Freed & Cain, 2021). Research comparing viewing videos with reading has had more mixed results (Kendeou et al., 2008; Venneker et al., 2024; Wannagat et al., 2017). One study found effects depended on age, with four-year-old participants showing somewhat better comprehension when listening to narratives than when viewing them, but six-year-old participants showing little to no effect of format (Kendeou et al., 2008). In a different study (Wannagat et al., 2017), 8-year-old participants comprehended audio and audiovisual narratives better than written ones, but 10-year-old and adult participants showed no difference among formats. In contrast, Venneker and colleagues (2024) found that children in grades 4–6 (average age of 10 years) comprehended video narratives better than either written or audio narratives, especially for children with weaker reading comprehension skills. Moreover, Venneker et al. found that video stimulated more background knowledge activation in children than did written and audio narratives. Nonetheless, in all three studies, they also found considerable similarities in comprehension across media; that is, inferencing and comprehension across media formats were highly correlated. Finally, research suggests that skill at inferencing can transfer across different media with instruction, suggesting that video may be a particularly effective medium for inference-making instruction (e.g., Kendeou et al., 2020; van den Broek et al., 2011).

However, delivering instructional intervention depends on our ability to detect when readers have a weakness in inference-making. That is where it becomes important to have assessments sensitive to individual differences in inferencing.

ASSESSING INFERENCING

While inference questions have traditionally been included in assessments of listening comprehension and reading comprehension, recently, assessment developers have worked to isolate and deepen how we assess a student's ability to make inferences. Assessing inference-making ability, apart from listening or reading comprehension more broadly, is essential because there are several types of inferences, and generic reading comprehension measures tend to treat all inferences equally. In other words, while they may produce an inference score, they do not yield insight into what types of inferences may be more or less difficult for specific students. In contrast, this chapter reviews several newer assessments specific to inferencing for students in grades K–6. These assessments include the Language and Reading Research Consortium Inference Making Task (LARRC Inference Making Task), the Minnesota Inferencing Assessment (MIA), the Multiple-choice Online Causal Comprehension Assessment (MOCCA), the Bridging Inferences Test (Bridge-IT), and the Connect-IT Inferential Reading Comprehension Assessment (CIRCA).

One of the biggest challenges in assessing the inferencing of young readers is that their decoding skills are a limiting factor. That is, the texts appropriate for early-grade students who are just learning to decode (i.e., kindergarten to grade 2) provide limited scope for inference-making (Kendeou, 2015). As a result, assessing the inference-making ability of such students is best supported by formats that do not require reading. As a result, we start our review with exactly such assessments before moving on to ones that require reading.

LARRC INFERENCE MAKING TASK

The LARRC Inference Making Task (LARRC & Muijselaar, 2018) comprises two stories presented aurally, followed by eight questions each, with different story sets for grade levels from prekindergarten through grade 3. Derived from earlier studies (Cain & Oakhill, 1999; Oakhill & Cain, 2012), the LARRC Inference Making Task is individually administered. Four of the questions per story tap local coherence inferences, and the other four tap global coherence inferences. An excerpt from one story with a few sample questions is presented in Box 7.2, where Question 1 requires a global coherence inference, and Question 2 requires a local coherence inference. Answers to questions are scored as correct (2 points), partially correct (1 point), or incorrect (0 points).

Box 7.2. LARRC Inferencing Task Sample Item Excerpt

The Game

Today was the last game of the season. There was only a minute left and the score was tied. Jake ran toward the goal and kicked the ball past the goalie. He had scored a goal. The crowd cheered. Jake's team had won the game.

1. What sport was Jake playing?
2. By how many goals did Jake's side win?

Note. From LARRC and Muijselaar (2018, p. 134).

Internal consistency (Cronbach's alpha; see Box 7.3) for the LARRC Inference Making Task was acceptable and ranged from a low of .64 for kindergarten to a high of .78 for prekindergarten. Reliabilities for the local and global coherence scores were lower. Factor analyses exploring whether local and global coherence inferences could be reliably distinguished proved equivocal; that is, while they were statistically distinguishable, the distinction explained only modest variance in scores. As a result, the LARRC Inference Making Task can be best thought of as assessing coherence inference making broadly through its overall score, and the factor analytic estimate of reliability was strong, ranging from .78 in grade 1 to .85 in prekindergarten. Correlations of the total score with criterion measures of listening comprehension were moderate to strong across all grades but were strongest in prekindergarten (r = .61 to .72) and weakest in grade 1 (r = .37 to .48). When correlated with a composite of three listening comprehension measures, all correlations were strong, ranging from r = .56 in grade 1 to r = .76 in prekindergarten.

Box 7.3. Assessing Assessments

For scores on an assessment to be considered meaningful, they must be both *reliable* and *valid*. *Reliability* is often determined by correlating item scores with total scores (i.e., internal consistency), correlating total scores from one administration to another, or through factor analysis. While internal consistency is usually reported as Cronbach's alpha, other correlations are reported as *r*. Values of .80 or higher are generally deemed sufficient for making moderate stakes decisions about individuals, like determining the time or content of Tier 2 instruction (Truckenmiller et al., 2024). *Validity* is often determined by how well an assessment's scores correlate with similar assessments. The more similar the assessments, the stronger (i.e., closer to 1.00) the correlation is expected to be. Values of .50 or better are generally deemed sufficient for low stakes decisions about individual students (Truckenmiller et al., 2024).

MINNESOTA INFERENCE ASSESSMENT

The MIA (Kendeou et al., 2021) is a web-based measure of inference-making for students in grades K–2. Similar to the LARRC Inference Making Task, it does not require students to read but rather presents them with two short (5-minute) videos, one nonfiction and one fiction. Each video includes 16 multiple-choice inference questions of two types: bridging or local inferences, which connect ideas within a text, and elaborative or global inferences, which connect ideas in a text with background knowledge from outside the text. Questions are administered aurally using an animated, gamified agent that interrupts the videos at key points to ask questions. Requiring about 20 minutes to complete, the MIA can be individually or group administered, assuming headsets are available. There are four forms that can be used for assessment.

Internal consistency (Cronbach's alpha) for the MIA was .88, and a range of alternative reliability indices also revealed strong internal consistency (e.g., Guttman L2 = .88; Feldt–Brennan = .88; Feldt–Gilmer = .88; Rasch person separation index = .85). When examined by form, internal consistency was uniformly high (alpha = .87–.90). To establish the unidimensionality of MIA scores, a confirmatory factor analysis was run and indicated that a one-factor model produced adequate fit (Comparative Fit Index = .90; root mean square error of approximation = .02). As a result, the MIA assessment reports a single total score rather than scores for each type of inference. Correlations of the total score with a criterion measure of listening comprehension were moderate, ranging from .32 to .40.

Correlations with reading comprehension measures were also moderate, ranging from .22 to .39. Finally, the instructional sensitivity of MIA was also evaluated by examining change in scores as a result of an eight-week inferencing intervention. Effect sizes ranged from small to medium, indicating good instructional sensitivity.

MULTIPLE-CHOICE ONLINE CAUSAL COMPREHENSION ASSESSMENT

The MOCCA (Biancarosa et al., 2019; Carlson et al., 2014; Davison et al., 2023) is another web-based measure, but it targets students in grades 2–6. Originally developed with a single paper form (Carlson et al., 2014), it is now offered online using computerized adaptive technology (CAT; Davison et al., 2023; see Box 7.4) and can support multiple administrations per year across second through sixth grade. Unique to MOCCA is its provision of two scores: a reading comprehension score based on the ability to make global causal inferences and a diagnostic score for students who struggle with making those inferences. The diagnostic score is a classification of readers into one of three groups: paraphrasing, elaborating, or inconclusive comprehenders. MOCCA is able to accomplish this classification because each MOCCA item has consistent distractors representing cognitive processes that think-aloud research has shown poor comprehenders rely on: paraphrasing and elaborating (Carlson et al., 2014; Kraal et al., 2018; McMaster et al., 2012; Rapp et al., 2007). Specifically, when asked to think aloud, poor comprehenders tend to either sound a lot like Ms Lin's student Pablo in that they strictly paraphrase what they read or like Ellie in that they produce a lot of unnecessary inferences. MOCCA tracks patterns in readers' incorrect responses such that readers who reliably choose the paraphrase response get classified as paraphrasing comprehenders, those who reliably choose the elaborative response get classified as elaborating comprehenders, and those who do not demonstrate a reliable pattern of responses get classified as inconclusive comprehenders. MOCCA also offers modest instructional advice for each of these groups.

Box 7.4. Computerized Adaptive Tests

In contrast to traditional tests where the same items are encountered in the same order by all test-takers, computerized adaptive test (CAT) technology assigns test-takers items based on how they perform. When a test-taker gets an item correct, the next item is a little harder; when a test-taker gets an item incorrect, the next item is a little easier. The test continues to adjust to a test-taker's level of performance until their score is reliable enough to discontinue the test. Because of CAT, test-takers not only receive an individualized score but an individualized confidence interval for that score that indicates the range of scores at the test-taker's ability level.

MOCCA items consist of very short passages, five to ten sentences long, with the next to last sentence missing. Students are asked to select the missing sentence from three to five options provided below the passage. The incorrect options always represent a paraphrase or an elaborative but unnecessary inference. See Box 7.5 for a sample item with answer choices labeled; the coherence inference is the correct answer. Since MOCCA is offered as a CAT, the number of items varies between 15 and 25 depending on student ability.

Box 7.5. Sample MOCCA Item

Pony Ride

The farm was an exciting place because of the new ponies.
Erin was excited because she was the first to ride one of the new ponies.
She wasn't sure how to mount the pony.
Erin thought she could climb up, but she was too short.
Erin looked around the barn for something to help her.
[Missing sentence.]
Happily she rode around the barnyard on the new pony.

Select the best sentence to complete the story.

She grabbed a step ladder and used it to climb onto the pony. [Coherence Inference]
She wanted to find something to help her climb on the pony. [Paraphrase]
She saw many things like saddles, rakes, and buckets. [Elaborative Inference]

Note. From the University of Oregon, the University of Minnesota, California State University, Chico, Georgia State University, and the University of North Dakota (2019).

Internal consistency reliability for the CAT version of MOCCA was estimated using item response theory and yielded moderate to strong marginal reliability for the reading comprehension score (.71 in grade 2, .81 in grade 3, .84 in grade 4, .85 in grade 5, and .87 in grade 6). Marginal reliability for the classification score was more modest (.72 in grade 2, .71 in grade 3, .67 in grade 4, .66 in grade 5, and .76 in grade 6; Davison et al., 2024). A wide range of criterion validity correlations were reported from a low of .41 for the DIBELS oral reading fluency accuracy score (University of Oregon, 2018–2019), which is a fairly dissimilar and widely used assessment that requires students to read aloud for one minute, to a high of .77 with Measure of Academic Progress (Northwest Education Association, 2019), which is a more similar and widely used assessment of broad reading comprehension, with similar magnitudes observed regardless of grade level.

BRIDGE-IT

The Bridge-IT is similar to the MIA in that it taps both local and global coherence inferences, though the assessment developers describe these inferences as *near* and *far* bridging inferences for inferences that bridge text content located close together and further apart, respectively (Barnes et al., 2024; Barth et al., 2015; Martinez-Lincoln et al., 2021; Pike et al., 2010, 2013). Available in a Picture Version for grades 2–6 and a text-only version for grades 6–12, the assessment requires students to read a very short story and then turn the page, losing direct access to the story, and choose the best sentence to come next in the story. In the Picture Version, a supportive or unsupportive picture appears below the story. See Box 7.6 for a sample item with the correct answer in italics. In the supportive picture condition, the picture shows a young boy with a cast and a crutch, while in the unsupportive picture condition, it shows boys using a tire swing to jump into water. The grade 2–6 Picture Version includes 24 items, while the grade 6–12 text-only version has 32 items. The grade 6–12 version is available in a computerized format, while the lower grades version is available in paper format.

Box 7.6. Bridge-IT Sample Item

John has a broken leg from falling off his skateboard last week. John's friend Andrew invited him to go to his cottage for the weekend. The first day it rained and the boys watched movies inside. The second day it was sunny and Andrew wanted to swim in the lake. The boys loved to jump from the tire swing into the lake.

A) John was the first to jump in from the tire swing and had fun swimming.
B) *John played in the sand and watched Andrew play on the tire swing.*
C) The boys decided to leave the cottage early to finish their homework.

Note. From Pike et al. (2010, p. 248).

While no internal consistency or other forms of reliability are available for the Picture Version, the text-only version of Bridge-IT has an average internal consistency of .86 for near inference items and .85 for far inference items (Barth et al., 2015). Alternate form reliability was also reported for an earlier paper version of the text-only Bridge-IT, which was .73 (Pike et al., 2013). Bridge-IT total scores correlated with CIRCA (Clemens & Barnes, 2018; described in the next section) at .60 and with the Weschler Individual Achievement Test (WIAT, Weschler, 2009) reading comprehension subtest scores at .54 (Barnes et al., 2024). Validity of Bridge-IT scores has also been explored using subscores for near and far inferences. Bridge-IT near inference scores correlated with the CIRCA at .71 to .75, while Bridge-IT far inference scores correlated with CIRCA at .23–.33. Bridge-IT scores were also correlated with the WIAT reading comprehension subtest scores at .53 to .63 for the near score and .22 to .37 for the far score (Martinez-Lincoln et al., 2021).

CONNECT-IT INFERENTIAL READING COMPREHENSION ASSESSMENT

CIRCA (Clemens & Barnes, 2018) was designed as an intervention-aligned assessment of four types of inferences for students in grades 6–8. These inferences include anaphoric, or pronoun, inferences (e.g., understanding that "he" in the Toby story refers to Toby and not to Chris); text-connecting inferences, or what other assessments and researchers have called local coherence inferences; word-meaning inferences (e.g., determining the meaning of a new word from context); and global coherence inferences focused on causal relations. There are 11 pronoun- and text-connecting inference questions each, while there are 10 word-meaning and global inference questions each, for a total of 42 items. The format of the items differs by the inference type targeted and includes both short response and multiple-choice formats. For example, pronoun inference items consist of short two- to three-sentence passages in which a pronoun is presented in bold font, and students are asked to write the correct referent for the pronoun in a blank space. In contrast, text-connecting inference questions were multiple-choice and true–false and followed short passages between 50 and 90 words long. See Box 7.7 for a sample multiple-choice text-connecting question with the correct answer italicized.

Box 7.7. CIRCA Sample Text-Connecting Inference Item

During the winter of 2012 a record amount of snow fell on the city, but without any snowplows, the city could not clear the massive amounts of snow from the streets. The next year, before the winter of 2013, the city bought 10 brand new snowplows. However, that winter only a very small amount of snow fell. People were angry that the city had spent so much money on them.
What happened to the snowplows during the winter of 2013 that made people so angry?

A) They were loud and their exhaust caused the air to be polluted.
B) They broke down and needed expensive repairs.
C) There were not enough workers available to drive them.
D) *They were not used.*

Note. From Barnes et al. (2024, p. 439).

Internal consistency reliability for the CIRCA as measured by Cronbach's alpha ranged from .88 to .89 (Barnes et al., 2024). Correlations with criterion measures of reading comprehension were strong. Specifically, CIRCA correlated with WIAT at .68 and the Bridge-IT total score at .52 (Barnes et al., 2024). When correlated with Bridge-IT near and far subscores, correlations were strong with Bridge-IT near scores (.71–.75) and weak with Bridge-IT far scores (.23–.33; Martinez-Lincoln et al., 2021). As the newest of the measures reviewed in this chapter, the evidence supporting the validity of the CIRCA is expected to expand in the next few years.

SUMMARY

In this chapter, we have reviewed what constitutes an inference, why inferencing is so critical to reading comprehension (and comprehension more broadly), and a range of measures that can be used to assess students' inference-making abilities. To reiterate, inference-making is how students establish a coherent mental model of what they are reading (or listening to or viewing). In the absence of inference-making, texts function as lists of disconnected facts. Readers must make both local and global coherence inferences to establish and maintain a reasonable understanding of what is being read. While there are other sorts of inferences that can be made, coherence inferences best distinguish readers with good comprehension from those without.

Table 7.2 summarizes some basic features of each assessment, as well as contact information for learning more about each assessment. It's worth noting that each of the assessments reviewed in this chapter started its life as a researcher-developed measure, and each is in a differing state of readiness for wide use. The one most easily available to teachers at the current time is MOCCA, which maintains a website and has the ability for teachers to self-register and enroll their students in the assessment. MIA is also available by reaching out through a contact form on their website. However, all of the assessments are available if one is willing to reach out to the developers.

As noted earlier, coherence inferences are what best differentiate better and poorer comprehenders (Cain et al., 2001). Thus, it is unsurprising that all of the assessments reviewed measure coherence inferencing ability. A highlight of the assessments reviewed here is that, collectively, they cover development from prekindergarten through high school, enabling teachers at any level to assess this critical ability in their students.

As noted earlier, assessing the inference-making ability of very young students is best supported by formats that do not require reading. Both the LARRC assessment and MIA offer just such formats, with LARRC using an aural format and MIA using video and aural formats, although the LARRC assessment must be individually administered. The availability of these two assessments allows teachers to catch weaknesses in coherence inference making early. Moreover, the creators behind both assessments have also produced curricula that foster better inference-making in young students. While the LARRC group has developed the Let's Know! curriculum for grades PreK–3 (LARRC et al., 2022; *https://larrc.ehe.osu.edu/curriculum*), as described by Piasta et al. (Chapter 3, this volume), the MIA makers have developed Early Language Comprehension Individualized Instruction

TABLE 7.2. Assessments of Inferencing Available for Use in Grades K–12

Measure	Grades	Format	Setting	Time	Items	Type	Contact
LARRC	P–3	Aural	Individual	15–20 min	16	Local coherence, global coherence	k.cain@lancaster.ac.uk
MIA	K–2	Video and aural	Group	20 min	32	Local coherence, global coherence	*http://inferencegalaxy.com*
MOCCA	2–6	Written	Group	15–25 min	15–25	Global coherence	*http://mocca.uoregon.edu*
Bridge-IT Picture Version	2–6	Written with picture support	Group	20 min	24	Local coherence, global coherence	marcia.barnes@vanderbilt.edu
CIRCA	6–8	Written	Group	30 min	42	Pronoun, vocabulary, local coherence, global coherence	nathan.clemens@austin.utexas.edu
Bridge-IT	6–12	Written	Group	20 min	32	Local coherence, global coherence	marcia.barnes@vanderbilt.edu

(ELCII; *https://inferencegalaxy.com/page/elcii*) for kindergarten and Technology-based Early Language Comprehension Intervention (TeLCI; *https://inferencegalaxy.com/page/telci*) for grades 1 and 2 (McMaster et al., 2019, 2024).

Unfortunately, it is not always possible to catch inferencing difficulties early, which is where the other assessments reviewed here come in. MOCCA and the Picture Version of Bridge-IT are designed for use in grades 2–6, while Bridge-IT and CIRCA are designed for use in grade 6 and beyond. Like the LARRC and MIA assessments, CIRCA has an aligned intervention called Connect-IT (*https://meadowscenter.org/program/project-connect-it*) for grades 6–8 (Barnes et al., 2024; Martinez-Lincoln et al., 2021). Of course, many other inferencing interventions with positive effects exist beyond those mentioned here (e.g., Elleman, 2017; Hall, 2016; Rice & Wijekumar, 2024), but the existence of interventions aligned to specific assessments is worth highlighting here as they provide an important method for monitoring response to intervention.

Reconsider Ms Lin's fourth-grade class. How fruitful it would be for her to use one of the assessments reviewed here! The two assessments suited to her grade level are the Picture Version of Bridge-IT and MOCCA. Sherisa, her student who made the necessary coherence inferences about the Toby story, would likely do very well on both assessments, confirming Ms Lin's suspicion that Sherisa is a good comprehender. With the Picture Version of Bridge-IT, she might learn that Pablo and Ellie both struggle with making bridging inferences, but that Pablo struggles even with near inferences. With MOCCA, she would learn that both Pablo and Ellie are failing to make coherence inferences, but that Pablo is doing so because he is paraphrasing when reading, while Ellie is doing so because she is making inferences but not the necessary ones. Armed with these results, Ms Lin knows she needs to work with both students on making coherence inferences.

Given the role that inference-making difficulties play in poor reading comprehension and the existence of several assessments of inferencing ability for readers in a wide range of grades, it is surprising that more use is not made of these assessments. This chapter is an effort to help spread the word about not only the importance of inferencing to comprehension but also the availability of tools that can help teachers meet the needs of their students with comprehension difficulties.

Reflection Questions

1. How has this chapter changed how you think about reading comprehension and inferencing?
2. How have you assessed inference-making ability in your students in the past?
3. Which of the reviewed assessments seems most useful to you and why?

REFERENCES

ACT. (2019). *The condition of college and career readiness 2019.* Author.

Albrecht, J. E., & O'Brien, E. J. (1993). Updating a mental model: Maintaining both local and global coherence. *Journal of Experimental Psychology: Learning, Memory, and Cognition, 19*(5), 1061–1070.

Barnes, M. A., Clemens, N. H., Simmons, D., Hall, C., Fogarty, M., Martinez-Lincoln, A., et al. (2024). A randomized controlled trial of tutor- and computer-delivered inferential comprehension interventions for middle school students with reading difficulties. *Scientific Studies of Reading, 28*(4), 411–440.

Barth, A. E., Barnes, M., Francis, D., Vaughn, S., & York, M. (2015). Inferential processing among adequate and struggling adolescent comprehenders and relations to reading comprehension. *Reading and Writing: An Interdisciplinary Journal, 28*, 587–609.

Barth, A. E., Daniel, J., Roberts, G., Vaughn, S., Barnes, M. A., Ankrum, E., & Kincaid, H. (2021). The role of knowledge availability in forming inferences with rural middle grade English learners. *Learning and Individual Differences, 88*, 102006.

Biancarosa, G., Kennedy, P. C., Carlson, S. E., Yoon, H. J., Seipel, B., Liu, B., & Davison, M. L. (2019). Constructing subscores that add validity: A case study of identifying students at-risk. *Educational and Psychological Measurement, 79*, 65–84.

Cain, K., & Oakhill, J. (2006). Profiles of children with specific reading comprehension difficulties. *British Journal of Educational Psychology, 76*, 683–696.

Cain, K., & Oakhill, J. V. (1999). Inference making ability and its relation to comprehension failure in young children. *Reading and Writing: An Interdisciplinary Journal, 11*, 489–503.

Cain, K., Oakhill, J. V., Barnes, M. A., & Bryant, P. E. (2001). Comprehension skill, inference-making ability, and their relation to knowledge. *Memory & Cognition, 29*(6), 850–859.

Carlson, S. E., Seipel, B., & McMaster, K. L. (2014). Development of a new reading comprehension assessment: Identifying comprehension differences among readers. *Learning and Individual Differences, 32*, 40–53.

Clemens, N. H., & Barnes, M. A. (2018). *Connect-IT Reading Comprehension Assessment (CIRCA).* University of Texas at Austin.

Davison, M. L., Weiss, D. J., DeWeese, J. N., Cinar, O. E., Biancarosa, G., & Kennedy, P. C. (2023). A diagnostic tree model for adaptive assessment of complex cognitive processes using multidimensional response options. *Journal of Educational and Behavioral Statistics, 48*(6), 914–941.

Davison, M. L., Weiss, D. J., DeWeese, J. N., Wong, Y. L., Biancarosa, G., Kennedy, P. C., & Lee, S. (2024). *MOCCA computer-adaptive test technical manual: MOCCA technical Report MTR-2024-1.* University of Oregon.

Elbro, C., & Buch-Iversen, I. (2013). Activation of background knowledge for inference making: Effects on reading comprehension. *Scientific Studies of Reading, 17*(6), 435–452.

Elleman, A. M. (2017). Examining the impact of inference instruction on the literal and inferential comprehension of skilled and less skilled readers: A meta-analytic review. *Journal of Educational Psychology, 109*(6), 761–781.

Freed, J., & Cain, K. (2021). Assessment of inference-making in children using comprehension questions and story retelling: Effect of text modality and a story presentation format. *International Journal of Language & Communication Disorders, 56*(3), 637–652.

Gauche, G., & Pfeiffer Flores, E. (2022). The role of inferences in reading comprehension: A critical analysis. *Theory & Psychology, 32*(2), 326–343.

Graesser, A. C., Singer, M., & Trabasso, T. (1994). Constructing inferences during narrative text comprehension. *Psychological Review, 101*(3), 371–395.

Hall, C. S. (2016). Inference instruction for struggling readers: A synthesis of intervention research. *Educational Psychology Review, 28*, 1–22.

Johnson-Laird, P. N. (1983). *Mental models: Towards a cognitive science of language, inference, and consciousness* (No. 6). Harvard University Press.

Kendeou, P. (2015). A general inference skill. In E. J. O'Brien, A. E. Cook, & R. F. Lorch, Jr (Eds.), *Inferences during reading* (pp. 160–181). Cambridge University Press.

Kendeou, P., Bohn-Gettler, C., White, M. J., & van den Broek, P. (2008). Children's inference generation across different media. *Journal of Research in Reading, 31*(3), 259–272.

Kendeou, P., McMaster, K. L., Butterfuss, R., Kim, J., Bresina, B., & Wagner, K. (2020). The inferential language comprehension (iLC) framework: Supporting children's comprehension of visual narratives. *Topics in Cognitive Science, 12*, 256–273.

Kendeou, P., McMaster, K. L., Butterfuss, R., Kim, J., Slater, S., & Bulut, O. (2021). Development and validation of the Minnesota inference assessment. *Assessment for Effective Intervention, 47*(1), 47–52.

Kintsch, W. (1988). The role of knowledge in discourse comprehension: A construction-integration model. *Psychological Review, 95*(2), 163–182.

Klingner, J. K. (2004). Assessing reading comprehension. *Assessment for Effective Intervention, 29*(4), 59–70.

Kraal, A., Koornneef, A. W., Saab, N., & van den Broek, P. W. (2018). Processing of expository and narrative texts by low- and high-comprehending children. *Reading & Writing, 31*, 2017–2040.

Language and Reading Research Consortium (LARRC), Lo, M.-T., & Xu, M. (2022). Impacts of the let's know! Curriculum on the language and comprehension-related skills of prekindergarten and kindergarten children. *Journal of Educational Psychology, 114*(6), 1205–1224.

Language and Reading Research Consortium (LARRC) & Muijselaar, M. M. L. (2018). The dimensionality of inference making: Are local and global inferences distinguishable? *Scientific Studies of Reading, 22*(2), 117–136.

Lee, J., & Wu, Y. (2017). Is the common core racing America to the top? Tracking changes in state standards, school practices, and student achievement. *Education Policy Analysis Archives, 25*(35), 1–23.

Magliano, J. P., Loschky, L. C., Clinton, J. A., & Larson, A. M. (2013). Is reading the same as viewing? An exploration of the similarities and differences between processing text- and visually based narratives. In B. Miller, L. Cutting, & P. McCardle (Eds.), *Unraveling the behavioral, neurobiological and genetic components of reading comprehension* (pp. 78–90). Brookes.

Martinez-Lincoln, A., Barnes, M. A., & Clemens, N. H. (2021). The influence of student engagement on the effects of an inferential reading comprehension intervention for struggling middle school readers. *Annals of Dyslexia, 71*, 322–345.

McMaster, K., Kendeou, P., Bresina, B. C., Slater, S., Wagner, K., White, M. J., Butterfuss, R., Kim, J., & Umana, C. (2019). Developing an interactive software application to support young children's inference-making. *L1-Educational Studies in Language and Literature, 19*(4), 1–30.

McMaster, K. L., Kendeou, P., Kim, J., & Butterfuss, R. (2024). Efficacy of a technology-based early language comprehension intervention: A randomized control trial. *Journal of Learning Disabilities, 57*(3), 139–152.

McMaster, K. L., van den Broek, P., Espin, C. A., White, M. J., Rapp, D. N., Kendeou, P., et al. (2012). Making the right connections: Differential effects of reading intervention for subgroups of comprehenders. *Learning and Individual Differences, 22*, 100–111.

Murnane, R., Sawhill, I., & Snow. C. (2012). Literacy challenges for the twenty-first century: Introducing the issue. *The Future of Children, 22*(2), 3–16.

National Governors Association Center for Best Practices, Council of Chief State School Officers. (2010). *Common core state standards*. Author.

Northwest Education Association. (2019). *MAP growth technical report*. Author.

Oakhill, J., & Cain, K. (2018). Children's problems with inference making: Causes and consequences. *Bulletin of Educational Psychology, 49*(4), 683–699.

Oakhill, J. V., & Cain, K. (2012). The precursors of reading ability in young readers: Evidence from a four-year longitudinal study. *Scientific Studies of Reading, 16*(2), 91–121.

Pearson, P. D., & Hamm, D. N. (2005). The assessment of reading comprehension: A review of practices—Past, present, and future. In S. G. Paris & S. A. Stahl (Eds.), *Children's reading comprehension and assessment* (pp. 13–69). Routledge.

Pearson, P. D., Palincsar, A. S., Biancarosa, G., & Berman, A. I. (2020). *Reaping the rewards of the reading for understanding initiative*. National Academy of Education.

Pearson, P. D., Valencia, S. W., & Wixson, K. (2014). Complicating the world of reading assessment: Toward better assessments for better teaching. *Theory into Practice, 53*(3), 236–246.

Pike, M. M., Barnes, M. A., & Barron, R. W. (2010). The role of illustrations in children's inferential comprehension. *Journal of Experimental Child Psychology, 105*, 243–255.

Pike, M., Swank, P., Taylor, H., Landry, S., & Barnes, M. A. (2013). Effect of preschool working memory, language, and narrative abilities on inferential comprehension at school-age in children with spina bifida myelomeningocele and typically developing children. *Journal of the International Neuropsychological Society, 19*(4), 390–399.

RAND Reading Study Group. (2002). *Reading for understanding: Toward and R&D program in reading comprehension*. RAND Corporation.

Rapp, D. N., Broek, P. V. D., McMaster, K. L., Kendeou, P., & Espin, C. A. (2007). Higher-order comprehension processes in struggling readers: A perspective for research and intervention. *Scientific Studies of Reading, 11*, 289–312.

Rice, M., & Wijekumar, K. (2024). Inference skills for reading: A meta-analysis of instructional practices. *Journal of Educational Psychology, 116*(4), 569–589.

Rice, M., Wijekumar, K., Lambright, K., & Bristow, A. (2023). Inferencing in reading comprehension: Examining variations in definition, instruction, and assessment. *Technology, Knowledge, and Learning, 29*, 1169–1190.

Snyder, L., Caccamise, D., & Wise, B. (2005). The assessment of reading comprehension: Considerations and cautions. *Topics in Language Disorders, 25*(1), 33–50.

Thurlow, R., & van den Broek, P. (1997). Automaticity and inference generation during reading comprehension. *Reading & Writing Quarterly: Overcoming Learning Difficulties, 13*(2), 165–181.

Truckenmiller, A. J., Cho, E., Bourgeois, S., & Friedman, E. (2024). Uses and misuses of commercial reading assessment: An applied framework for decision making in Grades K through 6. *The Reading Teacher, 77*(5), 609–623.

U.S. Department of Education, Institute of Education Sciences, National Center for Education Statistics. (2022). *National Assessment Educational Progress (NAEP): 2022 NAEP*

van den Brook, P., Kendeou, P., Lousberg, S., & Visser, G. (2011). Preparing for reading comprehension: Fostering text comprehension skills in preschool and early elementary school children. *International Electronic Journal of Elementary Education, 4*(1), 259–268.

Venneker, D., Helder, A., & van den Broek, P. (2024). Understanding narratives in different media formats: Processes and products of elementary-school children's comprehension of texts and videos. *Reading & Writing*. Advance online publication.

Wannagat, W., Waizenegger, G., & Nieding, G. (2017). Multi-level mental representations of written, auditory, and audiovisual text in children and adults. *Cognitive Processing, 18*, 491–504.

Weschler, D. (2009). *Wechsler individual achievement test* (3rd ed.). Pearson Clinical Assessments.

Wixson, K. K., Valencia, S. W., & Lipson, M. Y. (1994). Issues in literacy assessment: Facing the realities of internal and external assessment. *Journal of Reading Behavior, 26*(3), 315–337.

8

Effects of Language Components on Language and Reading Comprehension

Doris Luft Baker, Yixian Huang, Cinthia Berenice Herrera, Sholeh Moradibavi, and Hanyue Sha

Guiding Questions

1. Which language component or components have the largest effect on the English reading comprehension of culturally and linguistically diverse (CLD) students?
2. Which types of activities that address these language components are particularly effective to build the English reading comprehension of CLD students from preschool to grade 6?

To answer these questions, in this chapter we (1) explain our conceptual framework; (2) review findings from intervention studies summarized in several meta-analyses, including the one we describe more in depth in this chapter; and (3) describe specific activities and pedagogical models included in effective interventions designed to improve language and reading comprehension. We conclude the chapter with reflections to encourage application.

CONSIDER THIS VIGNETTE

Ms Perez is a reading coach at Juarez school. Juarez is an established school, grades preschool to 6, that has experienced a significant amount of change in the school population. Currently, 35% of students are native English speakers with various dialects, including African American Vernacular English and Texas English, 40% are Spanish speakers from many different countries in Latin America with different Spanish dialects, and 25% come from countries where the national language is Mandarin Chinese, Vietnamese, and Arabic, among others. Ms Perez is concerned about how she will address the needs of her students and, at the same time, meet the demands of the academic curriculum. She is particularly worried about those students with low English language proficiency either because they speak a different dialect or language at home, they just arrived in the country, or because they might have a language disability.

The district where Ms Perez works is concerned about students' low reading scores across grades, and administrators in the district have put a lot of effort into making sure that teachers teach decoding and word reading to their students in the early grades. However, very little professional development and support has been given to language development besides reminding teachers to teach vocabulary every day, creating lists of words students should know at the end of each grade, and emphasizing words that students are learning by putting them on a Word Wall. In addition, because of the large demand of students with low language proficiency, the English as a second language teacher (ESL) struggles to find time to support all students and teachers across grades. To tackle the difficult job of coaching teachers across grades on best practices to enhance reading comprehension in English, Ms Perez decides to learn more about how to address the different language components that support reading comprehension. What did Ms Perez learn?

Supporting CLD students in developing strong language and reading comprehension skills is essential for their academic success, especially in content-heavy subjects such as math, science, and social studies (Baker et al., 2018; Baker, Ma, et al., 2021). Moreover, research over the years has shown that language interventions can have a positive impact on CLD students (Silverman et al., 2020), but there is still much to learn about which specific components of language interventions—such as phonology, morphology, syntax, semantics, and pragmatics are most effective and how they should be combined to maximize students' reading comprehension across different subjects and across different grades. Table 8.1 provides definitions of specific concepts used in this chapter.

WHAT IS LANGUAGE AND WHAT ARE ITS CORE COMPONENTS?

Language is made of words and rules that govern the production of sounds, words, and sentences and how to use them (Moats, 2020). All human languages share universal characteristics such as (1) a certain number of sounds in words that can

TABLE 8.1. Definitions of Key Concepts

Concept	Definition
Culturally and linguistically diverse students	Culturally and linguistically diverse students (CLD) refers to students from a variety of cultural, social, and economic backgrounds who speak a language other than English at home.
Academic English	Academic English is defined broadly as the language used in schools to teach content and reading comprehension (e.g., teaching the meaning of *character, plot,* and *sequence* in fictional text or strategies such as cause and effect, prediction, answering and asking *wh-* questions in informational text) (What Works Clearinghouse [WWC], 2014).
Background knowledge	Refers to the knowledge derived from experiences and making connections to other knowledge obtained by listening to books, social interactions, and experiencing the world.
Meta-analysis	A meta-analysis is a review of the literature on a specific topic that uses statistical methods to calculate the effects of an intervention on a specific outcome (e.g., reading comprehension).
Effect size	Effect size is a standardized measure of the impact of an intervention that can be synthesized across outcome measures and studies. A large effect size means that the effect has practical implications while a small effect size has limited practical implications (WWC, 2022).
Metalinguistic awareness	Refers to the conscious knowledge of the structure of a language (Moats, 2020).

be said and understood (i.e., phonology); (2) words that are composed of meaningful units that sometimes can be combined to create new words, phrases, and sentences that have a meaning (i.e., morphology); (3) the specific rules of sentence structures (i.e., syntax); (4) words, phrases, and sentences that have meaning (i.e., semantics); and (5) a rule system that tells the speaker how to use language in different contexts and with different listeners (i.e., pragmatics). Later in the chapter, we provide specific activities for different grades. Most of the examples of activities will be particularly appropriate for Spanish-speaking CLD students, given that they are the majority group of CLD students in the United States (National Center for Education Statistics, 2023).

CONCEPTUAL FRAMEWORK

We use the Simple View of Reading (SVR; Hoover & Gough, 1990) to help us understand how language and reading are connected. In this model, reading comprehension is the product of two key skills: decoding and language comprehension (see Box 8.1).

Box 8.1. Definitions of Decoding and Language Comprehension

Decoding refers to the ability to recognize letter sounds automatically and combine them to read words accurately and with prosody when they are encountered in a text. The goal of decoding is for the reader to build a mental representation of the word that can be recognized or named immediately (Ehri, 2014; Moats, 2020).

Language comprehension is the ability to understand spoken language. It includes the interpretation of words, phrases, sentences, and connected text. Language comprehension also requires the ability to connect ideas within a text, the association of the ideas in a text to the reader's background knowledge and to other outside sources. Moreover, understanding language requires the reader to identify the meaning of words that are spelled the same such as *can* (i.e., both as a noun and an auxiliary verb) or words that sound the same but are spelled differently (e.g., *their* versus *there*; Baker et al., 2023; Moats, 2020).

HOW DO LANGUAGE COMPONENTS SUPPORT READING COMPREHENSION?

Although several meta-analyses have contributed to a better understanding of how spoken language supports reading comprehension (e.g., Brady & Mason, 2024; Silverman et al., 2020; Zhang et al., 2023). Few studies have examined closely how language components by themselves or in combination affect reading comprehension. A better understanding of how these components interact can provide practitioners with evidence to inform different ways of creating activities that enhance student knowledge of language and reading comprehension. In addition, understanding the language components can also be used with CLD students who are trying to make sense of their native linguistic repertoire and, at the same time, learn the rules of the English linguistic system. Given that English is one of the most widely spoken languages in the world and that it consists of very specific complex characteristics (Moats, 2020), understanding how language affects reading comprehension has been widely researched. Below, we summarize the results of five reviews. We then describe in more detail the results of our own meta-analytic review that has focused on understanding how different language components affect language and reading comprehension. To our knowledge, this is the first meta-analysis that examines more closely how language components in isolation or in combination increase reading comprehension.

In the meta-analysis by Silverman et al. (2020), researchers examined 43 language comprehension interventions, finding positive effects of the interventions reviewed on CLD students' reading and vocabulary development. While Silverman et al. underscored the importance of language comprehension, the study did not isolate the effects of individual language components or investigate their combined impact, leaving a gap in understanding which specific components are most effective in improving language and reading comprehension. Nonetheless, the authors did suggest, as part of their future research recommendations, the importance of reviewing the effects of language components on reading comprehension and on how to best support CLD students.

Other reviews, such as Brady and Mason (2024) and Zhang et al. (2023), for instance, highlighted the importance of morphological awareness in reading comprehension. However, they did not address other language components such as phonology, semantics, syntax, or pragmatics that can also contribute to reading comprehension. In studies focused on students with language disorders, such as the review by Cirrin and Gillam (2008), researchers found positive effects of language interventions, but they note that the lack of research on older students and more complex language interventions leaves teachers without clear guidance on how to support CLD students in middle and high school. Similarly, Vishnu et al. (2023) explored interventions for bilingual children with developmental language disorders, finding promising results for vocabulary interventions, though there was limited evidence of the effects of interventions targeting phonology and syntax on reading comprehension.

Taken together, these studies suggest that while language interventions can be effective, there is still much to learn about how different language components can work together to support reading comprehension and content learning for CLD students. Our recent meta-analysis systematically analyzed language interventions on both reading and language comprehension, focusing on the combined effects of multiple language components to provide a clearer picture of what works best for CLD students at different stages of learning (Huang et al., 2025). Specifically, we looked at how different interventions targeting various language components compare in improving language and reading comprehension. We applied a Bayesian Network Meta-Analysis, a statistical method that allowed us to compare multiple interventions at once, even those not directly compared in individual studies (van Valkenhoef et al., 2012).

WHAT DOES THE RESEARCH SAY ABOUT INTERVENTIONS THAT ADDRESS LANGUAGE COMPONENTS TO INCREASE READING COMPREHENSION?

In this section, we summarize the main findings of our meta-analytic review on CLD students ages 3–12 learning to read in English as a second, third, or fourth language. We focused on identifying rigorous studies that have examined the effects of a language intervention on reading and listening comprehension. Specifically, we wanted to know whether an intervention using one or more language components (i.e., phonology, morphology, semantics, syntax, and pragmatics) would increase student reading comprehension compared to business as usual or other interventions. By focusing on how different language components, such as phonology, morphology, semantics, syntax, and pragmatics, work together, we aim to offer a more nuanced view of how to design effective instruction and intervention to address the unique needs of CLD students. Although we also included in our search interventions that focused on pragmatics, we could not find any language interventions that included pragmatics as one of their language components.

Next, we provide a summary of the interventions with the largest effects, breaking them by grade: prekindergarten to kindergarten, lower elementary (grades 1 to 3), and upper elementary (grades 4 to 6). By analyzing the effectiveness of language interventions across these grades, we aim to provide targeted teaching strategies with which educators can best tailor their language instruction to meet the needs of all students, but particularly to meet the developmental needs of their CLD students. We include activities from studies with significant effect sizes to provide teachers with examples of what works for CLD students in different grades.

Overall, our research findings highlight the importance of integrating multiple language components (e.g., semantics, phonology, and syntax) to support language and reading comprehension. For language comprehension, we found that combining semantics and translation activities had a strong positive effect, helping CLD students make connections between words in their native language and English. (See Box 8.2 for the definition of translation activities.) For reading comprehension, however, addressing a broader mix of language components is essential. The most effective interventions that increase reading comprehension involved phonology, morphology, semantics, and syntax, as well as decoding words and understanding sentences. This comprehensive approach is essential for reading because it supports not only the ability to recognize and decode words but also the ability to understand the meaning of words within the text. Results from our analyses indicate that combining components is highly effective for developing language and reading comprehension.

Box 8.2. Definition of Translation Activities

Translation activities are broadly defined in this chapter as the use of the native language to support the learning of the English language and/or reading comprehension (e.g., students learn the sounds of words in Spanish, Chinese, Arabic, and so on, either at the same time or before learning the sounds of words in English). Translation activities support CLD student development of language and reading comprehension in English (Baker, Basaraba, et al., 2016; Baker & Santoro, 2023).

Next, we describe in more detail activities across grades that were very successful in supporting language and reading comprehension.

WHAT LANGUAGE ACTIVITIES ARE THE MOST EFFECTIVE IN PREKINDERGARTEN AND KINDERGARTEN?

Three primary studies informed what we found to be the best teaching approaches for improving listening and reading comprehension in prekindergarten and kindergarten (Farver et al., 2009, Neuman & Kaefer, 2018, and Pile et al., 2010). All three studies utilized a shared book reading intervention with large effects. Farver et al. (2009) implemented shared book reading in Spanish, the child's native language, while Neuman and Kaefer (2018) and Pile et al. (2010) conducted the shared book reading activities in English with CLD students. Shared book reading, an activity that includes an adult reading together with the child by interacting with the book during the read-aloud, is the most common and effective reading strategy practiced in mainstream classrooms by teachers, paraprofessionals, and parents at home (What Works Clearinghouse, 2010).

As shown by Farver et al. (2009) and others, shared book reading activities can also be conducted in the students' native language. Extensive research has shown that reading books aloud at home in the child's native language fosters deeper conversations and builds more semantic and syntactic awareness because the adult (and the child) can express themselves in the language they are most familiar with

(Dixon & Wu, 2014; Richards-Tutor et al., 2016). To illustrate how to carry out shared book reading activities, we provide suggestions for before, during, and after reading from the studies reviewed for our meta-analysis.

With shared book reading, the goal is for the adult to converse with the child about the book, focusing on the details of the pictures, and drawing the child's attention to their own experiences and background knowledge (Ciornei & Dina, 2015; Neuman & Kaefer, 2018). Prereading activities include "wh-" questions about the cover of the book and making predictions of what will happen in the book. As illustrated in Figure 8.1, during the reading activities, the adult (i.e., practitioner, parent, research staff) asks literal questions ("What do you see?"), inferential questions (e.g., "Why do you think . . .?"; "How do you know . . .?"),

Literal Questions	Inferential Questions	Open-Ended Questions
Refers to questions about ideas and concepts that appear directly from the images or written text of the book.	Questions that are *not* directly related to images or the written text of the book. The text may help infer or refer to external information. These questions ask the child to think beyond the information presented.	These questions cannot be answered with a *yes* or *no*. They involve a conversation of one sentence or more about the opportunity to express what they think and feel.
Examples:	*Examples:*	*Examples:*
What expression did the character show?	What would happen if this character came to our house?	What happened in the beginning?
Who has a green hat?	How would you say goodnight to the moon?	What happened at the end?
What day did the caterpillar hatch from the egg?	What do you think it would be like if the character in the story became your friend?	Why did the character do that?
		What would you change in the story?

Note. Although the Pile et al. (2010) study used literal, inferential, and open-ended questions in their curriculum for their intervention, their study did not provide examples. We adapted questions from Zucker et al. (2010).

FIGURE 8.1. Literal, inferential, and open-ended questions with examples.

and open-ended questions (e.g., "What expression did the character demonstrate?"; Pile, 2010). The after-reading activities involve asking questions that help the child make connections to other books the child has read or to their own experiences (Whitehurst et al., 1994). Additionally, post-story role-playing or reenacting stories using cutouts of characters and various props can be very engaging for children (Pile et al., 2010).

For shared book reading, teachers can choose books with vibrant illustrations that are popular with children and that also include topics that are particularly interesting and appealing to CLD students (Pile et al., 2010). Involving the parents in shared book reading by providing them with the Spanish (or other native language) versions of the books read in class is particularly motivating and engaging for the children, who will be able to participate actively in shared book reading activities in the classroom if they have read and discussed the books before they listen to them in school (Baker, Mogna, et al., 2016; Neuman & Kaefer, 2018; Zucker et al., 2010). Given that semantic activities with phonology are also particularly effective whether they are used in English or in Spanish, shared book reading can also be used to develop children's semantic knowledge (Farver et al., 2009; Neuman & Kaefer, 2018). In general, CLD students have higher vocabulary scores in their native language than in English, given their lack of exposure to English. Shared book reading can be paired with semantic activities and word games to further develop CLD students' English language proficiency. Semantic games can be embedded within the shared book reading activity, or they can be played at the end of a shared book reading session. Examples that can be used to develop student semantic knowledge can be the use of picture word cards to provide examples versus non-examples of the use of a word, picture sort games (e.g., sorting pictures into categories), and making connection word webs (i.e., semantic networks of words related to emotions; Baker et al., 2015; Coyne et al., 2009; Neuman & Kaefer, 2018). In addition, as illustrated in Figure 8.2, strategies that support language comprehension and later reading comprehension are: compare–contrast questions, release control, stepping back to support open-ended responses, and encouraging children to use familiar and content-specific words (Neuman & Kaefer, 2018).

Table 8.2 has examples of activities of phonology, semantics, and decoding that teachers may typically use in the classrooms. As our meta-analysis indicated, phonology and semantics are a particularly effective combination of language components. In the early grades, phonology plays an important role given its reciprocal relation with decoding and spelling (Moats, 2020). In Farver et al. (2009), teachers used picture puzzles and manipulatives in activities to help children recognize that

Compare and contrast:

- **Comparing,** Focuses on similarities between two or more objects or animals or between before and after events. For example: Look at the caterpillar now! Is it small or big compared to the beginning of the story?
- **Contrasting.** Focuses on the differences between two or more objects or animals. What are the differences between a caterpillar and an earth worm?

Release control:

- **Popcorn reading.** After a brief teacher-led reading, there should be a transition to a release control popcorn reading activity, allowing students to take turns reading aloud.
- **Choral reading.** To scaffold students' reading of a complex text, using a release control strategy such as charcoal reading, lets the teacher gradually release responsibility to the students. In the early grades, books for these activities should be simple and include many decodable words the student has already learned and internalized. Pictures of key vocabulary should be presented prior to students reading the book.

Stepping back to support open-ended responses:

- **Guiding conversation and modeling ways of thinking -** Allow students to think before responding and let **children** pause to encourage thoughtful answers as well as provide children with a safe place to make mistakes.
- **Encouraging children to use familiar and content-specific words** - Using picture word cards and other games.

FIGURE 8.2. Examples of supporting reading comprehension as suggested by Neuman and Kaefer (2018).

words are made up of smaller sound units. Phonological activities can begin with larger, concrete sound units (e.g., compound words) and progress to smaller ones (e.g., syllables, onsets, rhymes, and phonemes). Phonological activities should take between 5 and 15 minutes and should be taught explicitly. They can be combined with decoding activities, such as manipulating objects and puzzles that teach letter names and letter-sound knowledge, and various matching and oddity games to help children identify capital and lowercase letters.

TABLE 8.2. Phonology, Semantics, and Decoding Activities for Prekindergarten and Kindergarten Students

Activities for . . .	Description
Phonology	• Activities focused on initial sound identification and sound matching through engaging games, such as fishing and sorting (Pile, 2015). • Phonology is sequenced along the developmental continuum, starting with hearing rhyming sounds and progressing to syllable awareness and initial sound awareness (Farver et al., 2009).
Semantics	• Activities that focus on picture card categories, definitions, and relationships between words (e.g., *camel* and *scorpion* are both desert animals; Neuman & Kaefer, 2018).
Decoding	• Activities to recognize letter sounds and letter names build the foundation for understanding the relation between letters (graphemes) and sounds (phonemes; Farver et al., 2009). • Associating a letter with a key word (e.g., the child's name) reinforces letter recognition (Farver et al., 2009). • Singing the alphabet helps children learn the sequence of letters. • Activities that use objects and puzzles to teach letter names and letter-sound relationships, along with matching and oddity games to help children recognize capital and lowercase letters (Farver et al., 2009).

WHAT LANGUAGE ACTIVITIES ARE THE MOST EFFECTIVE IN GRADES 1–3?

Results from our meta-analysis suggest that language components such as semantics, phonology, syntax, and the use of students' native language have a large positive effect on language and reading comprehension for CLD students in grades 1–3. Thus, interventions that address multiple components of language are far more effective than those that exclude any of these components. In addition to teaching these language components, all studies that used structured and sequenced lessons provided in small groups were the most effective (see Busse et al., 2021; Kamps et al., 2007; Sun & Dong, 2004; Vaughn et al., 2006).

Using a student's native language to teach semantics, syntax, and phonology enhances comprehension, builds cognitive bridges between the languages, and reduces learning anxiety, allowing students to grasp complex ideas in the language they understand best (Richards-Tutor et al., 2016). Furthermore, learning language components in the native language enables the transfer of literacy skills from the native language to the new language, expanding the student's phonology, morphology, and semantics through connections between languages and the promotion of metalinguistic awareness (Moats, 2020).

Accordingly, educators are encouraged to prioritize foundational reading skills in early instruction, particularly through the integrated development of semantics and syntax. Together, these language components form a strong basis for reading comprehension. Fostering these skills early on allows students to build confidence in their reading abilities and develop the tools they need to engage with more complex texts as they progress through their reading trajectory.

Teaching Phonology

In their 2006 study, Vaughn et al. used two main activities: phoneme discrimination and phoneme segmentation with blending to develop student phonological awareness. In the initial stage, students were asked to isolate the initial sounds of words or identify whether a word began with a specific sound. For example, the teacher introduces a target sound (e.g., /m/) and then guides students in identifying this sound in various words. As shown in Table 8.3, activities should be carefully sequenced to ensure that students learn all sound patterns from simple to more complex ones. Phonological activities help students develop their metalinguistic awareness and their spelling.

Teaching Semantics

The activity in Table 8.4 shows a set of strategies to teach semantics through a specific science topic. The teacher begins by selecting an expository book appropriate for first graders (e.g., *Bugs*) and identifying two to three key vocabulary words relevant to the topic (e.g., *antennae, hive, flutter*). The lesson starts with the teacher introducing and teaching the meanings of the key vocabulary using sentences and visuals to provide context. The teacher then reads a passage from the selected book, pausing to ask simple comprehension questions and incorporating the new vocabulary in context. Following this, the teacher encourages students to retell the story by using sentence prompts and emphasizing the integration of the new vocabulary. Finally, the lesson concludes with a vocabulary practice activity, where students use the newly learned words in complete sentences (Vaughn et al., 2006).

Teaching Semantics with L1 Instruction

In the study by Sun and Dong (2004), the activity to learn semantics using the native language included a 6-minute animated segment taken from a Disney

TABLE 8.3. Phonological Activities

Activities	Description
Isolating initial sounds	Children are asked to identify the initial sounds in words or determine if a word begins with a particular sound: "What is the initial sound in *dog*?"
Isolating final and medial sounds	After students master initial sound recognition, the focus shifts to isolating final and middle sounds in words: "What is the final sound in *cat*?" "What is the middle sound /a/?"
Sound-discrimination activities	In these activities, students become sensitive to the differences in vowel sounds: "Tell me the middle sound in *book*." If the teacher has taught students the sound of two *o*'s together (i.e., /u/), the teacher can ask students, "Now write the word *book*. Remember, the sound /u/ in *book* is spelled with two *o*'s."
Segmenting one-syllable words	Children learn to segment one-syllable words: "What is the first sound [i.e., onset] in *fog?* What are the last sounds in *fog* [i.e., rime]? /f/, /og/. Now, let's change the first sound in *fog* to an /l/. What is the new word?" (*log*)
Reconstituting words from phonemes	Children practice putting together words from separately spoken phonemes: "What word do these sounds make: /l/ /e/ /g/?"
Blending/segmenting words with more complex sounds	Children learn to blend and segment more complex sounds, such as words with consonant blends (e.g., *black, cream*) or diphthongs (e.g., *sound, book*).

cartoon. The cartoon features a family of ducks and contains 29 sentences and 19 words, including six nouns, two adjectives, four pronouns, two adverbs, two articles, and three auxiliary verbs. A native English speaker read the sentences, and a computer program provided an oral Chinese translation. The activity instructions state: "You will watch an interesting cartoon with some English sentences. A translation of each sentence will be provided to help you understand. Please watch carefully." By providing a context for translation, simple vocabulary and visual aids are particularly suitable for newcomers to the English language. (See Box 8.3 for the importance of the use of native language to build student's English reading comprehension.) Four words from the animation—baby, family, sad, and happy—were selected for first and second graders as target words in this activity because learning many second-language words in a short time can be difficult for students in the early elementary grades. Each target word appeared in different contexts within the animation, serving as clues to help children infer their meanings (Sun &

TABLE 8.4. Semantics Activities

Activities	Description
Book selection	Teacher selects an appropriate expository book for first grade (e.g., pets, bugs).
Vocabulary selection	Teacher selects two to three vocabulary words that are relevant to the topic.
Introduction of key vocabulary	Teacher introduces and teaches key vocabulary (e.g., *antennae, hive, flutter*) using sentences that provide context.
Reading and comprehension	Teacher reads the passage from an expository book about bugs, pauses to ask comprehension questions, and uses new vocabulary in context.
Story retelling	Teacher encourages students to retell the story using sentence prompts while incorporating the new vocabulary.
Vocabulary practice	Teacher concludes the lesson with vocabulary practice where students use the new words in sentences.

Dong, 2004). Table 8.5 provides examples of semantics activities using the native language.

Box 8.3. Importance of Native Language

Teachers of CLD students in grades 1 through 3 are encouraged to incorporate students' native languages when teaching language components such as semantics, syntax, and phonology. This can include providing translations of vocabulary and sentences (Sun & Dong, 2004; Baker et al., 2016). For example, lessons can highlight which language features are transferable between languages and which are not.

Practicing Syntax

To enhance syntactic structures, students can practice forming basic English questions and responses through the song "Do You Like Broccoli?" (Busse et al., 2021). This activity begins with introducing body parts with flashcards and phrases such as "Do you have a hand? Yes, I do," and "Does she have three hands? No, she doesn't." These sample phrases emphasize the question-response structure. Next, students will sing along with the adapted song and repeat each stanza to reinforce learning through call-and-response. Finally, they are encouraged to work in pairs and ask and answer questions (e.g., "Does he have two heads? No, he doesn't").

TABLE 8.5. Semantics Activities Using the Native Language

Activities	Description
Cartoon viewing	A 6-minute animated segment from a Disney cartoon featuring a family of ducks.
Bilingual presentation	A native English speaker reads the sentences aloud, accompanied by a computer-generated oral Chinese translation for each sentence.
Clear instructions	Instructions emphasize careful observation: "You will watch an interesting cartoon with some English sentences. A translation of each sentence will be provided to help you understand."
Target words	The focus is on four target words—*baby, family, sad,* and *happy*—selected because early elementary students may struggle to learn basic words when being exposed to a second language.
Contextual learning	Target words appear in different contexts within the animation, allowing children to infer their meanings from the story's clues.

Note. From Sun and Dong (2004).

Transferable features might include consonant letter sounds that are the same in both languages (e.g., /m/ has the same sound in Spanish and in English). Nontransferable features also need to be taught, such as the different vowel sounds in English, where vowels have many different sounds based on their position and letter-sound combinations in a word. For example, the vowel "*a*" has only one sound in Spanish, but it has many different sounds in English as pronounced in the following words: *cat, cake, sofa, father, boat, ball, many, artist.*

Additionally, lessons can provide scaffolding to help CLD students understand key instructional terms. For instance, during phonemic awareness instruction, students can be taught that the English word for *sonido* is sound. Incorporating the native language in these ways can reduce student anxiety and help them form cognitive connections between their first language and English.

WHAT LANGUAGE ACTIVITIES ARE THE MOST EFFECTIVE IN GRADES 4–6?

Language instruction is especially critical for CLD students in the upper elementary grades. While some students are still struggling and need instruction on reading words, most studies focus more on unconstrained skills such as semantics and syntax with the assumption that CLD students have already mastered foundational skills such as phonology and decoding (Hopp & Thoma, 2021; Jones et al., 2019;

Kieffer & Lesaux, 2012; Lesaux et al., 2010; Snow & Matthews, 2016). (See Box 8.4 for expectations for students in grades 4 to 6.) In our meta-analysis, we found that in the upper elementary grades, the combination of "semantics and syntax" had the largest impact on CLD students' language comprehension, while the integration of "morphology, semantics, and syntax" was most effective in improving reading comprehension (Carlo et al., 2004; Hopp & Thoma, 2021).

Box 8.4. Expectations for Students in Grades 4–6

According to the requirements of the Common Core State Standards (National Governors Association Center for Best Practices and Council of Chief State School Officers [NGA & CCSSO], 2010), for English language arts (ELA), the expectations for students in grades 4–6 are to (1) use grade-appropriate vocabulary and recognize word relationships; (2) demonstrate command of English grammar and spelling; and (3) write narratives with effective techniques and details. Most activities in the studies we reviewed included practicing detailed meanings of target words in presentations and discussions, reviewing words using cooperative games, building sentences, and using the target words in writing (Lesaux et al., 2014; Proctor et al., 2009).

In grades 4 to 6, CLD students read to acquire new concepts across various contexts, making robust language proficiency supports essential for reading comprehension. In the Lesaux et al. (2014) study, for example, researchers taught incremental learning strategies by first introducing the new target vocabulary words, then modeling how students carry out a morphological breakdown. In Lesaux et al. (2010), the intervention focused on enhancing students' semantic and syntactic awareness and reinforcing their understanding of syntactic rules. Teachers engaged students in peer discussions, mock interviews, and crossword puzzles to achieve these goals.

In the study by Kieffer and Lesaux (2012), researchers implemented detailed morphological decomposition instruction to teach sixth-grade CLD and native English-speaking students the meanings and functions of target suffixes. (See Box 8.5 for the importance of morphological awareness in grades 4 to 6.) For example, in a lesson on the suffix *-al,* students learned how this suffix contributes to understanding the meanings of complex words such as *accidental, analytical, emotional*) and how to use them in sentences. Teachers then guided students in practicing how to distinguish learned suffixes in new semantic contexts based on their background knowledge and what they had learned in school and then engaged students in peer discussions to identify inappropriate suffix usage when reading a new text.

Box 8.5. Morphological Awareness in Grades 4–6

By developing students' morphological awareness and providing multiple opportunities to use, identify, and apply affixes to unknown words in sentences and texts, students enhance their word knowledge and word learning strategies. Over time, this increases their ability to understand texts and improves their overall reading comprehension (Kieffer & Lesaux, 2012).

Tables 8.6 and 8.7 include suggestions for activities, as well as an example of peer-group and partner discussions to practice the syntactical use of target words. The lesson breakdown and activities are adapted from multiple published examples of effective vocabulary and reading comprehension interventions in the upper elementary grades and middle school developed by Lesaux and Kieffer, whose studies have been included in our meta-analysis.

Small groups and paired reading can be powerful approaches for language development, particularly in building both semantics and syntax. (See Box 8.6 for the importance of small-group and paired-reading activities.)

TABLE 8.6. Morphological Awareness, Syntax, and Semantics Activities in Grades 4–6

Activities	Description
Warm-up with morphology	• Review of prefixes and suffixes
Building morphological awareness	• Introduce two new prefixes and suffixes using explicit modeling and guided practice. Students work with a partner to build words using a list of prefixes, suffixes, and base words.
Learning morphology by analogy	• Demonstrate how to use suffixes and combine them with target words by using meaningful sentences taken from the unit text. Students then work in pairs to discuss and identify additional examples of words that include the suffix they learned.
Practicing semantics and syntactics	• Teacher uses guided reading to focus on main ideas for each paragraph. She then reviews vocabulary learned in text, asks students to practice partner reading, and checks for comprehension. • Teacher reminds students to use vocabulary learned in the lesson in their writing activities.

Note. Example activities adapted from Kieffer and Lesaux (2012).

TABLE 8.7. Examples of Teacher-Initiated Group and Partner Discussion and Syntactic Practice

Activity type	Prompt example	Student response example
Group discussion	• Discuss whether single-gender classrooms should be mandatory in public schools. Use evidence from the unit text to support your view.	• One student argued that single-gender classrooms reduce distractions, while another countered that they limit social development.
Partner discussion	• Assign word definition task and let students share target words with partner.	• Students defined *mandatory* as "required by rule" and created a sentence: "Attending math tutoring is mandatory for students failing the course."
Syntactic practice	• Correct the following sentence by applying the correct suffix: "The man is a great tranter."	• Corrected response: "The man is a great translator." (The suffix *-or* indicates a person who translates.)

Note. Activities adapted from Kieffer and Lesaux (2012) and Lesaux et al. (2010).

Box 8.6. Importance of Small-Group and Paired-Reading Activities

Small-group and paired-reading activities expand students' semantic knowledge by promoting vocabulary acquisition and precise language use. In the example provided above, students were also encouraged to actively use and internalize new academic vocabulary such as *regulation, mandatory,* and *implementation* when forming arguments and defending positions (Jones et al., 2019).

Through conversations and interactions during small group or pair reading, CLD students are exposed to English syntactic rules, helping them understand the structure of sentences and the relationships between words (Lesaux et al., 2014). In the study by Jones et al. (2019), fourth- and fifth-grade CLD students practiced using academic language and argumentation skills by engaging in small-group and whole-class discussion activities, and debating controversial, but relevant and engaging topics such as "Should the government impose a mandatory year of service after high school?" or "Should junk food be banned from school cafeterias?" (See Box 8.7 for the importance of text selection.)

Box 8.7. Text Selection

Selecting engaging passages that spark thoughtful discussion encourages students to delve deeper into the text, promoting comprehension beyond surface-level understanding. When students analyze, synthesize, or evaluate information, they engage in higher-order thinking which builds their ability to interpret and connect complex ideas.

Discussing and using these structures with peers allows CLD students to build academic language and vocabulary, analyze different text structures, interpret, explain, and defend their ideas, and ultimately increase their reading comprehension abilities.

Similarly, Lesaux et al. (2014) found that teaching academic vocabulary in context improved linguistically diverse students' understanding of word meanings and their ability to apply these words in reading and writing tasks. (See Box 8.8 for the description of vocabulary instruction.)

Box 8.8. Vocabulary Instruction

In structured vocabulary instruction, teachers help students engage meaningfully by modeling and providing sentence frames. Teachers also supervise the content of students' discussion, ensuring students stay on task and use correct structures (Lesaux et al., 2014).

This integrated approach involved contextualized word study, allowing students to practice vocabulary in meaningful settings, supporting better word retention and application in reading comprehension. Thus, collaborative reading activities enable students to discuss and refine their ideas using newly learned words, enhancing both vocabulary and semantic precision essential for reading comprehension (Kelley et al., 2010). In vocabulary interventions, incorporating syntactic exercises is essential for enhancing student outcomes, particularly through teacher-facilitated group discussions and self-composition exercises based on key vocabulary (Kieffer & Lesaux, 2012; Lesaux et al., 2014).

The suggested strategies and activities support reading and language skills for CLD students in grades 4 to 6 by encouraging active engagement, structured dialogue, and targeted feedback, which together foster comprehension, vocabulary, and critical thinking (Jones et al., 2019). The teacher-directed small groups or paired discussion activities, which include prompts and probing questions, scaffold the conversation, providing students with a framework to navigate challenging text elements and enhancing their reasoning and argumentation skills (Lesaux et al., 2014).

Partner interactions, with Partner 2 restating, agreeing/disagreeing, providing examples, and building on Partner 1's ideas, reinforce a critical component for comprehension and syntactic development. By restating and expanding on their partner's points, students practice using precise language and correct syntactic structures, such as relative clauses or compound sentences, while also reinforcing understanding of the content. Teachers can ensure students use precise sentence structures by modeling their think-aloud about explaining a word, by providing sentence stems and offering feedback when students use a phrase improperly (Lesaux et al., 2010).

Additionally, peer feedback routines help students focus on both content and language, as they learn to highlight strengths and offer constructive suggestions. This routine supports students in reflecting on their language use, understanding the content more deeply, and improving their critical thinking and language skills. Through these structured activities, CLD students not only enhance their reading comprehension but also build the language skills necessary for effective communication and academic success.

BACK TO MS. PEREZ

After Ms. Perez attended several professional learning community sessions where she learned more about the different language components and how they contribute to language and reading comprehension, she decided to share this knowledge with her teachers and work together on building daily language activities that include and combine the language components that seem to have the largest impact on CLD students' reading comprehension across the grades.

For teachers in grades preschool to kindergarten, she emphasized teachers conducting interactive book reading activities daily. She particularly made sure teachers understood that the goal of interactive reading is for children to eventually narrate the story and lead the conversation about the book. Ms. Perez also reminded teachers that they could train parents to carry out shared book reading at home in their native language or their English dialect to engage in rich conversations that lead to developing children's language comprehension.

Ms. Perez suggested that teachers select words they thought were important to understand the stories and build vocabulary before and after reading the book using word games. Spending time on semantics activities is important and necessary to develop a mental representation of words children are likely to hear in school.

For teachers in grades 1 to 3, Ms. Perez reminded them that research indicated that the use of the students' native language is a strategy that can help students who are being exposed to English for the first time. In addition, Ms. Perez also reminded teachers that language activities are not a substitute for phonological awareness and decoding instruction to build word automaticity (i.e., reading words fluently, without hesitation) and that all decoding and language activities should occur daily. The absence of building word automaticity reduces student opportunities to understand the written word. The absence of developing student understanding reduces their opportunities to develop their expressive and receptive vocabulary, their background knowledge, and their ability to recognize how the sound system and syntactic system work in English.

For students in grades 4 to 6, the emphasis should be on morphology, semantics, and syntax. Teachers should also make sure that newcomers who cannot read in English also receive support in phonology and decoding to make sure they understand the English phonological system and the English syntactic rules. If teachers speak the students' native language, they should be encouraged to use it to explicitly show students the differences and similarities between languages.

CONCLUSION

Our students in the U.S. school system are becoming increasingly diverse. Recognizing the similarities and differences between languages as well as the role language components play in communicating and expressing ideas, beliefs, and knowledge can support the English language and reading comprehension of CLD students. As Moats (2020) indicates, "literacy is an achievement that rests primarily on language processing at all levels, from elemental sounds to the most overarching structures of text" (p. 2). Developing and practicing the components of language (i.e., phonology, morphology, semantics, syntax, and pragmatics) will lead to better reading comprehension and to reading for learning.

Reflection Questions

1. What are the five language components and how can you practice them in the classroom?

2. Based on the age group you teach, what are examples of routines you can use to develop each or a combination of language components?
3. If you have CLD students in your classroom, what are some questions you have about their native language and about their family background? Why is that information important?

REFERENCES

Baker, D. L., Basaraba, D. L., & Richards-Tutor, C. (2018). *Second language acquisition: Methods, perspectives and challenges.* Nova Science.

Baker, D. L., Basaraba, D., & Polanco, P. (2016). Connecting the present to the past: Furthering the research on bilingualism and bilingual education. *Review of Research in Education, 40*(1), 821–883.

Baker, D. L., Ma, H., Polanco, P., Conry, J. M., Kamata, A., Al Otaiba, S., et al. (2021). Development and promise of a vocabulary intelligent tutoring system for Second-Grade Latinx English learners. *Journal of Research on Technology in Education, 53*(2), 223–247.

Baker, D. L., Mogna, V., Rodriguez, S., Farmer, D., & Yovanoff, P. (2016). Building the oral language of young Hispanic Children through interactive read alouds and vocabulary games in preschool and at home. *Journal of International Special Needs Education, 19*(2), 81–94.

Baker, D. L., Park, Y., & Andress, T. T. (2023). Longitudinal predictors of bilingual language proficiency, decoding, and oral reading fluency on reading comprehension in Spanish and in English. *School Psychology Review, 52*(4), 421–434.

Baker, D. L., & Santoro, L. (2023). Quality Read Alouds Matter: **How** you teach is just as Important as **What** you Teach. *The Reading Teacher,* 77(3), 310–320.

Baker, D. L., Santoro, L., Ware, S., Cuellar, D., Oldham, A., Cuticelli, M., et al. (2015). Understanding and implementing the common core vocabulary standards in kindergarten. *Teaching Exceptional Children,* 47(5), 264–271.

Brady, S., & Mason, L. H. (2024). A literature review of morphological awareness interventions and the effects on literacy outcomes. *Learning Disability Quarterly,* 47(1), 16–29.

Busse, V., Hennies, C., Kreutz, G., & Roden, I. (2021). Learning grammar through singing? An intervention with EFL primary school learners. *Learning and Instruction, 71,* 101372.

Carlo, M. S., August, D., Mclaughlin, B., Snow, C. E., Dressler, C., Lippman, D. N., et al. (2004). Closing the gap: Addressing the vocabulary needs of English-language learners in bilingual and mainstream classrooms. *Reading Research Quarterly, 39*(2), 188–215.

Ciornei, S. I., & Dina, T. A. (2015). Authentic texts in teaching English. *Procedia – Social and Behavioral Sciences, 180,* 274–279.

Cirrin, F. M., & Gillam, R. B. (2008). Language intervention practices for school-age children with spoken language disorders: A systematic review. *Language, Speech, and Hearing Services in Schools, 39*(1), S110–137.

Coyne, M. D., McCoach, D. B., Loftus, S., Zipoli Jr., R., & Kapp, S. (2009). Direct vocabulary instruction in kindergarten: Teaching for breadth versus depth. *The Elementary School Journal, 110*(1), 1–18.

Dixon, L. Q., & Wu, S. (2014). Home language and literacy practices among immigrant second-language learners. *Language Teaching, 47*(4), 414–449.

Ehri, L. C. (2014). Orthographic mapping in the acquisition of sight word reading, spelling memory, and vocabulary learning. *Scientific Studies of Reading, 18*(1), 5–21.

Farver, J. A. M., Lonigan, C. J., & Eppe, S. (2009). Effective early literacy skill development for young Spanish-speaking English language learners: An experimental study of two methods. *Child Development, 80*(3), 703–719.

Hoover, W. A., & Gough, P. B. (1990). The simple view of reading. *Reading and Writing, 2*(2), 127–160.

Hopp, H., & Thoma, D. (2021). Effects of plurilingual teaching on grammatical development in early foreign-language learning. *The Modern Language Journal, 105*(2), 464–483.

Huang, Y., Baker, D. L., Herrera, C. B., Sha, H., Moradibavi, S., & Peng, P. (2025, February 5–7). *Language interventions for English learners in grades preK–6: A network meta-analysis* [Conference presentation]. The 33rd Annual Pacific Coast Research Conference (PCRC). Coronado, CA.

Jones, S. M., LaRusso, M., Kim, J., Yeon Kim, H., Selman, R., Uccelli, P., et al. (2019). Experimental effects of word generation on vocabulary, academic language, perspective taking, and reading comprehension in high poverty schools. *Journal of Research on Educational Effectiveness, 12*(3), 448–483.

Kamps, D., Abbott, M., Greenwood, C., Arreaga-Mayer, C., Wills, H., Longstaff, J., et al. (2007). Use of evidence-based, small-group reading instruction for English language learners in elementary grades: Secondary-tier intervention. *Learning Disability Quarterly, 30*(3), 153–168.

Kelley, J. G., Lesaux, N. K., Kieffer, M. J., & Faller, S. E. (2010). Effective academic vocabulary instruction in the urban middle school. *The Reading Teacher, 64*(1), 5–14.

Kieffer, M. J., & Lesaux, N. K. (2012). Effects of academic language instruction on relational and syntactic aspects of morphological awareness for sixth graders from linguistically diverse backgrounds. *The Elementary School Journal, 112*(3), 519–545.

Lesaux, N. K., Kieffer, M. J., Faller, S. E., & Kelley, J. G. (2010). The effectiveness and ease of implementation of an academic vocabulary intervention for linguistically diverse students in urban middle schools. *Reading Research Quarterly, 45*(2), 196–228.

Lesaux, N. K., Kieffer, M. J., Kelley, J. G., & Harris, J. R. (2014). Effects of academic vocabulary instruction for linguistically diverse adolescents: Evidence from a randomized field trial. *American Educational Research Journal, 51*(6), 1159–1194.

Moats, L. C. (2020). Teaching reading "is" rocket science: What expert teachers of reading should know and be able to do. *American Educator, 44*(2). *www.aft.org/sites/default/files/moats.pdf*

National Center for Education Statistics. (2023). English learners in public schools. In *Condition of Education 2023. https://nces.ed.gov/programs/coe/indicator/cgf#1*

National Governors Association Center for Best Practices & Council of Chief State School Officers. (2010). *Common core state standards for English language arts & literacy in history/social studies, science, and technical subjects. https://learning.ccsso.org/wp-content/uploads/2022/11/ELA_Standards1.pdf*

Neuman, S. B., & Kaefer, T. (2018). Developing low-income children's vocabulary and content knowledge through a shared book reading program. *Contemporary Educational Psychology, 52*, 15–24.

Pile, E. J., Girolametto, L., Johnson, C. J., Chen, X., & Cleave, P. L. (2010). Shared book reading intervention for children with language impairment: Using parents-as-aides in language intervention. *Canadian Journal of Speech-Language Pathology & Audiology, 34*(2), 96–109.

Richards-Tutor, C., Baker, D. L., Gersten, R., Baker, S. K., & Smith, J. M. (2016). The effectiveness of reading interventions for English learners: A research synthesis. *Exceptional Children, 82*(2), 144–169.

Silverman, R. D., Johnson, E., Keane, K., & Khanna, S. (2020). Beyond decoding: A meta-analysis of the effects of language comprehension interventions on K–5 students' language and literacy outcomes. *Reading Research Quarterly, 55*(S1), S207–S233.

Snow, C. E., & Matthews, T. J. (2016). Reading and language in the early grades. *Future of Children, 26*(2), 57–74.

Sun, Y., & Dong, Q. (2004). An experiment on supporting children's English vocabulary learning in multimedia context. *Computer Assisted Language Learning, 17*(2), 131–147.

van Valkenhoef, G., Lu, G., de Brock, B., Hillege, H., Ades, A. E., & Welton, N. J. (2012). Automating network meta-analysis. *Research Synthesis Methods, 3*(4), 285–299.

Vaughn, S., Mathes, P., Linan-Thompson, S., Cirino, P., Carlson, C., Pollard-Durodola, S., et al. (2006). Effectiveness of an English intervention for first-grade English language learners at risk for reading problems. *The Elementary School Journal, 107*(2), 153–180.

Vishnu, K. K. N., Clark, G. T., Siyambalapitiya, S., & Reuterskiöld, C. (2023). Language intervention in bilingual children with developmental language disorder: A systematic review. *International Journal of Language & Communication Disorders, 58*(2), 576–600.

What Works Clearinghouse. (2010). *Early childhood education for children with disabilities intervention report: Dialogic reading. https://ies.ed.gov/ncee/wwc/InterventionReport/136*

What Works Clearinghouse. (2014). *Teaching academic content and literacy to English learners in elementary and middle school. https://ies.ed.gov/ncee/WWC/PracticeGuide/19*

What Works Clearinghouse. (2022). *What works clearinghouse procedures and standards handbook, version 5.0. https://ies.ed.gov/ncee/wwc/Handbooks*

Whitehurst, G. J., Epstein, J. N., Angell, A. L., Payne, A. C., Crone, D. A., & Fischel, J. E. (1994). Outcomes of an emergent literacy intervention in Head Start. *Journal of Educational Psychology, 86*(4), 542–555.

Zhang, D., Ke, S., & Mo, Y. (2023). Morphology in reading comprehension among school-aged readers of English: A synthesis and meta-analytic structural equation modeling study. *Journal of Educational Psychology, 115*(5), 683–699.

Zucker, T. A., Justice, L. M., Piasta, S. B., & Kaderavek, J. N. (2010). Preschool teachers' literal and inferential questions and children's responses during whole class shared reading. *Early Childhood Research Quarterly, 25*(1), 65–83.

9

Hearing Themselves in Books

Using Authentic Children's Literature to Support the Language of African American Students

Ramona T. Pittman, Endia Lindo, Whitney N. McCoy, and Jasmine Rogers

Guiding Questions

1. What are the unique structures and rules of African American English (AAE), and what is its cultural significance?
2. How can teachers support speakers of AAE in the areas of language and literacy in their classrooms?

In the United States, a plethora of media outlets (magazines, blogs, television, etc.) and mental health care professionals suggest that each person be his, her, or their authentic self. This is not a new phenomenon, as in 1603 Shakespeare wrote in *Hamlet* (1982), "This above all: to thine own self be true." Yet, in an era of social media filters and cosmetic surgery, a message of being authentic still resonates. In fact, many professional and career resources have commenced around the topic of the "authentic self" (Ladkin & Taylor, 2010). This authenticity has become prominent in education, as well. Many educational institutions, from prekindergarten to higher education, call for authentic learning experiences (Stanley, 2018), assessments (Villarroel et al., 2018), and teaching materials (Guo, 2012). For example, many teachers use resources, such as authentic children's literature (i.e., children's literature from popular presses that are not leveled text or decodable text), to explain a concept or skill and to provide students opportunities to listen to the text and read texts for learning and enjoyment.

Effective strategies for using children's literature emphasize the importance of selecting authentic texts (Piper et al., 2017) and ensuring inclusivity (Heineke & Papola-Ellis, 2022a). To integrate authentic, "real-life" materials, teachers should choose texts that reflect the diversity of their students, as this inclusivity helps students see their own identities represented (Bishop, 1990; Heineke et al., 2022b). Even in classrooms without a wide range of student backgrounds, the recommended best practice is to include diverse, authentic texts to expose students to various cultures and perspectives (National Governors Association Center for Best Practices & Council of Chief State School Officers, 2010; Piper et al., 2017).

Given the prominence of the inclusion of children's literature that is authentic and diverse, this chapter seeks to disrupt the idea of what it means for children's literature to be authentic. For instance, books about enslaved Africans may inaccurately depict characters as using General American English (GAE)[1] upon their forced arrival in America. This portrayal is historically implausible, as enslaved Africans spoke a range of West African languages rather than GAE. Even if they provide a "real-life" storyline, books that portray slaves as speaking GAE lack linguistic authenticity for the period they portray (Pittman et al., 2024a) and reinforce the hegemonic notion that, in the United States, GAE is the preferred language (Metz, 2018).

Across the United States, teachers have been focused on deepening their understanding of evidence-based reading practices through the Science of Reading. This is critically important because, currently, over 60% of U.S. students read below proficiency. Even more concerning is that over 80% of African American students fall below proficiency, a rate higher than any other racial or ethnic group (National Center for Education Statistics, 2024). This significant gap—more than 20% above the national average—raises essential questions. Could it be that African American English (AAE),[2] a language most African American students speak at home and in their community, is undervalued in the classroom? Perhaps teachers are unaware that many African American students use a distinct language dialect that differs from the language dialect emphasized in schools. Alternatively, some teachers might recognize this linguistic difference but, as some research suggests, may misinterpret it as laziness or "slang" and, consequently, set low expectations for students who speak this language variation. Research consistently shows that low expectations are detrimental to academic achievement, reinforcing barriers to success (Delpit, 1995). Addressing these gaps requires a broader recognition of students' linguistic backgrounds and a commitment to fostering high expectations for all learners.

Recently, proponents of the Science of Reading have been focused on the need to support students' decoding through phonics-based instruction and decodable texts. There has been much less attention to the importance of using authentic children's literature to promote language and literacy. In fact, there is a substantial amount of research that calls for the use of read-alouds of authentic children's literature to facilitate vocabulary and comprehension development, enable the exploration of diverse text structures, and cultivate a love of reading (e.g., Lennox, 2013). Read-alouds also allow teachers to model fluent reading, engage in think-alouds, and prompt higher-order thinking through literal and inferential questions. Importantly, including read-alouds of text that reflect children's lived experiences helps children draw on their background knowledge as they learn new concepts and skills. Yet, many African American students do not find their language or life experiences reflected in the texts chosen for read-alouds in many classrooms. Consequently, they may struggle to "see" themselves (Bishop, 1990) or "hear" themselves (Pittman et al., 2024a) in the literature, limiting the potential impact of these valuable learning opportunities.

In this chapter, we outline strategies for teachers to use children's texts that feature AAE and to use these texts to facilitate the language and literacy of African American children in U.S. classrooms. We begin with a brief overview of authentic literature. We then introduce AAE, highlighting its history and common linguistic features. Additionally, we provide an overview of culturally relevant teaching and its importance within this context. We conclude the chapter with practical implications and resources that teachers can use to support the language of their African American students. To start, consider the vignette about Mr. Sims in Box 9.1.

Box 9.1. Vignette: Mr. Sims

Mr. Sims sat at his desk after school, a notebook open in front of him and a slightly bewildered look on his face. He had just returned from a professional development session on AAE, where he had learned about its unique structure, rules, and cultural significance. Much of the information had been new to him, and he was captivated. He thought about his classroom, where the majority of his fifth graders were African American. He realized that many of them spoke in AAE with one another, slipping comfortably between it and GAE, the language he required them to speak during class and use in their written language. With a new understanding, Mr. Sims wanted to support their language and make his classroom a place where they felt their voices were respected and understood, but he wasn't quite sure where to begin. He tapped his pen against his notebook, where he had jotted down terms like "style-shifting" and "culturally relevant teaching." Each sounded meaningful, yet implementing them felt daunting. He didn't want to make a misstep or unintentionally come across as patronizing. What are some ways Mr. Sims can make his students feel their language is respected?

As Mr. Sims reflected, he recalled something the presenter had emphasized: start with listening. "Listen to your students," she had said. "Let their voices guide you and show them you value their language as part of who they are." Inspired by this, Mr. Sims decided his first step would be to create opportunities for open discussion. He would invite students to share stories from home, allowing them to speak in whatever way felt most natural. He would also choose literature that reflected their experiences and language, starting with books they could see and hear themselves in. Mr. Sims still had much to learn, but he knew he was on the right path. He realized that supporting his students' language meant more than any single strategy; it was about making space for their voices and letting them know they were truly heard.

AUTHENTIC CHILDREN'S LITERATURE

Authentic children's literature presents complex and culturally rich narratives, allowing children to both understand their own experiences and develop empathy for others (Bishop, 1990). Authentic children's literature is characterized by its accurate, respectful, and culturally genuine representations of diverse backgrounds, experiences, and perspectives that resonate with children from varied backgrounds. Unlike superficial diversity, authentic literature delves deeply into the nuanced traditions, languages, values, and narratives of the communities it portrays. This authenticity is often achieved when authors either belong to the depicted culture or possess a profound understanding and respect for it, ensuring that characters and settings are presented with cultural integrity rather than relying on stereotypes or generalized tropes.

The importance of authentic literature for children is multifaceted, as it supports the following:

- *Identity formation and affirmation:* Authentic literature can reflect underrepresented children's experiences, fostering pride and validating their identities.
- *Empathy and cultural understanding:* Authentic stories offer all children windows into other lives, building empathy and promoting inclusivity through diverse perspectives.

- *Combating stereotypes and biases:* Authentic literature breaks stereotypes by portraying diverse, complex characters, thus reducing bias and supporting equity.
- *Linguistic representation:* Proper representation affirms languages like AAE and avoids negative portrayals that may shame students (Brooks & McNair, 2009).

In 2023, the Cooperative Children's Book Center (CCBC) noted 15% of children's books featured African American characters and 39% featured BIPOC characters (Cooperative Children's Book Center, CCBC, 2024). Though there have been gradual increases in diverse representation in children's literature, many of these titles still reflect limited or concerning representations and issues of fairness. Since a key aim of multicultural education is to create learning experiences that respect and affirm students from diverse backgrounds, fostering positive attitudes toward racial, ethnic, and cultural diversity (Banks, 1993), accurate and respectful representation of African Americans in literature is essential. It is also important to handle the linguistic representation of AAE with care, requiring teachers to understand its rule-governed structure and affirm its use. Research indicates that students who engage with authentic literature show higher academic achievement and a stronger motivation to read, as these texts feel relevant and engaging, sparking curiosity and imagination (Wooten et al., 2018).

AFRICAN AMERICAN CHILDREN'S LITERATURE

The history of African American children's literature reflects the broader struggle for representation and self-definition within American culture. This genre has evolved to challenge stereotypes and celebrate African American heritage, providing children with empowering stories that reflect their lives and the diversity of the African American experience.

Early Beginnings and the Push for Representation

African American children's literature dates to the 19th century when works such as *The Child's Story of the Negro* by Jane Dabney Shackelford (1938) sought to provide young readers with historical and cultural narratives reflecting African American achievements. However, the genre remained limited well into the 20th century, with most children's books featuring Black characters being written by White authors and perpetuating harmful stereotypes. African Americans were often depicted as subservient, happy servants or comical figures, reflecting the prevailing racist attitudes of the time.

African American Children's Literature in the 20th Century

The early 20th century, influenced by the Harlem Renaissance, saw a focus on stories and poetry that affirmed African American identity, community, and culture with works such as *The First Book of Rhymes* (1954) by Langston Hughes. The Civil Rights movement and the push for racial equality influenced the growth of African American children's literature in the 1960s and 1970s. Nancy Larrick's (1965) article "The All-White World of Children's Books" criticized the lack of representation of African Americans in children's literature. This period prompted a growing demand for children's books accurately portraying African American history and daily life, often aimed at dismantling stereotypes and promoting positive self-identity among African American children. Ezra Jack Keats's portrayal of an African American boy experiencing everyday life in *The Snowy Day* (1962) broke new ground for inclusivity in children's literature and authors like Virginia Hamilton, who wrote *M. C. Higgins, the Great* (1974), became pivotal figures during this period. Her work, along with that of other authors such as Mildred Taylor (*Roll of Thunder, Hear My Cry,* 1976), showcased African American protagonists with depth and complexity, addressing themes of resilience and social justice. These books offered Black children relatable heroes and validated their experiences, fostering a stronger sense of identity and self-worth. Furthermore, pioneers such as Charlemae Rollins, Augusta Baker, and Dr. Rudine Sims Bishop played critical roles in advocating for authentic and diverse representation of African Americans in children's literature, shepherding the rise of multicultural literature focused on themes of family, community, and resilience.

Modern Developments and Increased Diversity

From the late 20th century to the present, African American children's literature has continued to expand, with a growing emphasis on diversity within the Black experience, offering stories that cover a wide range of genres and perspectives. Authors such as Jacqueline Woodson (*Brown Girl Dreaming,* 2014) and Christopher Paul Curtis (*Bud, Not Buddy,* 1999) have enriched the genre with stories that celebrate African American culture, history, and language. Scholars like Dr. Rudine Sims Bishop (1990) have emphasized the importance of African American children's literature as a means to foster understanding, empathy, and racial pride among all children, serving as mirrors (reflecting the reader's own world), windows (introducing readers to the experiences of others), and sliding glass doors (walking into the story and becoming a part of the world created).

A BRIEF HISTORY OF AAE

During the transatlantic slave trade, Africans were forcibly removed from their homeland and brought to the United States, where they encountered stymying language barriers, as they did not speak the language of their enslavers, and, among the enslaved, they did not all speak the same language. Additionally, slaves were denied formal education and often punished for using their native languages. Subversively, they developed a means of communication to understand one another across language backgrounds that grew into what is now referred to as AAE. After emancipation, African Americans continued to face discrimination and segregation, limiting access to education and economic opportunities. Despite these obstacles, they cultivated rich cultural and linguistic traditions, including distinct speech patterns and vocabulary. The Great Migration of the early 20th century, during which millions of African Americans moved from the rural South to urban Northern areas, further diversified and spread AAE nationwide (Smitherman, 1991, 2021).

In academic settings, however, AAE has faced considerable challenges. In December 1996, the Oakland Unified School District in California passed a resolution recognizing AAE as a legitimate language with its own linguistic features (Oakland Unified School District, 1996). This resolution sparked controversy, with critics arguing it reinforced segregation and implied AAE was inferior to GAE, while others misinterpreted the intent as promoting AAE over GAE. The Linguistic Society of America responded in 1997, affirming AAE as a systematic, rule-governed language (Linguistic Society of America, 1997). Although the debate initially fueled criticism from educators, parents, political figures, and the media, it ultimately sparked essential conversations about language diversity, education, and social justice, increasing awareness of linguistic variation and the value of culturally relevant teaching (Ladson-Billings, 1995, 2021). Despite the growing visibility of AAE in mainstream media and public platforms across racial groups, its use in classrooms remains stigmatized, and debates on language, race, and identity in academic settings continues.

AAE FEATURES

Most African American children in the United States begin school speaking AAE (Washington, 2001). AAE is a structured language, defined by unique patterns in phonology, morphology, syntax, semantics, and vocabulary (Green, 2002; Pittman et al., 2024b). Known by various names—such as Black Language, African American Language, Black English, and Ebonics—AAE is spoken by an estimated

80% of African Americans (Rickford, 1999). We use AAE in this chapter to reflect the lineage of students whose ancestors came to the United States as enslaved Africans. It is important to distinguish AAE-speaking students from other Black students who come from countries such as Jamaica or Haiti, where students may speak languages like Jamaican Patois or Haitian Creole and may or may not use AAE.

Box 9.2. Vignette: Ms. Salazar

Ms. Salazar, a fourth-grade teacher, noticed how her students often spoke with familiar phrases she had come to recognize. "Ms. Salazar, can we go to the baf-room?" they'd ask. Or, "Are we taking a tess today?" And, on most days, "Can we have mo' time at recess?" These expressions, rich with the unique sounds and patterns of AAE, were a part of her students' language. She loved the energy and authenticity her students brought to the classroom, and she knew it was essential to respect and value their language. But Ms. Salazar also wanted to ensure they could decode and encode (spell) in GAE, especially for tasks like retelling stories orally or in writing after they read together, so they could have success across contexts. How should Ms. Salazar approach her students' language since she knows that her students will be evaluated on various literacy assessments in GAE?

Though multiple theories exist regarding the origins of AAE (see Lanehart, 2015), the most widely accepted is the theory described above, referred to in scholarship as the Creole Theory, that enslaved Africans brought to the United States spoke various West African languages and had to develop a means of communication among themselves and with English-speaking colonizers, and, therefore, blending English vocabulary and African grammatical and phonological structures, developed the language variation that became what we now know of as AAE (Smitherman, 1991, 2021). Table 9.1 lists phonological distinctions between AAE and GAE and Table 9.2 presents morphosyntactic differences. Notably, other features of AAE, such as semantic and rhetorical features, are not included in these tables (Baker-Bell, 2020).

It is important to note, as mentioned above, that not all African Americans speak AAE, and individuals who live or work near African American communities may also use AAE (Wolfram & Schilling-Estes, 2006). Additionally, speakers of AAE vary in their usage over time and in different contexts. Some speakers of AAE use AAE exclusively, others use AAE minimally, and still others shift fluidly between AAE and GAE as needed. In the United States, schools enforce GAE as

TABLE 9.1. Phonological Features of AAE and GAE

Feature	AAE	GAE
Final consonant blend variation	lif, frien	*lift, friend*
Unvoiced /th/ variation	Bef, boof	*Beth, booth*
Voiced /th/ variation	breave, deir	*breathe, their*
Final /r/ variation	sco, fo	*score, four*
Variation in "l"	toe, pia	*toll, pill*
Final *g* in the suffix *-ing* variation	drivin', smilin'	*driving, smiling*
Cognates /t/ and /d/ reversal	salat, toiled	*salad, toilet*
Initial consonant blend *str-* variation	skreet, skraw	*street, straw*

Note. The initial consonant blend *str-* variation is mostly used by younger AAE speakers (Green, 2002). For more features, see Green (2002).

TABLE 9.2. Morphosyntactic (Grammatical) Features of AAE and GAE

Feature	AAE	GAE
Copula variation	He smart.	*He is smart.*
Habitual "be" variation	She be reading during lunch.	*She is always reading during lunch.*
Modal perfect variation	The teacher should'a laughed.	*The teacher should have laughed.*
"Gonna"-future tense marker	She gonna win the spelling bee.	*She is going to win the* spelling bee.
Dən	He done finished his homework.	*He has already finished his homework.*
Negation variation	Don't nobody talk during class.	*Don't anybody talk during class.*
Agreement patterns	They wasn't happy with their grades.	*They weren't happy with grades.*
Possessive variation	Zoe backpack	*Zoe's backpack*

Note. "She be reading during lunch" can also mean that she should not be reading during lunch. "He done finished his homework" can also mean that maybe he should not have (if he was told not to work on it in class, etc.). For more features, see Green (2002).

the standard for curriculum, instruction, and assessment in reading and writing instruction (Washington & Seidenberg, 2021). GAE has historically been associated with social privilege and power (Lippi-Green, 2012), creating a division between those who are perceived to speak it "correctly" and those who do not.

AAE AND LITERACY

AAE plays a significant role in the language development of many African American students, as displayed in students' oral language, decoding (reading), spelling, and writing. Students whose oral language has a higher "dialect density," which refers to the more frequent use of AAE features, may face challenges with literacy, as their oral language differs from the classroom's GAE-based curriculum, instruction, and assessment. The more difficult it is for a student to style shift (Wolfram & Schilling-Etse, 2006) to GAE, the more problems the student may face with reaching reading proficiency (Washington & Seidenberg, 2021). Additionally, the student may experience difficulty in spelling. Spelling involves the student segmenting the sounds or phonemes of words and matching them to corresponding graphemes (Pittman et al., 2023). If a student orally pronounces *smooth* as /s/ /m/ /oo/ /v/, consistent with AAE, the student might write the word as *smoov,* which would be considered incorrect in assessment protocols that require GAE (Read, 1971). Moreover, AAE's morphosyntactic (and phonological) features can appear in students' writing, as well. For example, a student might write, "Bef play all day," versus the GAE agreement pattern of "Beth plays all day."

Now, let's revisit Box 9.2's question: How should Ms. Salazar approach her students' language since she knows that her students will be evaluated on various literacy assessments in GAE? For best practice, she must not "correct" her students' language while they are speaking. Students should have a free license to communicate (Lee, 2022) and preventing them from using their natural language is linguistic injustice (Baker-Bell, 2020).

Educators can effectively support African American students' use of AAE in the classroom by affirming their linguistic identity and demonstrating an understanding of their communication (Wynter-Hoyte et al., 2020). Ms. Salazar's instructional approach reflects this affirmation. When a student asks, "Are we taking a tes today?" Ms. Salazar can respond, "yes, my hope is that you can show everything you've learned this semester. I know you'll do great." In this interaction, the teacher not only acknowledges the student's communication but also provides positive reinforcement, affirming the student's academic abilities and expressing confidence in their potential for success.

If Ms. Salazar notices that her students who speak AAE use GAE when they write and spell, this is evidence that her students know how to style shift to GAE for the purposes of progressing through GAE-required schools. If she notices a student does not know how to style shift, Ms. Salazar can implement some strategies and practices that will respect the students' language and teach them skills to style shift if they choose to do so. For example, when using Elkonin or sound boxes to support phonemic awareness (i.e., the ability to distinguish between the smallest spoken sounds in words or phonemes), Ms. Salazar can notice how students segment words and guide students on the similarities and differences between AAE and GAE. For example, when she asks a student to place counters down for each sound they hear in the word "left," she can ask the student to repeat the word after her as they place the sounds. If she hears the student say "lef" and place three counters, she can note that the student may be using AAE and, if so, has correctly segmented the sounds in the word as they say it. Using a similar approach when asking a student to spell the word "math," Ms. Salazar can hear if the student says /m/ /a/ /f/ and spells the word as maf, which would be consistent with AAE. In these cases, the student has segmented the words correctly in AAE, but, in GAE-governed assessments, would be scored as though their segmenting were incorrect. In these instances, the teacher can call attention to the fact that the student has correctly segmented the words as they use them, and she can point out that, after introducing the concepts of AAE and GAE, which will be discussed in more detail below, she can explain that, in texts that use GAE, *left* has a /t/ at the end and the final sound in *math* is spelled with *th*.

To affirm students' linguistic identities, educators must familiarize themselves with the specific linguistic patterns students use. Teachers who invest time in understanding their students' language and consult linguistic resources can identify these patterns in real-time interactions. Recognizing these patterns requires that teachers provide ample opportunities for students to engage in oral language practices, such as through strategies like turn-and-talk, think-pair-share, and other interactive methods that promote active communication. When engaging with students, it is crucial for teachers to be aware of the broader social, political, and historical contexts surrounding the use of AAE. Research suggests that children as young as 3 years old are conscious of race (Katz & Kofkin, 1997), and by the second grade, some students reduce their use of AAE in the classroom, despite higher usage in earlier years (Washington & Seidenberg, 2021). This shift in linguistic style is cause for concern if students feel part of their identity is unwelcome in school and, consequently, become disengaged. To ensure students remain engaged in classroom instruction, it is important to validate students' home language while simultaneously expanding their linguistic repertoire. Instruction should connect to students' home language without demanding its suppression or reduction.

SUPPORTING AFRICAN AMERICAN STUDENTS' LANGUAGE THROUGH CHILDREN'S LITERATURE

One of the most significant ways to enable students to see (Bishop, 1990) and hear (Pittman et al., 2024) themselves in text is through the use of culturally relevant, authentic children's literature in classroom instruction. Culturally relevant children's literature values the cultural and linguistic strengths that African American students bring to the classroom. Educators can create inclusive environments that foster engagement and support positive identity development by incorporating African American students' language into literature and classroom discussions. This is a crucial component of culturally relevant pedagogy. Recognizing and valuing AAE as a legitimate and rich linguistic form allows students to see their language as an asset rather than a deficit. When their language is included in educational settings, students are more likely to feel respected and validated, fostering a sense of belonging and encouraging active participation. Embracing students' linguistic identities in the classroom builds their self-efficacy and supports positive identity development. If AAE is disregarded or seen as inferior, students may hesitate to share their ideas in an oral discussion, which can limit their educational engagement and confidence. When teachers embed students' language into the classroom context through discussions, they can express themselves authentically and feel empowered in academic spaces. This approach not only enhances literacy skills but also empowers students to view their language as a tool for self-expression, learning, and identity formation.

Selecting books that reflect diverse Black experiences allows African American students to feel seen and valued. Literature that resonates with their everyday lives and cultural heritage fosters a sense of belonging, while stories of empowerment and social justice help them understand their role as agents of change. Culturally relevant books that affirm African American identity build self-worth and pride, encouraging students to resist stereotypes and connect with reading on a personal level.

When educators create spaces for open discussions on race, culture, and identity, students feel validated and empowered to express themselves. Incorporating African American storytelling traditions further enhances literacy by connecting students to their heritage and valuing oral expression. Additionally, literature that challenges stereotypes expands students' understanding of Black identity, celebrating a wide range of achievements and contributions. Integrating culturally relevant literature into the classroom not only strengthens literacy skills but also supports meaningful engagement, affirming students' identities and empowering them to see and hear themselves positively represented.

Box 9.3. Vignette: Ms. Resnek

Ms. Resnek, a dedicated third-grade teacher, gazed at the stack of books on her desk. She had carefully chosen each one, hoping they would resonate with her students. Although Ms. Resnek took pride in creating an inclusive classroom, she was aware of her limitations; she didn't speak AAE, which many of her students spoke, yet she wanted to share a book that used AAE. She was mindful of being respectful of her students' language. One book in particular, *Sweet Clara and the Freedom Quilt*, seemed to interest her students as a book that could be shared to discuss her students' history. She knew that the language in the text would enhance the vivid storyline in a way she knew her students would connect with deeply. Yet as she practiced reading it aloud, Ms. Resnek felt the words didn't flow as naturally for her as she had hoped. She worried that her attempt might come across as forced—or worse, disrespectful. She knew that language was personal, a part of identity. She wanted her students to hear the story as it was meant to be heard, with the richness and cadence that only familiarity with AAE could provide. Additionally, she wanted to have a rich discussion with her students about the text. She knew these discussions would be critical conversations because of the historical content of the text she used. In this instance, what should Ms. Resnek do?

PRACTICAL IMPLICATIONS

Literature can serve as a valuable resource for celebrating and affirming students' linguistic competence. Teachers can select texts that reflect the languages spoken by students in the classroom. This practice can mitigate the cognitive load faced by students who routinely navigate between two language systems. Incorporating texts in students' home languages allows them to focus on meaning, comprehension, and making connections to their prior knowledge. When teachers are not proficient in the language featured in a text, they should seek out native speakers for support or utilize electronic resources such as audiobooks or video platforms like YouTube to provide an authentic reading experience. Seeking out native speakers would be a great opportunity to partner with families for a home-to-school connection or partner with community members to establish community partnerships. This allows students to see that their families and community members are invested in their learning in culturally relevant ways.

It is very important to use native speakers or genuine recordings because students are likely to recognize if a read-aloud does not sound authentic, and attempting to read in AAE without fluency may unintentionally come across as humorous or even mocking of their language. Although a teacher who does not speak AAE might be able to read the words, certain elements of the language require the teacher to know how to say particular words. For example, in AAE, the word *police* as in the sentence "the *police* siren was flashin," would be pronounced as "poh-lice," with the stress on the first syllable. Other words that are pronounced with different stress patterns in AAE compared to GAE include "De-troit," "gui-tar" (regionally, it could be "git-ar"), and "ho-tel." See Box 9.4 for AAE features in the book *Sweet Clara and the Freedom Quilt*. Using a native speaker or genuine recording ensures respect for the language and enhances students' engagement with the story. When teachers use stories that showcase AAE's distinct linguistic structures, they can point the features out in a positive light and explain that these features are rule-governed and systematic, which helps affirm the value of AAE. For further books that include AAE, see Pittman et al. (2024).

Box 9.4. AAE Features in *Sweet Clara and the Freedom Quilt*

Phonological features: 'cause (because); never gon' (going to) eat; eatin (eating); dreamin' (dreaming); But don't you start thinkin' (thinking) bout (about) it; sewin' (sewing); teachin' (teaching); comin' (coming); Missus; gettin'; helpin' (helping); 'cept (except); yo (your); streamin (streaming); goin (going); askin' (asking); makin' (making); patchin' (patching); goin' (going)

Morphosyntactic features: I got (was) sent; Missus' (Misses') daughter Ella be (is) gettin' (getting) married come (in the) spring; You aine (are not) gone (going to) last in the fields; You gon' be (going to become) a real seamstress; Where you gon' (Where are you going); You growed (grew) so big; What cabin my momma at (what cabin my momma is at)

Further, engaging in critical discussions about language to cultivate students' linguistic consciousness is essential for fostering a strong sense of identity and self-awareness among AAE-speaking students (Baker-Bell, 2020). Such critical conversations deepen students' understanding of standard language ideology and empower them to enact change within their communities. Critical language awareness pedagogy supports students as they examine the connections between language, power, and society (Smitherman, 2017). This pedagogy "seeks to heighten their awareness of the stakes involved in language attitudes and policies of correctness and strives to impart knowledge about their language, its social and linguistic rules, its history and cultural connection" (Smitherman, 2017, p. 10).

Engaging in these conversations requires educators to thoroughly understand the historical, social, and cultural dimensions of AAE, including its distinctive linguistic features. Using asset-based language when discussing AAE is crucial, as much of the vocabulary found in educational contexts—such as textbooks, research articles, and professional seminars—often reflects deficit-based perspectives (Hamilton, 2018). AAE is frequently described in such contexts with terms like *omission* (e.g., *be* verb omission: "He loud"), *deletion* (e.g., final consonant blend in a consonant blend deletion: *frien* for *friend*), or *reduction* (e.g., final *r* reduction: *doe* for *door*). This deficit-oriented language can be likened to "an assault on the cultural identity of a speaker" (Hamilton, 2018, p. 112). Supporting students' linguistic consciousness and advancing educators' understanding of AAE as a distinct linguistic system requires adopting affirming language that recognizes its structure without comparing it unfavorably to other language systems.

Box 9.5. Vignette: Ms. Resnek (*continued*)

After some thought, Ms. Resnek reached out to Mr. Carter, a fourth-grade teacher known for his engaging storytelling and his natural ability to connect with students through language. She asked if he might record himself reading *Sweet Clara and the Freedom Quilt*. To her delight, he agreed and was happy to help bring the story to life. The next day, as her students gathered on the reading rug, Ms. Resnek introduced the story and told them they'd be hearing Mr. Carter read it. She noticed the way her African American students' faces lit up, recognizing the familiar patterns and rhythm in his voice. They leaned in, engaged and attentive, as the story unfolded with authenticity and warmth. After the recording finished, Ms. Resnek invited the class to discuss the story. Her students eagerly shared their thoughts, even relating parts of the story to oral stories they heard from elders in their family. That afternoon, Ms. Resnek reflected on the experience. She realized that supporting her students' language meant more than just choosing the right books—it meant ensuring those books were presented in ways that honored her students' language. With this small but meaningful adjustment, she felt she had taken a step toward creating a classroom that not only celebrated diversity but also respected the unique voices of each student.

Mr. Carter was able to help Ms. Resnek introduce *Sweet Clara and the Freedom Quilt* to her students in a way that was meaningful and impactful. Mr. Resnek and Mr. Carter could have, also, co-taught *Sweet Clara and the Freedom Quilt* utilizing the lesson plan in Figure 9.1.

African American families have a wealth of literacy knowledge via oral language. Historically, enslaved African Americans were prohibited from reading and writing; therefore, they passed many stories down from generation to generation via oral language. Teachers can connect with families by encouraging families to share their favorite stories that reflect African American culture or history. Incorporating these stories into the classroom provides students with a sense of cultural pride and reinforces language connections between home and school. Teachers can also create assignments where students can create their books with their own stories with their families. These books can be added to the classroom library and ensure students have access to a variety of books in their language.

Teachers can also use this approach to support early reading. Teachers can have families and students coauthor decodable texts in their home language (Lawson, 2024). For example, in one study, Lawson (2024) integrated cognitive, linguistic, and sociocultural aspects of reading by incorporating students' natural speech patterns into phonics-aligned texts. This approach enhanced word recognition and supported word reading proficiency. It also reflected culturally relevant pedagogy (Ladson-Billings, 1995) by utilizing students' linguistic and cultural strengths in decoding tasks.

TRANSLANGUAGING

Recently, there has been a focus on recognizing and encouraging translanguaging as a natural form of communication for dual-language learners (Garcia & Wei, 2014). While much of the research on translanguaging has focused on English and Spanish, translanguaging across AAE and GAE can be a powerful tool to support AAE speakers in the classroom, as it validates their linguistic identity while enhancing their engagement and learning. By encouraging students to use AAE alongside GAE, translanguaging allows them to draw from their full linguistic repertoire, fostering deeper comprehension and expression. For example, students might read a text in GAE and discuss it or summarize it in AAE, which can boost confidence and help them connect new concepts to familiar language patterns.

Other examples can include pairing students to read a book in GAE and then having them rewrite specific sections or dialogues in AAE or vice versa.

This lesson plan supports AAE speakers by honoring their language, engaging students in culturally relevant literature, and encouraging personal expression through language and art.

Subject: Integrated English Language Arts and Social Studies

Grade Level: 4th-5th grades **Duration: 60 minutes**

Objectives

- Students will explore AAE as a unique and rule-governed language
- Students will analyze language use in *Sweet Clara and the Freedom Quilt* and discuss how it reflects the characters' cultural and historical background.
- Students will understand the historical context of the Underground Railroad and how the freedom quilt symbolized hope and resilience.
- Students will create a "quilt square" based on their own experiences and language to contribute to a classroom "freedom quilt."

Materials

Sweet Clara and the Freedom Quilt by Deborah Hopkinson; chart paper or whiteboard; quilt square templates (paper or fabric, about 6 x 6 inches); crayons or markers; quilt or blanket for classroom display (optional)

Vocabulary

- African American English: A language spoken by many African American people. Give examples (see Tables 9.1 and 9.2).
- Freedom quilt: A coded quilt used as a map or guide for enslaved people seeking freedom.
- Underground Railroad: A network of secret routes and safe houses used by enslaved African Americans to escape to free states and Canada.

Lesson Activities

1. Introduction to the book (10 minutes)

Introduce *Sweet Clara and the Freedom Quilt* and provide a brief overview of the story's setting in the context of slavery and the Underground Railroad. Explain the concept of the "freedom quilt" as a tool for guidance and hope for those seeking freedom.

(continued)

FIGURE 9.1. Lesson plan for exploring language and history with *Sweet Clara and the Freedom Quilt*.

2. Read-Aloud and Language Exploration (20 minutes)

Read select passages from *Sweet Clara and the Freedom Quilt*, focusing on sections that feature AAE. See Box 9.6 for the AAE features from the text. As you read, pause to point out specific examples of AAE in the dialogue. Then, discuss with students why the author might have chosen to use AAE for Clara and other characters. *Questions to prompt discussion:* How does the language in the story make the characters feel more real and what does the language tell us about where Clara is from and her experiences?

3. Understanding AAE (15 minutes)

Provide a student-friendly definition and explanation for AAE. Next, show how certain words or phrases in AAE are different from GAE but follow a consistent pattern. (See Box 9.6 for the AAE words and phrases from the text.) Then, encourage students to share if they have heard language like this in their own communities or families.

4. Creating Quilt Squares (15 minutes)

Explain to students that they will create their own quilt squares, inspired by Clara's freedom quilt. On their square, students will write a short phrase or sentence in their own words that represents their culture, family, or something important to them. Then, the students can decorate their square with symbols, patterns, or colors that reflect their personal story or identity.

5. Class Quilt and Reflection (5 minutes)

Collect the squares and assemble them on a classroom wall or display, creating a collective "freedom quilt." Next, discuss with the class how their squares, like Clara's quilt, reflect each of their unique identities and stories. Then, conclude with a reflection question: "How can using our own words and language make our stories stronger and more meaningful?"

Extensions

- *Writing extension:* Invite students to write a journal entry about what freedom or hope means to them, encouraging them to express their thoughts in the language they feel most comfortable using.
- *Social studies connection:* Explore more about the Underground Railroad, allowing students to map routes that freedom-seekers might have taken, reinforcing the historical context of the story. Invite students to give an oral presentation on their maps in the language that they feel most comfortable using.

FIGURE 9.1. *(continued)*

Books with familiar narratives, like *The Snowy Day* by Ezra Jack Keats, can provide simple structures that students can adapt, practicing language flexibility. Journal reflections offer an effective way for students to think about language choices in texts. For example, after reading *Crown: An Ode to the Fresh Cut* by Derrick Barnes, students could journal about the main character's experiences, expressing thoughts in both AAE and GAE. Alternatively, they could read a book like *Goin' Someplace Special* by Patricia McKissack, analyzing which characters use AAE or GAE and exploring the author's reasons for these language choices for each character.

Translanguaging creates opportunities for bidialectal development. By allowing students to move fluidly between AAE and GAE, teachers can support students in learning the contrasts and applications of each language without devaluing one over the other. This approach not only respects students' cultural and linguistic backgrounds but also enhances metalinguistic awareness, helping students develop skills to adapt language use to various contexts, a skill that benefits both academic and social interactions.

CONCLUSION

In summary, we provide some dos and don'ts for implementing children's literature with AAE.

Dos

1. Use authentic children's literature and ensure the language is genuine. If unsure about a text, consult a colleague or community member who speaks AAE.
2. Allow AAE speakers to use their language in class to support strong communication skills. Encourage translanguaging to expand their linguistic repertoire.
3. As with any text, pre-teach unfamiliar vocabulary. Also, preview AAE-specific terms to support non-AAE speakers' understanding.

Don'ts

1. Don't assume all African American students speak AAE or that others don't.
2. Avoid books with AAE or African American stereotypes; ensure language is authentic.
3. Don't "correct" students' language during key tasks like retelling; this reinforces dominant language ideologies (Metz, 2018).

Reflection Questions

1. How does AAE in children's literature help children understand language as a marker of identity by reflecting themselves and their communities?
2. How does the inclusion of AAE in literature impact your perception of a book's authenticity?
3. How can educators discuss AAE in literature without stigmatizing it as "incorrect" or "improper" English, and how should educators approach explaining AAE in literature to students who may be unfamiliar with it?

NOTES

1 *General American English* refers to a variety of English that is codified, taught, and used in conventional writing in most schools in the United States.

2 *African American English* refers to a rule-governed variety of English spoken by many African Americans in the United States.

REFERENCES

Baker-Bell, A. (2020). *Linguistic justice: Black language, literacy, identity, and pedagogy.* Routledge.

Banks, J. A. (1993). Multicultural education: Historical development, dimensions, and practice. *Phi Delta Kappan, 75*(1), 22–28.

Bishop, R. S. (1990). Mirrors, windows, and sliding glass doors. *Perspectives: Choosing and Using Books for Classrooms, 6*(3), 9–12.

Brooks, W., & McNair, J. C. (2009). "But This Story of Mine Is Not Unique": A review of research on African American children's literature. *Review of Educational Research, 79*(1), 125–162.

Cooperative Children's Book Center. (2024). *Books by and/or about Black, Indigenous and People of Color (All Years).* Retrieved November 7, 2024 from *https://ccbc.education.wisc.edu/literature-resources/ccbc-diversity-statistics/books-by-about-poc-fnn*

Curtis, C. P. (1999). *Bud, not buddy.* Delacorte Press.

Delpit, L. D. (1995). *Other people's children: Cultural conflict in the classroom.* The New Press.

García, O., & Wei, L. (2014). *Translanguaging: Language, bilingualism and education.* Palgrave Macmillan.

Green, L. (2002). *African American English: A linguistic introduction.* Cambridge University Press.

Guo, S.-c. (2012). Using authentic materials for extensive reading to promote English proficiency. *English Language Teaching*, 5(8), 196–206.

Hamilton, M.B., Mont, E., & McLain, C. (2018). Deletion, omission, reduction: Redefining the language we use to talk about African American English. *Perspectives of the ASHA Special Interest Groups, 3*(1), 107–117.

Hamilton, V. (1974). *M.C. Higgins, the great.* Simon & Schuster Books for Young Readers.

Heineke, A. J., & Papola-Ellis, A. (2022a). *Inclusive texts in elementary classrooms. Developing literacies, identities, and understandings.* Teachers College Press.

Heineke, A. J., Papola-Ellis, A., & Elliott, J. (2022b). Using texts as mirrors: The power of readers seeing themselves. *The Reading Teacher, 76*(3), 1–8.

Hughes, L. (1954). *The first book of rhythms.* Franklin Watts.

Katz, P. A., & Kofkin, J. A. (1997). Race, gender, and young children. In S. S. Luthar, J. A. Burack, D. Cicchetti, & J. R. Weisz (Eds.), *Developmental psychopathology: Perspectives on adjustment, risk, and disorder* (pp. 51–74). Cambridge University Press.

Keats, E. J. (1962). *The snowy day.* Viking Press.

Ladkin, D., & Taylor, S. S. (2010). Enacting the "true self": Towards a theory of embodied authentic leadership. *The Leadership Quarterly, 21*(1), 64–74.

Ladson-Billings, G. (1995). Toward a theory of culturally relevant pedagogy. *American Educational Research Journal, 32*(3), 465–491.

Ladson-Billings, G., & Dixson, A. (2021). Put some respect on the theory: Confronting distortions of culturally relevant pedagogy. In C. Compton-Lilly, T. L. Ellison, K. Perry, & P. Smagorinsky (Eds.), *Whitewashed critical perspectives: Restoring the edge to edgy ideas* (pp. 16–31). Routledge.

Lanehart, S. (Ed.). (2015). *The Oxford handbook of African American language.* Oxford University Press.

Larrick, N. (1965). The all-white world of children's books. *Saturday Review, 48*(11), 63–65.

Lawson, A. (2024). Make it make sense: Fostering children of color from minoritized communities' comprehension through student-generated decodable readers. *Education Sciences, 14*(11), 1191.

Lee, A. Y. (2022). Free license to communicate: Licensing black language against white supremacist language assessments in a preK classroom. *Research in the Teaching of English, 57*(2), 133–155.

Lennox, S. (2013). Interactive read-alouds—an avenue for enhancing children's language for thinking and understanding: A review of recent research. *Early Childhood Education Journal, 41*(5), 381–389.

Linguistic Society of America. (1997, January 3). *Resolution on the Oakland "Ebonics" issue unanimously adopted at the annual meeting of the Linguistic Society of America, Chicago, IL.* Retrieved April 23, 2024, from *https://websites.umich.edu/~jlawler/ebonics.lsa.html#top*

Lippi-Green, R. (2012). *English with an accent: Language, ideology, and discrimination in the United States* (2nd ed.). Routledge.

Metz, M. (2018). Challenges of confronting dominant language ideologies in the high school English classroom. *Research in the Teaching of English, 52*(4), 455–477.

National Center for Education Statistics. (2024). *The nation's report card: 2024 Mathematics and reading assessments.* U.S. Department of Education, Institute of Education Sciences. *www.nationsreportcard.gov*

National Governors Association Center for Best Practices & Council of Chief State School Officers. (2010). *Common core state standards for English language arts.* Authors. *www.corestandards.org*

Oakland Unified School District. (1996, December 18). Resolution recognizing Ebonics as the primary language of African American students and directing the superintendent to take steps to fully utilize the language in the educational program. Retrieved April 23,

2024, from *www.edweek.org/leadership/full-text-of-ebonics-resolution-adopted-by-oakland-board/1997/01*

Piper, R. E., Vice, T. A., & Pittman, R. T. (2017). Using multicultural children's literature to address social issues: The power of interactive read aloud. *Read: An Online Journal for Literacy Educators, 3*(5), 15–25.

Pittman, R. T., Rice, D., Garza, J., & Guerra, N. (2023). The importance of phonemic awareness instruction for African American students. *The Reading League Journal, 4*(2), 27–32.

Pittman, R. T., O'Neal, L., Wright, K., & White, B. R. (2024a). Elevating students' oral and written language: Empowering African American students through language. *Education Sciences, 14*(1191).

Pittman, R. T., Piper, R. E., McCoy, W., & Alanis, M. (2024b). African American language in children's literature. *Journal of Literacy Research, 56*(2), 157–183.

Read, C. (1971). Pre-school children's knowledge of English phonology. *Harvard Educational Review, 41*(1), 1–34.

Rickford, J. R. (1999). *African American Vernacular English: Features, evolution, educational implications.* Blackwell Publishers.

Shackelford, J. D. (1938). *Child's story of the Negro.* The Associated Publishers.

Shakespeare, W. (1982). *Hamlet* (H. Jenkins, Ed.). Methuen.

Smitherman, G. (1991). "What is Africa to me?": Language, ideology, and African American. *American Speech, 66*(2), 115–132.

Smitherman, G. (2017). Raciolinguistics, "mis-education," and language arts teaching in the 21st century. *Language Arts Journal of Michigan, 32*(2), 4–12.

Smitherman, G. (2021). *Word from the mother: Language and African Americans.* Routledge.

Stanley, T. (2018). *Authentic earning: Real-world experiences that build 21st-century s kills* (1st ed.). Routledge.

Taylor, M. (1976). *Roll of thunder, hear my cry.* Dial Press.

Villarroel, V., Bloxham, S., Bruna, D., Bruna, C., & Herrera-Seda, C. (2018). Authentic assessment: Creating a blueprint for course design. *Assessment and Evaluation in Higher Education,* 43(5), 840–854.

Washington, J. A., & Seidenberg, M. S. (2021). Teaching reading to African American children: When home and school language differ. *American Educator, 45,* 26–31.

Wolfram, W., & Schilling-Estes, N. (2006). *American English: Dialects and variation* (2nd ed.). Blackwell.

Woodson, J. (2014). *Brown girl dreaming.* Penguin.

Wooten, D. A., Liang, L. A., & Cullinan, B. E. (Eds.). (2018). *Children's Literature in the reading program: Engaging young readers in the 21st Century.* Guilford Press.

Wynter-Hoyte, K., Braden, E. G., Rodriguez, S., & Thornton, N. (2020). Humanize Blackness in early childhood education: Supporting teachers to see beyond a single story about Blackness. *Journal of Early Childhood Literacy, 20*(4), 532–561.

10

Language and Reading Assessment Practices for Multilingual Learners from Spanish-Speaking Homes

Jeannette Mancilla-Martinez, Bhabika Joshi, and Phoebe J. Ahn

Guiding Questions

1. What is the difference between multilingual learners and English learners?
2. What are some of the key challenges teachers face in supporting multilingual learners' English language and reading achievement?
3. What are promising directions for teachers to support multilingual learners' English language and reading achievement?

U.S. READING ACHIEVEMENT TRENDS

Language and reading abilities are foundational for academic, professional, and personal success. However, when these skills are not effectively developed, individuals may face challenges such as compromised high school completion, reduced earning potential, and health-related issues (Aro et al., 2019; Eloranta et al., 2019; Gubbels et al., 2019). Results from extant studies help inform research-, practice-, and policy-based efforts aimed at ensuring that all children, including students from multilingual homes in the United States, are provided with a foundation that allows them to meet their potential. As we have learned more about how to best support all students' reading achievement, language comprehension, often overlooked in the past, has increasingly received attention for its critical role in the development of reading (Hattan & Kendeou, 2024; Mancilla-Martinez, 2020).

Specifically, researchers have called for school-based assessments to include attention to language comprehension (Silverman et al., 2021), which is not typical in the current context. There is a need for a paradigm shift in school-based assessments to focus not only on decoding but also on language comprehension with linguistically sensitive measures that can help guide reading instruction. Such a shift also has strong potential for informing the complex decision-making process of identifying the types of reading instructional supports students need, such as additional academic English language support, more intensified reading interventions, referral for potential special education eligibility for reading difficulties, or a combination of supports. Language comprehension assessments are particularly important for the especially complicated decision-making process for how best to support multilingual learners, as a key consideration is whether they possess the required English proficiency to access the curriculum in English.

MULTILINGUAL LEARNERS AND SPECIAL EDUCATION

Significant disproportionality refers to the unequal distribution of students in special education by race and ethnicity. Prior to 2016, states used different approaches to identify significant disproportionality. However, the 2016 Equity Regulations under the Individuals with Disabilities Education Act (IDEA) required that all states adopt a standard approach to identify significant disproportionality with the goal of addressing the root cause(s). Unfortunately, misrepresentation (i.e., over- and under-representation) of students in special education by race and ethnicity has long been reported (e.g., Constantino et al., 2020; Cruz & Firestone, 2022; Morgan et al., 2012). Despite the large and growing population of multilingual learners in the United States, the Equity Regulations in IDEA focus on disproportionality by racial and ethnic groups—not language groups. Nonetheless, the growing body of research anchored in the representation of students from multilingual homes in special education is similarly mixed and contentious.

Disproportionality of multilingual learners has been reported across grades and across disability types (e.g., Artiles & Ortiz, 2002). However, multilingual learners continue to be particularly disproportionately represented in the subcategory of specific learning disabilities (SLD; Office of English Language Acquisition [OELA], 2020), which includes reading difficulties or dyslexia (20 U.S.C. § 1401). Some studies report overrepresentation (e.g., Sullivan, 2011), some underrepresentation (e.g., Mancilla-Martinez et al., 2022; Morgan et al., 2012, 2015, 2017), and others a shift in the disproportionality pattern, such that students are initially underrepresented and later overrepresented (e.g., Hibel & Jasper, 2012; Samson &

Lesaux, 2009; Umansky et al., 2017; Yamasaki & Luk, 2018). Recent cross-sectional findings across a 10-year span point to underrepresentation of multilingual learners in special education (Mancilla-Martinez et al., 2024). These mixed findings are not entirely unexpected given that SLD has been identified as a relatively subjective disability category, largely relying on educators' judgment (Donovan & Cross, 2002) and encompassing learning disabilities that do not fit into other official categories of special education (Counts et al., 2018; Hibel & Jasper, 2012; U.S. Commission on Civil Rights, 2009). It is also important to acknowledge that many educators have not received adequate training in this area.

Ultimately, whether multilingual learners are over- or underrepresented is concerning, as special education identification should be separately evaluated from second language proficiency. Supporting multilingual students' reading comprehension development necessitates a comprehensive approach to assessment and instruction that takes into consideration the heterogeneity of this population of students. Therefore, we begin by providing an overview of the sociodemographic characteristics of students from multilingual homes in the United States. We then explain how typical school-based assessment practices are limited and constrain the extent to which educators can support multilingual students' language and reading achievement. We end the chapter by offering educators practical guidance on ways to address the limitations of school-based assessment so that they have the information they need to provide multilingual students appropriate and equitable academic support.

ALL ENGLISH LEARNERS ARE MULTILINGUAL LEARNERS, BUT NOT THE OTHER WAY AROUND

In the simplest terms, multilingual learners in the United States are students who are *not* from English-only homes. In other words, multilingual learners are students who come from homes in which a language other than or in addition to English is used. The number of U.S. school-age (ages 5–17) students from homes in which a language other than or in addition to English is used currently stands at nearly 12 million (Annie E. Casey Foundation, 2024). Hundreds of languages are represented in the homes of multilingual students, and these students have a wide range of proficiency in English and in the home language(s).

Perhaps the most well-known subgroup of multilingual learners is English learners (ELs). EL is the official term used by the U.S. Department of Education's Office of English Language Acquisition (OELA, 2024) for students whose primary language is not English and who are formally identified by their schools as being in the process of acquiring academic English language proficiency. At school entry, families are asked to complete a Home Language Survey that includes questions to help schools identify students who may be ELs. If families indicate that a language other than English is used at home, the student is screened for EL status eligibility (Sugarman & Geary, 2018). Students who score below a certain cut point on the academic English language proficiency screener are identified as ELs. This subgroup, formally referred to as ELs, is legally eligible for academic English language services to support academic success in English. A second subgroup refers to students who were ELs and were subsequently reclassified as proficient in English, referred to as *former ELs*. Students are reclassified if they meet state-specific criteria, which typically include performance on standardized language assessments, academic achievement, and teacher evaluations. The final subgroup of multilingual learners, and the least researched subgroup, is referred to as *never ELs*. As the term implies, never ELs are students from multilingual homes who entered school already proficient in English. This subgroup was *never* classified as EL because they scored above the cut point on the academic English language proficiency screener and were thus never eligible for academic English language support services.

In summary, ELs are one subgroup of the multilingual learner population, and not all multilingual learners are in the process of developing academic English language proficiency. Former ELs attained English proficiency after having been identified as eligible for academic English language support services, and never ELs entered school already proficient in English and were never eligible for academic English language support services. It is also the case that multilingual learners vary widely in their home language proficiency. The key point is that students from multilingual homes are exposed to a language other than or in addition to English only, even if multilingual students themselves are fully proficient in English. Thus, the language environment of multilingual learners is distinct from that of students from homes in which English is the only language.

Notwithstanding the vast heterogeneity of the multilingual learner population in the United States, multilingual learners are too often broadly characterized as a population that has limited academic English language proficiency and limited academic success. This is an essential point for educators to understand. Some multilingual learners effectively have language profiles that are indistinguishable from their English-only peers, with the difference being that multilingual learners have been exposed to another language(s) at home. It is also the case that some multilingual learners may have academic English language skills that surpass those of their English-only peers, and yet other multilingual learners may surpass the English academic achievement of their English-only peers (Mancilla-Martinez et al., in revision). However, multilingual learners who have not yet attained academic English proficiency are generally more susceptible to risk factors for English academic under-achievement (Mavrogordato et al., 2024). National data consistently find limited English academic success among students in the process of acquiring English, particularly in English reading, such that they tend to lag their non-EL peers (e.g., Mancilla-Martinez, 2020a; National Center for Education Statistics [NCES], 2024a; Villegas, 2023). This should come as no surprise as this subgroup of learners is effectively still in the process of acquiring academic English language proficiency to access the curriculum in English. However, it is essential to underscore that the non-English language(s) spoken in students' homes is(are) not the risk factor(s) for compromised academic achievement (Mancilla-Martinez, 2020b).

Poverty, however, is a well-known risk factor for compromised academic achievement, and multilingual learners in the United States tend to experience poverty at higher rates than their English-only peers (Ashcraft, 2023). If a multilingual learner is experiencing academic struggles, it is essential for educators to disentangle whether their challenges are related to academic English language proficiency, limited learning opportunities due to poverty and other systemic barriers, and/or a disability (we return to the intersection of language and disability status in the discussion). Unfortunately, the processes, procedures, and policies meant to guide educators in meeting multilingual learners' academic needs remain limited. Thus, educators may not be adequately prepared to best support multilingual learners' academic development. In this chapter, we aim to provide guidance for educators on tangible actions to support the language and reading achievement of multilingual students despite systemic barriers. Based on space limitations and on the prevalence of the population, we focus on multilingual learners from Spanish-speaking homes in the sections that follow.

MULTILINGUAL LEARNERS FROM SPANISH-SPEAKING HOMES

Spanish is the most common home language of multilingual learners in the United States (NCES, 2024a), and the Latino population remains the fastest-growing segment of U.S. public school enrollment (NCES, 2024b). Multilingual learners from Spanish-speaking homes in the United States trace their origins to numerous countries, though the largest numbers come from Mexico (Moslimani et al., 2023). Importantly, and with direct implications for educators, multilingual learners from Spanish-speaking homes reside in all regions of the United States. For decades, states such as California, Texas, Illinois, Florida, and New York have educated large numbers of multilingual learners from Spanish-speaking homes. Yet, the largest growth rates of multilingual learners have been so-called new immigrant destination states such as Georgia, Louisiana, North Dakota, South Dakota, and Alabama (Singer, 2004). Many questions remain as to how best to support the language and academic development of multilingual learners, including in historical immigrant destination states. However, new immigrant destination states face an arguably more daunting task given the more limited experience in educating multilingual learners.

In brief, multilingual learners from Spanish-speaking homes are generally more susceptible to risk factors for compromised English reading achievement (Bedore et al., 2023; Mancilla-Martinez et al., 2020a), but not due to their language status per se. Yet, a persistent misconception is that speaking or being instructed in a language other than English interferes with multilingual learners' academic English language development and, in turn, English academic achievement. Not only is there no empirical evidence of negative effects of bilingual programming on academic outcomes, but research has also shown positive effects of bilingual programming on students' academic English language development (August & Shanahan, 2006; Morita-Mullaney et al., 2020; Porter et al., 2023). However, the fact is that most multilingual learners in the United States are educated in English-only classrooms: a mere 7% of multilingual learners in the United States are educated in dual immersion programs (August & Shanahan, 2006; Porter et al., 2023). Given that most multilingual learners in the United States are educated in English-only classrooms, it is essential to examine how to best support them in these settings. A major factor in this discussion is assessment—ensuring that language and reading assessments accurately capture multilingual learners' abilities is critical for making informed instructional decisions and providing appropriate instructional support. Below, we briefly outline three persistent assessment problems educators consistently contend with.

PERSISTENT PROBLEMS: TYPICAL SCHOOL-BASED ASSESSMENT PRACTICES

It is generally agreed that the ability to read the printed words that appear in text (i.e., word reading) and to simultaneously understand the meanings of the printed words (i.e., language comprehension) is the goal of reading. Indeed, word reading and language comprehension represent two nonnegotiable reading comprehension contributors, as described in the well-known and empirically supported Simple View of Reading model (SVR; Hoover & Gough, 1990). But typical U.S.

school-based assessment practices complicate the identification of the causes of reading difficulty for all learners, and especially for multilingual learners. This limits the extent to which educators can support this population's reading comprehension achievement. Below, we outline three persistent problems educators consistently contend with.

Problem 1: English-Only Assessments

Despite the diverse linguistic experiences of the U.S. school-age population, school protocols and procedures under the jurisdiction of the education system remain largely homogeneous, such that nearly all assessments are administered only in English for all learners (Gándara & Escamilla, 2016; Sugarman & Villegas, 2020). Furthermore, standardized assessments typically rely on norms established from monolingual samples, often overlooking the diverse language experiences of multilingual learners (O'Connor et al., 2019). Indeed, standardized assessments rarely report the proportion of the norming sample who speak more than one language (Luk & Christodoulou, 2016). This is a crucial point for educators to understand. Assessment developers select a sample of individuals (referred to as the norming sample) that is representative of a larger population the assessment is intended to measure. If students from English-only homes comprise the norming population for an English reading comprehension assessment, the norms that are derived reflect "normal" performance on the assessment for students from English-only homes. If this same English reading comprehension assessment is used with multilingual learners (who do *not* come from English-only homes), the validity of the results may be compromised. Thus, at minimum, caution must be exercised in interpreting the results because the norms were derived from an English-only population. When performance scores of multilingual learners are compared against their age-matched English-only peers, English reading comprehension scores are persistently lower for multilingual learners compared to that of their English-only peers (Mancilla-Martinez & Lesaux, 2011; NCES, 2024a). This is particularly concerning for ELs as—by definition—English is the developing language. However, even for former ELs (i.e., students who were classified as EL and have been reclassified as English-proficient) and never ELs (i.e., students from multilingual homes who entered school proficient in English and were never classified as EL), performance on English-only assessments reflects their skills in only one language, not their full linguistic abilities.

A related, but additional, concern is that reliance on language and reading assessments normed on monolingual populations only captures students' skills in one language. For example, when multilingual learners are assessed in Spanish, these measures are also typically designed for Spanish-only speakers, raising the same norming sample concerns previously discussed. It is thus not uncommon to find that multilingual learners from Spanish-speaking homes evidence low Spanish and low English vocabulary knowledge (Gross et al., 2014; Hammer et al., 2008; Mancilla-Martinez & Lesaux, 2011, 2017; Mancilla-Martinez & Vagh, 2013). The key point is that, by relying on monolingually designed measures for multilingual learners, we inevitably tap only partial knowledge of what multilingual learners know. This contributes to a persistent deficit orientation toward multilingual learners' linguistic knowledge and academic potential, as well as to potential suspicions of a learning disability. Of course, it is also possible that multilingual learners who evidence low performance when assessed in both languages require more comprehensive language and reading assessment to determine their instructional needs. But this can only happen if the home language is accounted for. By relying on monolingually normed assessments (typically English only), schools risk making inaccurate assumptions about multilingual students' abilities. This can lead to inappropriate placements, misidentifications, or missed opportunities for meaningful instructional support.

Problem 2: Word Reading Assessments Prioritize Speed and Convenience

Multilingual learners from Spanish-speaking homes in the United States tend to particularly struggle with English language comprehension and English reading comprehension, even though their English word reading skills are often, though not always, comparable to those of their monolingual English-speaking peers (Mancilla-Martinez & Lesaux, 2017; Mancilla-Martinez, Hwang, Oh, & McClain, 2020a). Yet, English word reading assessment remains the primary means by which schools identify reading difficulties (Adlof & Hogan, 2018, 2019; Gee, 2015; Lesaux, 2012; Mancilla-Martinez & Lesaux, 2017; Nation, 2019; Spencer & Wagner, 2017). To be clear, word reading is a robust predictor of future reading achievement (Scarborough, 1998; Cutting & Scarborough, 2006; Peng et al., 2019). It is thus unsurprising that word reading assessments play a central role in screeners for reading difficulties and/or characteristics of dyslexia. However, word reading is not the *only* pathway to reading difficulties, but there are numerous interrelated reasons for the reliance on word reading assessment.

First, there is a finite set of letter-sound correspondences, such that word reading is often referred to as a "constrained" skill (Ehri, 1998; Paris, 2005). In other words, there is a limited range of letter-sound correspondence possibilities, and an accompanying finite set of phonics rules. In fact, word reading skills are expected to be mastered toward the end of the primary grade years (though educators are fully aware that this is not always the case). The point is that the developmental expectation is for students to reach full word reading proficiency by the upper elementary grade years. Second, word reading assessment can appear to be relatively straightforward. Students are asked to read printed words—whether they are real words (which may be recognized automatically or require decoding, including both regular and irregular words) or non-words (which all require decoding but vary in complexity). Many word reading assessments also include a fluency component, providing information on accuracy, rate, and expression. Finally, regardless of the specifics of the word reading assessment, progress on single or connected word reading can be tracked over short periods of time, as students systematically build on a finite set of skills. This can be accomplished using brief and frequently administered assessments that can take as little as one minute to administer.

Taken together, the fact that there is a finite set of letter-sound correspondences, guidance on how to teach word reading skills, and wide availability of word reading assessments that can be administered quickly and regularly as screeners and to track progress has led to an uneven emphasis on word reading compared to language comprehension (Castles et al., 2018; Mancilla-Martinez, 2023; Nation & Snowling, 1997; Spencer & Wagner, 2017). Again, word reading development is nonnegotiable for reading comprehension, but so is language comprehension.

Problem 3: Language Comprehension Assessment Flag Students as ELs

Language comprehension is essential for reading comprehension (Scarborough, 1998), including for multilingual learners from Spanish-speaking homes (Mancilla-Martinez & Lesaux, 2017; Oh, Basma, Bertone, & Luk, 2023). But a key challenge for educators is that language comprehension is not straightforward to test and teach for a variety of reasons (Mancilla-Martinez, 2020b). To begin with, language comprehension encompasses multiple linguistic components—such as vocabulary (knowledge of word meanings), syntax (sentence structure and grammar), morphology (the structure and formation of words), and retelling (narrative cohesion and recall)—that contribute to a student's ability to understand and use language. These components can be measured separately, highlighting specific strengths and weaknesses, or collectively, as a single construct representing overall language comprehension. Language comprehension assessments can also focus on receptive skills (e.g., listening comprehension, where students demonstrate understanding of spoken language) or expressive skills (e.g., oral language production, where students generate spoken responses). The complex nature of language comprehension results in a wide spectrum of measures that can be used to assess this construct. Furthermore, language comprehension development requires many opportunities for students to hear and use language—a process that begins well before students learn to read—and it is referred to as an "unconstrained" skill that does not reach a ceiling of mastery.

However conceptualized, assessing language comprehension is a time-consuming process, even when only a small universe of possible words is assessed. Most language comprehension assessments require one-on-one administration and specialized training. It is also the case that language comprehension measures are typically not sensitive to growth over short intervals of time, meaning that most of these measures cannot be used to monitor progress (Adlof & Hogan, 2019). It is thus no surprise that language comprehension is not commonly included in universal screening batteries. Put simply, language comprehension has not become a fabric of typical school-based assessment for informing reading instruction. But there is an exception: academic English language proficiency is thoroughly assessed for students who enter U.S. schools and whose parents/guardians report that a language other than English is used at home.

In brief, the Every Student Succeeds Act requires that all states have procedures to formally identify students who can benefit from academic English language support services (U.S. Department of Education, 2017). Specifically, a Home Language Survey is used to identify students who will be assessed on an academic English language proficiency screener. Based on the academic English language proficiency screener results, students may be deemed English-proficient upon school entry or may be identified as in need of specialized academic English language supports. Of note, the Home Language Survey varies from state to state. Without clear standards across the country, students are identified differently from one state to the next (Salerno & Andrei, 2021). One of the most significant points to underscore is that students whose parents report that only English is spoken in the home are *assumed* to be proficient in academic English. In other words, these students are not administered an academic English language proficiency screener that assesses academic English listening, speaking, reading, and writing to determine if students have the requisite language proficiency to succeed in English academic settings (i.e., they do not have to take this test and thus do not have to "pass" this test).

In sharp contrast, students whose parents report a language other than or in addition to English are subjected to academic English language proficiency screening. If students score below a certain cut point on the academic English language proficiency screener, they are identified as English learners (i.e., determined to not have sufficient English proficiency to succeed in English academic settings). The current system of identification risks missing supports for students whose guardians *report* (there is no way to verify this) that they are from English-only homes. Perhaps more concerning and however well-intended, this system of identification is ultimately an inequitable approach that sets the academic English language proficiency bar higher for students from multilingual homes, effectively serving as a gatekeeper. Students identified as ELs not only have to demonstrate English proficiency on a standardized assessment (i.e., they have to "pass" the test), but they must also meet other state-specific criteria to exit out of EL services and be reclassified as English-proficient.

PRACTICAL POSSIBILITIES: TRANSFORMING MINDSETS AND METHODS

The persistent challenges rooted in typical school-based assessment practices that disadvantage multilingual learners require a shift in mindsets and methods. By first recognizing the limitations of typical assessment practices that have long been a staple in U.S. classrooms, there is a real possibility of shifting toward equitable approaches to better support the achievement of all students. We offer educators three practical recommendations that can serve as a foundation for ensuring multilingual learners' language and reading development is supported.

Possibility 1: Recognizing the Limitations of an English-Only Lens

A first step is to recognize the limitations of an English-only lens that has dominated U.S. school-based assessment practices. Multilingual learners have long been viewed through a deficit-based lens, where their language abilities in a language other than English are considered a barrier in need of remediation rather than an asset (Allen, 2017; Bacon, 2017; Castro & Meek, 2022; Rossell & Baker, 1996). This deficit framework has implications for teachers' perception of students (Harris et al., 2009; Oh & Mancilla-Martinez, 2021; Mun et al., 2020; Umansky & Dumont, 2021) and for student achievement (Leo & Wilcox, 2023; Oh & Mancilla-Martinez, 2021; Shapiro, 2014).

A relatively recent study examined elementary school teachers' beliefs about dual-language development and its relation to ELs' reading achievement (Oh & Mancilla-Martinez, 2021). The study revealed that teachers' asset view (e.g., exposure to a home language does not interfere with English language development) and bilingual development understanding (e.g., language and literacy development occurs through natural exposure and use) positively predicted their ELs' English reading comprehension achievement. However, teachers who held lenient expectations for ELs (e.g., believing that teachers should wait until the child speaks on their own rather than actively supporting language use) and who emphasized English-only achievement (e.g., opposing accommodations for ELs) were associated with lower English reading comprehension outcomes for their EL students. In other words, when teachers de-emphasized bilingualism and took a passive approach to language development, their students showed lower English reading outcomes. This suggests that teachers' beliefs about language development—whether they view multilingualism as an asset or a barrier—can directly influence ELs' English academic trajectories. To support ELs' English reading comprehension achievement, these findings underscore the need for professional development and training programs to allow teachers the opportunity to evaluate their current beliefs about high-quality instruction for ELs (Rangnes, 2019; Torff & Murphy, 2020) against research-grounded understandings.

Indeed, viewing bilingualism as a strength has the potential to allow educators to tap into multilingual learners' full potential, fostering an environment where language diversity is a tool for learning. However, despite the benefits of bilingualism, the dominant approach in U.S. schools remains English-only instruction and, subsequently, English-only assessment. This approach fails to build on students' linguistic resources, undermining the complex language development process that many multilingual learners experience. Multilingual learners, especially ELs, acquire academic content while simultaneously developing their English language skills. This means that assessments conducted solely in English may not accurately capture their full knowledge or abilities. In fact, demonstrating thought and knowledge in English often underrepresents the depth of multilingual learners' understanding. Therefore, one key recommendation is to, at minimum, acknowledge the limitations of the current English-only assessment practices for multilingual learners. Educators must be cognizant of the fact that assessing in English only will provide partial insight into their multilingual learners' knowledge. This insight can help shift deficit-oriented views and, most importantly, allow educators to understand that multilingual learners are as capable as students from English-only homes.

Possibility 2: Language Comprehension Assessment for All Students

There is an urgent need to assess language comprehension for all students, regardless of their home language. Word reading is a strong predictor of reading during the early elementary grades, but language comprehension becomes a stronger predictor over time (Cutting & Scarborough, 2006; Geva & Farnia, 2012; Mancilla-Martinez & Lesaux, 2017). It is thus imperative to implement universal language comprehension screening at school entry and throughout students' academic journeys. These assessments can help educators identify students—whether English-only or multilingual—who may need additional language-based support in the service of English reading comprehension.

To be clear, language comprehension screeners and ongoing progress monitoring to ensure appropriate language and reading support are essential for *all* students, regardless of English proficiency status. This is distinct from the current gatekeeping approach, where only students whose parents report speaking a language other than only English at home are assessed for academic English language proficiency. As noted, the current approach simply *assumes* students whose parents did not indicate a language other than only English at home effectively have the requisite academic English language skills. This is a misguided assumption that compromises the extent to which students can receive the reading supports they may need. It is also the case that simply identifying students as ELs does not mean they receive the language-based support they need to access the curriculum in English. Indeed, about one-third of ELs are not reclassified as English-proficient even after five–six years of EL support services, raising significant concerns about the quality of support ELs receive (U.S. Department of Education, 2024).

Although educators have minimal control over the scarcity of language comprehension assessments for informing instruction, the field is making strides in developing and testing language comprehension universal screeners for potential reading difficulties, including for multilingual learners (see *https://multitudesinfo.ucsf.edu/en-default/multitudes* and *https://roar.stanford.edu*). This represents an important step in providing valuable data to guide reading instruction and interventions, and, for now, educators can advocate for the need to assess students' language comprehension skills. By attending to language comprehension assessment without undermining the importance of word reading, we can better understand and address the specific reading needs of all students, ensuring their growth is supported across all grade levels (remember, there is no "ceiling" or final mastery of language comprehension skills).

Possibility 3: Conceptual Scoring for Multilingual Learners

For multilingual learners specifically, it is critical for educators to know that they often reach language acquisition milestones at different developmental stages relative to their monolingual peers (for a review, see Kovács, 2015). This difference is particularly evident in vocabulary development, as bilingual children distribute their vocabulary across languages rather than concentrating vocabulary knowledge on only one language (Pearson, 1998; Peña, Bedore, & Rappazzo, 2003). In other words, multilingual learners may know some words only in Spanish (e.g., home-specific words, such as *cocina* [kitchen] and *recamara* [bedroom]) and distinct words only in English (e.g., school-specific words, such as *desk* or *whiteboard*) rather than knowing the same words in both Spanish and English. As a result, and as noted earlier, traditional assessments that measure vocabulary in only one language run the risk of underestimating multilingual learners' abilities. If these learners' vocabulary performance is compared to monolingual norms on single language standardized vocabulary measures (e.g., Spanish-only or English-only), their performance may appear low in both languages (e.g., Mancilla-Martinez & Lesaux, 2011; Mancilla-Martinez, Hwang, Oh, & Pokowitz, 2020b). This is problematic for a variety of reasons, not the least of which is risking a deficit orientation in the instruction provided to multilingual learners. As previously underscored, teacher expectations and understanding of bilingual language acquisition matter (e.g., Oh & Mancilla-Martinez, 2021; Umansky & Dumont, 2021). It is also the case that the quality of instruction may differ for students deemed to have English proficiency compared to those labeled as ELs (Umansky, 2016). Measures that allow linguistically diverse students to demonstrate their language knowledge across both languages (referred to as conceptual knowledge) have strong potential to help inform instructional efforts, as well as help differentiate language differences from language disorders.

Currently, most assessments do not properly encapsulate the extent of multilingual learners' skills. Simply translating English-only language assessments into other languages also misses the mark on various fronts (e.g., improper translation across languages, lack of norms for accurate score interpretation). Instead, conceptual scoring is recommended and, fortunately, standardized conceptual vocabulary assessments are available. Conceptual scoring focuses on assessing known concepts, not on the language in which the concepts are known (Spanish or English). For example, and as noted earlier, multilingual learners from Spanish-speaking homes may know what a *kitchen* is but may only have the label in Spanish (*cocina*). Conceptually scored assessments allow students to respond in either language by giving credit for labeling the concept, whether the label is produced in Spanish (*cocina*) or in English (*kitchen*). This approach does not require knowledge of the label for the concept in both languages, as is the case with Spanish monolingual and English monolingual assessments. This assessment method has strong potential to serve as a basis for an equitable assessment framework for understanding language development among multilingual learners from Spanish-speaking homes, especially for multilingual learners in the process of developing English proficiency (ELs).

Conceptually scored measures have been found to have utility for preschool-age ELs from Spanish-speaking homes (e.g., Mancilla-Martinez et al., 2018), and more recent research likewise supports its promise in predicting English reading comprehension among elementary-age multilingual learners from Spanish-speaking homes, over and above the effects of English academic language (Hwang et al., 2020). A compelling implication of this line of research is that taking multilingual learners' first language proficiency into consideration may help shift from a subtractive, deficit view of bilingualism toward an additive, asset-oriented emphasis on what multilingual learners from Spanish-speaking homes bring to learning. Of course, despite the promise of conceptual scoring, like all learners, multilingual learners from Spanish-speaking homes need ample opportunities to develop their language skills in the service of later English reading comprehension. This means that assessment must inform quality instruction.

CONCLUSION

The future of language and reading assessment practices for multilingual learners from Spanish-speaking homes has direct implications for the overall large and growing population of multilingual learners in the United States. Despite increased research attention to the learning needs of multilingual learners in general and ELs in particular, the need for effective interventions tailored specifically for multilingual learners who struggle with reading remains a pressing one (Cho et al., 2019; Francis et al., 2019; Vaughn et al., 2019). A promising direction is for educators to move beyond (or at least acknowledge the limitations of) English-only measures for use with multilingual learners from Spanish-speaking homes. It is also imperative that, alongside word reading, language comprehension is assessed. Using measures that account for known concepts could improve educators' understanding of multilingual learners' language comprehension by providing a fuller picture of students' linguistic repertoires. By doing so, there is strong potential for elevating the knowledge this vastly diverse population of learners brings to school, thereby improving the quality of instruction and also informing the elusive special education identification process for this population of learners.

Indeed, more research is needed to examine how multilingual learners with reading difficulties are referred for and identified as needing special education services, particularly given the persistent misidentification rates (Mancilla-Martinez et al., 2022, 2024; National Academies of Sciences, Engineering, and Medicine [NASEM], 2017). The central issue is not just about assessment practices but the need for clearer guidance on how to provide appropriate instructional support that matches students' needs. An important consideration is that the 2016 Equity Regulations in IDEA only establish a system for identifying significant disproportionality in terms of overrepresentation, not underrepresentation (Office of Special Education Programs, 2017). This is problematic as all students, independent of their backgrounds, should receive the instructional services that align with their educational needs, necessitating accurate and timely placement decisions for equitable educational outcomes. Given the limitations of current school-based assessment practices, many students—including multilingual students—may not be provided with the language and reading instructional support they need. We hope that continued research can drive a paradigm shift in school-based assessment practices, leading to greater linguistic equity with linguistically responsive assessments that better inform reading instruction, intervention, and special education placement.

Reflection Questions

1. How are English learners identified in your school? What assessments and other kinds of information do you gather to identify ELs at your school?
2. What supports are in place at your school, and what supports do you provide for multilingual learners, especially in the areas of language and literacy?
3. What supports do you think your school or you could add for multilingual learners, especially in the areas of language and literacy?

REFERENCES

Adlof, S. M., & Hogan, T. P. (2018). Understanding dyslexia in the context of developmental language disorders. *Language, Speech & Hearing Services in Schools, 49*(4), 762–773.

Adlof, S. M., & Hogan, T. P. (2019). If we don't look, we won't see: Measuring language development to inform literacy instruction. *Policy Insights from the Behavioral and Brain Sciences, 6*, 210–217.

Allen, J. K. (2017). Exploring the role teacher perceptions play in the underrepresentation of culturally and linguistically diverse students in gifted programming. *Gifted Child Today, 40*(2), 77–86.

Annie E. Casey Foundation. (2024). *Kids count data center. https://datacenter.aecf.org/*

Aro, T., Eklund, K., Eloranta, A. K., Närhi, V., Korhonen, E., & Ahonen, T. (2019). Associations between childhood learning disabilities and adult-age mental health problems, lack of education, and unemployment. *Journal of Learning Disabilities, 52*(1), 71–83.

Artiles, A. J., & Ortiz, A. (2002). *English language learners with special education needs.* Center for Applied Linguistics.

Ashcraft, A. (2023). Effects of socioeconomic status on English language learners' success in school. *M.Ed. Literature Reviews,* 19. *https://digitalcommons.tacoma.uw.edu/med_theses/19*

August, D., & Shanahan, T. (Eds.). (2006). *Developing literacy in second-language learners: Report of the national literacy panel on language minority children and youth.* Erlbaum.

Bacon, C. K. (2017). Multilanguage, multipurpose: A literature review, synthesis, and framework for critical literacies in English language teaching. *Journal of Literacy Research, 49*(3), 424–453.

Bedore, L. M., Peña, E. D., Collins, P., Fiestas, C., Lugo-Neris, M., & Barquin, E. (2023). Predicting literacy development and risk in Spanish-English bilingual first graders. *Child Language Teaching and Therapy, 39*(2), 135–149.

Castles, A., Rastle, K., & Nation, K. (2018). Ending the reading wars: Reading acquisition from novice to expert. *Psychological Science in the Public Interest, 19*(1), 5–51.

Castro, D. C., & Meek, S. (2022). Beyond Castañeda and the "language barrier" ideology: Young children and their right to bilingualism. *Language Policy, 21*(3), 407–425.

Cho, E., Capin, P., Roberts, G., Roberts, G. J., & Vaughn, S. (2019). Examining sources and mechanisms of reading comprehension difficulties: Comparing English learners and non-English learners within the simple view of reading. *Journal of Educational Psychology, 111*(6), 982–1000.

Constantino, J. N., Abbacchi, A. M., Saulnier, C., Klaiman, C., Mandell, D. S., Zhang, Y., et al. (2020). Timing of the diagnosis of autism in African American children. *Pediatrics, 146*(3), Article e20193629.

Counts, J., Katsiyannis, A., & Whitford, D. K. (2018). Culturally and linguistically diverse learners in special education: English learners. *National Association of Secondary School Principals, 102*(1), 5–21.

Cruz, R. A., & Firestone, A. R. (2022). Understanding the empty backpack: The role of timing in disproportionate special education identification. *Sociology of Race and Ethnicity, 8,* 95–113.

Cutting, L. E., & Scarborough, H. S. (2006). Prediction of reading comprehension: Relative contributions of word recognition, language proficiency, and other cognitive skills can depend on how comprehension is measured. *Scientific Studies of Reading, 10*(3), 277–299.

Donovan, S., & Cross, C. T. (2002). *Minority students in special and gifted education / Committee on Minority Representation in Special Education, Division of Behavioral and Social Sciences and Education, National Research Council* (1st ed.). National Academy Press.

Ehri, L. C. (1998). *Grapheme–phoneme knowledge is essential for learning to read words in English.* In J. L. Metsala & L. C. Ehri (Eds.), *Word recognition in beginning literacy* (pp. 3–40). Erlbaum.

Eloranta, A. K., Närhi, V. M., Eklund, K. M., Ahonen, T. P., & Aro, T. I. (2019). Resolving reading disability—Childhood predictors and adult-age outcomes. *Dyslexia, 25*(1), 20–37.

Francis, D. J., Rojas, R., Gusewski, S., Santi, K. L., Khalaf, S., Hiebert, L., & Bunta, F. (2019). Speaking and reading in two languages: On the identification of reading and language disabilities in Spanish-Speaking English learners. *New Directions for Child and Adolescent Development, 2019*(166), 15–41.

Gándara, P., & Escamilla, K. (2016). Bilingual education in the United States. In O. García, O. Garcia, A. Lin, & S. May (Eds.), *Encyclopedia of language and education* (pp. 1–14). Springer.

Gee, J. P. (2015). *Literacy and education / James Paul Gee* (1st ed.). Routledge.

Geva, E., & Farnia, F. (2012). Developmental changes in the nature of language proficiency and reading fluency paint a more complex view of reading comprehension in ELL and EL1. *Reading and Writing, 25*(8), 1819–1845.

Gross, M., Buac, M., & Kaushanskaya, M. (2014). Conceptual scoring of receptive and expressive vocabulary measures in simultaneous and sequential bilingual children. *American Journal of Speech-Language Pathology, 23*(4), 574–586.

Gubbels, J., van der Put, C. E., & Assink, M. (2019). Risk factors for school absenteeism and dropout: A meta-analytic review. *Journal of Youth and Adolescence, 48*, 1637–1667.

Hammer, C. S., Lawrence, F. R., & Miccio, A. W. (2008). Exposure to English before and after entry into head start: Bilingual children's receptive language growth in Spanish and English. *International Journal of Bilingual Education and Bilingualism, 11*(1), 30–56.

Harris, B., Plucker, J. A., Rapp, K. E., & Martínez, R. S. (2009). Identifying gifted and talented English language learners: A case study. *Journal for the Education of the Gifted, 32*(3), 368–393.

Hattan, C., & Kendeou, P. (2024). Expanding the science of reading: Contributions from educational psychology. *Educational Psychologist, 59*(4), 217–232.

Hibel, J., & Jasper, A. D. (2012). Delayed special education placement for learning disabilities among children of immigrants. *Social Forces, 91*(2), 503–529.

Hwang, J. K., Mancilla-Martinez, J., McClain, J. B., Oh, M., & Flores, I. (2020). Spanish-speaking English learners' English language and literacy skills: The predictive role of conceptually-scored vocabulary. *Applied Psycholinguistics, 41*, 1–24.

Hoover, W., & Gough, P. (1990). The simple view of reading. *Reading & Writing, 2*(2), 127–160.

Kovács, Á. M. (2015). Cognitive adaptations induced by a multi-language input in early development. *Current Opinion in Neurobiology, 35*, 80–86.

Leo, A., & Wilcox, K. C. (2023). Beyond deficit and determinism to address the Latinx Attainment Gap. *Journal of Latinos and Education, 22*(2), 729–744.

Lesaux, N. K. (2012). Reading and reading instruction for children from low-income and Non-English-Speaking households. *The Future of Children, 22*(2), 73–88.

Luk, G., & Christodoulou, J. A. (2016). Assessing and understanding the needs of dual-language learners. In S. Jones & N. Lesaux (Eds.), *The leading edge of early childhood education: Linking science to policy for a new generation of pre-K* (pp. 41–51). Cambridge, MA: Harvard Education Press.

Mancilla-Martinez, J. (2020). Understanding and supporting literacy development among English learners: A deep dive into the role of language comprehension. *AERA Open, 6*(1), 1–7.

Mancilla-Martinez, J. (2023). Prioritizing dual language learners' language comprehension development to support later reading achievement. In S. Q. Cabell, S. B. Neuman, & N. P. Terry (Eds.), *Handbook on the science of early literacy* (chapter 3). Guilford Press.

Mancilla-Martinez, J., Greenfader, C. M., & Ochoa, W. (2018). Spanish-speaking preschoolers' conceptual vocabulary knowledge: Towards more comprehensive assessment. *NHSA Dialog, 21*(1), 22-.

Mancilla-Martinez, J., Hwang, J. K., Oh, M. H., & McClain, J. B. (2020a). Early elementary grade dual language learners from Spanish-speaking homes struggling with English reading comprehension: The dormant role of language skills. *Journal of Educational Psychology, 112*, 880–894.

Mancilla-Martinez, J., Hwang, J. K., Oh, M. H., & Pokowitz, E. L. (2020b). Patterns of development in Spanish-English conceptually scored vocabulary among elementary age dual language learners. *Journal of Speech, Language, and Hearing Research, 63*(9), 3084–3099.

Mancilla-Martinez, J., & Lesaux, N. K. (2011). The gap between Spanish speakers' word reading and word knowledge: A longitudinal study. *Child Development, 82*(5), 1544–1560.

Mancilla-Martinez, J., & Lesaux, N. K. (2017). Early indicators of later English reading comprehension outcomes among children from Spanish-Speaking homes. *Scientific Studies of Reading, 21*(5), 428–448.

Mancilla-Martinez, J., Oh, M. H., Luk, G., & Rollins, A. (2022). Language and special education status: 2009–2019 Tennessee trends. *Educational Researcher, 51*, 419–422.

Mancilla-Martinez, J., Oh, M. H., Luk, G., & Rollins, A. (2024). Special education representation trends vary by language status: Evidence of underrepresentation in Tennessee. *Journal of Learning Disabilities, 57*, 153–167.

Mancilla-Martinez, J., Oh, M, Zagata, E., & Wang, J. J. (in revision). Representation of linguistically diverse students in gifted and talented services: 2006 2019 Tennessee trends. *Gifted Child Quarterly.*

Mancilla-Martinez, J., & Vagh, S. B. (2013). Growth in toddlers' Spanish, English, and conceptual vocabulary knowledge. *Early Childhood Research Quarterly, 28*(3), 555–567.

Mavrogordato, M., Bartlett, C., Callahan, R., DeMatthews, D., & Izquierdo, E. (2024). Supports for multilingual students who are classified as English learners. Overview Brief# 15: Vulnerable Populations. Updated. *EdResearch for Action.*

Morgan, P. L., Farkas, G., Hillemeier, M. M., & Maczuga, S. (2012). Are minority children disproportionately represented in early intervention and early childhood special education? *Educational Researcher, 41*(9), 339–351.

Morgan, P. L., Farkas, G., Hillemeier, M. M., & Maczuga, S. (2017). Replicated evidence of racial and ethnic disparities in disability identification in U.S. schools. *Educational Researcher, 46*(6), 305–322.

Morgan, P. L., Farkas, G., Hillemeier, M. M., Mattison, R., Maczuga, S., Li, H., & Cook, M. (2015). Minorities are disproportionately underrepresented in special education: Longitudinal evidence across five disability conditions. *Educational Researcher, 44*(5), 278–292.

Morita-Mullaney, T., Renn, J., & Chiu, M. M. (2020). Obscuring equity in dual language bilingual education: A longitudinal study of emergent bilingual achievement, course placements, and grades. *TESOL Quarterly, 54*(3), 685–718.

Moslimani, M., Lopez, M. H., & Noe-Bustamante, L. (2023). *11 facts about Hispanic origin groups in the U.S. www.pewresearch.org/short-reads/2023/08/16/11-facts-about-hispanic-origin-groups-in-the-us*

Mun, R. U., Hemmler, V., Langley, S. D., Ware, S., Gubbins, E. J., Callahan, C. M., et al. (2020). Identifying and serving English learners in gifted education: Looking back and moving forward. *Journal for the Education of the Gifted, 43*(4), 297–335.

Nation, K. (2019). Children's reading difficulties, language, and reflections on the simple view of reading. *Australian Journal of Learning Difficulties, 24*(1), 47–73.

Nation, K., & Snowling, M. (1997). Assessing reading difficulties: The validity and utility of current measures of reading skill. *British Journal of Educational Psychology, 67*(3), 359–370.

National Academies of Sciences, Engineering, and Medicine. (2017). *Promoting the educational success of children and youth learning English: Promising futures*. National Academies Press.

National Center for Education Statistics. (2024a). English learners in public schools. *Condition of Education*. U.S. Department of Education, Institute of Education Sciences. *https://nces.ed.gov/programs/coe/indicator/cgf*

National Center for Education Statistics. (2024b). Racial/Ethnic enrollment in public schools. *Condition of Education*. U.S. Department of Education, Institute of Education Sciences. *https://nces.ed.gov/programs/coe/indicator/cge*

O'Connor, M., Geva, E., & Koh, P. W. (2019). Examining reading comprehension profiles of grade 5 monolinguals and English language learners through the lexical quality hypothesis lens. *Journal of Learning Disabilities, 52*(3), 232–246.

Office of English Language Acquisition. (2020). English learners: Demographic trends. U.S. Department of Education. *https://ncela.ed.gov/resources/fact-sheet-english-learners-demographic-trends-february-2020*

Office of English Language Acquisition. (2024). U.S. Department of Education. *www.ed.gov/about/ed-offices/oela*

Office of Special Education Programs. (2017). Significant disproportionality (Equity in IDEA) 81 FR 92376: Essential questions and answers.

Oh, M. H., & Mancilla-Martinez, J. (2021). Elementary schoolteachers' bilingual development beliefs and English learners' English reading comprehension achievement. *The Elementary School Journal, 122*(2), 165–190.

Oh, J. H. J., Basma, B., Bertone, A., & Luk, G. (2023). Assessments of English reading and language comprehension in bilingual children: A systematic review 2010 to 2021. *Canadian Journal of School Psychology, 38*(4), 373–392.

Paris, S. G. (2005). Reinterpreting the development of reading skills. *Reading Research Quarterly, 40*, 184–202.

Pearson, B. Z. (1998). Assessing lexical development in bilingual babies and toddlers. *The International Journal of Bilingualism: Cross-Disciplinary, Cross-Linguistic Studies of Language Behavior, 2*(3), 347–372.

Pena, E., Bedore, L. M., & Rappazzo, C. (2003). Comparison of Spanish, English, and bilingual children's performance across semantic tasks. *Language, Speech & Hearing Services in Schools, 34*(1), 5–16.

Peng, P., Fuchs, D., Fuchs, L. S., Elleman, A. M., Kearns, D. M., Gilbert, J. K., et al. (2019). A longitudinal analysis of the trajectories and predictors of word reading and reading comprehension development among at-risk readers. *Journal of Learning Disabilities, 52*(3), 195–208.

Porter, L., Vazquez Cano, M., & Umansky, I. (2023). *Bilingual education and America's future: Evidence and pathways*. Civil Rights Project/Proyecto Derechos Civiles, UCLA.

Rangnes, H. (2019). Facilitating second-language learners' access to expository texts: teachers' understanding of the challenges involved. *L1-Educational Studies in Language and Literature, 19, Running Issue* (Running Issue), 1–27.

Rossell, C. H., & Baker, K. (1996). The educational effectiveness of bilingual education. *Research in the Teaching of English, 30*(1), 7–74. *www.jstor.org/stable/40171543*

Salerno, A. S., & Andrei, E. (2021). Inconsistencies in English learner identification: An inventory of how home language surveys across U.S. States screen multilingual students. *AERA Open,* 7(1): 1–16.

Samson, J. F., & Lesaux, N. K. (2009). Language-minority learners in special education: Rates and predictors of identification for services. *Journal of Learning Disabilities, 42*(2), 148–162.

Scarborough, H. S. (1998). Predicting future achievement of second graders with reading disabilities: Contributions of phonemic awareness, verbal memory, rapid naming and IQ. *Annals of Dyslexia, 48,* 115–136.

Shapiro, S. (2014). "Words That You Said Got Bigger": English language learners' lived experiences of deficit discourse. *Research in the Teaching of English, 48*(4), 386–406.

Silverman, R. D., McNeish, D., Speece, D. L., & Ritchey, K. D. (2021). Early screening for decoding- and language-related reading difficulties in first and third grades. *Assessment for Effective Intervention, 46*(2), 99–109.

Singer, A. (2004). *The rise of new immigrant gateways.* Brookings Institution Reports.

Spencer, M., & Wagner, R. K. (2017). The comprehension problems for second-language learners with poor reading comprehension despite adequate decoding: A meta-analysis. *Journal of Research in Reading, 40,* 199–217.

Sullivan, A. L. (2011). Disproportionality in special education identification and placement of English language learners. *Exceptional Children,* 77(3), 317–334.

Sugarman, J., & Geary, C. (2018). *English learners in select states: Demographics, outcomes, and state accountability policies. Fact Sheet.* Migration Policy Institute.

Sugarman, J., & Villegas, L. (2020). *Native language assessments for K–12 English learners: Policy considerations and state practices. Policy file.* Migration Policy Institute.

Torff, B., & Murphy, A. F. (2020). Teachers' beliefs about English learners: Adding linguistic support to enhance academic rigor. *Phi Delta Kappan, 101*(5), 14–18.

Umansky, I. M. (2016). Leveled and exclusionary tracking: English learners' access to academic content in middle school. *American Educational Research Journal, 53*(6), 1792–1833.

Umansky, I. M., Thompson, K. D., & Díaz, G. (2017). Using an ever-English learner framework to examine disproportionality in special education. *Exceptional Children, 84*(1), 76–96.

Umansky, I. M., & Dumont, H. (2021). English learner labeling: How English learner classification in kindergarten shapes teacher perceptions of student skills and the moderating role of bilingual instructional settings. *American Educational Research Journal, 58*(5), 993–1031.

U.S. Commission on Civil Rights. (2009). *Minorities in special education. www.usccr.gov/files/pubs/docs/MinoritiesinSpecialEducation.pdf*

U.S. Department of Education, Office of Elementary and Secondary Education, ESEA Consolidated State Plans. (2024). *www.ed.gov/laws-and-policy/laws-preschool-grade-12-education/esea/esea-consolidated-state-plans*

U.S. Department of Education, Office of English Language Acquisition. (2017). *English learner tool kit* (2nd rev. ed.). Author.

Vaughn, S., Fall, A.-M., Roberts, G., Wanzek, J., Swanson, E., & Martinez, L. R. (2019). Class percentage of students with reading difficulties on content knowledge and comprehension. *Journal of Learning Disabilities, 52*(2), 120–134.

Villegas, L. (2023). Accountability for long-term English learners. *Phi Delta Kappan, 105*(2), 13–18.

Yamasaki, B. L., & Luk, G. (2018). Eligibility for special education in elementary school: The role of diverse language experiences. *Language, Speech & Hearing Services in Schools, 49*(4), 889–901.

11

The Role of Language in Reading Comprehension

Instructional Implications for Teachers of Multilingual Learners

C. Patrick Proctor and Rebecca D. Silverman

Guiding Questions

1. How can teachers leverage the language repertoires of multilingual learners to support reading comprehension?
2. What principles can be used to guide instruction to support multilingual learners' language and reading comprehension?

The linguistic diversity of classrooms across the United States continues to grow (National Center for Education Statistics, 2024), creating challenges and opportunities for educators charged with supporting reading development throughout elementary school. Indeed, many teachers feel underprepared to address challenges and take advantage of opportunities presented by the linguistic diversity in their classrooms (Deng et al., 2021). Theory and research have established that language is a critical component of reading, particularly for multilingual learners who are navigating two or more languages and/or dialects as they learn to read (Mancilla-Martinez, 2023). We use the term *multilingual learners* to broadly represent any students who speak more than one language or dialect, regardless of proficiency level. In the United States, multilingual learners typically speak English, the language of instruction in most school systems, and one or more other languages. For example, Spanish–English bilingual learners are multilingual learners, as are students who speak English and Zapotec, an indigenous language of Mexico. Multilingual learners include students who are considered to be developing English proficiency (English learners) as well as students who speak English with proficiency. Pedagogy focused on multilingual learners acknowledges and values multilingual students' varied linguistic repertoires that can support reading comprehension in English and other languages (e.g., Spanish in Spanish–English bilingual classrooms).

In our work over the past 15 years, we have been focused on understanding how various aspects of language proficiency affect reading comprehension, particularly for multilingual learners, and how instruction that focuses on language skills and language use may support the reading development of multilingual learners in elementary school. We started with a narrow focus on how specific components of language (i.e., vocabulary, morphology, and syntax) relate to reading and, over time, have developed an instructional approach that includes attention to the components of language within a broader focus on using language to make meaning from text. In this chapter, we review our work and the work of others on the intricate connections between language skills and reading comprehension, and we provide an overview of how instruction that highlights those connections supports multilingual learners. Our hope here is to equip educators with a deeper understanding of the language-to-reading comprehension connection and provide a set of principles and core instructional practices that can support multilingual learners in developing reading comprehension in English and other languages or dialects.

READING COMPREHENSION

Reading comprehension is a complex cognitive process that goes far beyond the mere decoding of words. Of course, reading cannot happen without the ability to recognize and read words accurately and fluently because this allows readers to access and process text. However, accurate and efficient decoding skills do not, by themselves, provide a free pass to reading comprehension. Without the presence of language comprehension, there can be no true reading comprehension (Hoover & Gough, 1990). Throughout our years working together, we have explored and tested the unique role of language in reading comprehension for multilingual learners in particular and what that means for instruction. We think about language as a dynamic system with interconnected component parts that interact with each other and are activated along with background knowledge and cognitive skills and strategies within larger social and educational contexts.

The interconnected component parts that we have examined in our work include vocabulary, morphology, and syntax. Vocabulary refers to the range of words, in any given language, that one can access for expressive and receptive purposes. Vocabulary knowledge is comprised of both breadth (i.e., knowing a lot *of* words) and depth (i.e., knowing a lot *about* words). Vocabulary depth can include knowing that words have more than one meaning or knowing the nuanced differences between semantically related words. Vocabulary is highly related to morphological knowledge or knowledge about how word parts affect meaning.

Morphology refers to breaking down words into their component morphemes, which can be inflections like plural and past-tense endings (adding *-s* or *-ed* to the word *adopt* to get *adopts* and *adopted*), compound words (combining *tooth* and *brush* to get *toothbrush*), and derivations (adding prefixes or suffixes like adding *-ion* to *adopt* to get *adoption*). Morphology is intricately connected to syntax, which refers to the grammatical arrangement of words (verbs, nouns, adjectives) and how that arrangement affects meaning. Words often change morphologically and syntactically when they serve different functions in phrases and sentences (e.g., *move* [present-tense verb], *moved* [past-tense verb], *mover* [noun]). For example, in the sentence *the mover moved the box,* the subject is *mover,* the verb is *moved,* and *the box* is the object of the sentence.

In comprehension, these interconnected component parts of language are activated along with background knowledge, sometimes referred to as "prior knowledge" or just "knowledge," derived from lived experiences and exposure to concepts and content through books, television, and conversations with family members, teachers, and peers. This background knowledge serves as a critical foundation that supports making sense of language (oral or written) and facilitates acquiring new knowledge and learning about new concepts (Hattan & Kendeou, 2024). Readers constantly draw upon prior information and experiences to make sense of new text, filling in gaps and making inferences. This aspect of comprehension is particularly significant for multilingual learners, who may bring knowledge and experiences that reside outside that of their teachers. This can affect the ways in which students actually comprehend text. Teachers need to be aware of how background knowledge affects text comprehension because comprehension that may appear "wrong" from one perspective may be completely reasonable from another. Along these lines, we have learned that students can be excellent instructors of their teachers, particularly when it comes to issues of language.

Coordinating language and background knowledge to make meaning is an active process that requires the use of cognitive skills (e.g., attention and memory) and strategies. Seminal research by Palinscar and Brown (1984) showed that cognitive strategies, which are internal procedures that help support attention and memory while doing complex tasks (Rosenshine & Meister, 1994), are particularly useful for reading comprehension. Cognitive strategies such as predicting, summarizing, clarifying, and questioning help with processing language, knowledge, and new information, and recent research suggests that they may be particularly important for multilingual learners who are drawing on multiple languages and unique background knowledge (Proctor et al., 2020).

Importantly, the interconnected component parts of language, along with background knowledge and cognitive skills and strategies, are activated in particular social contexts. In schools, students interact with their teachers and their peers, who are all affected by larger social contexts (e.g., the community and global contexts). When they read and discuss texts in schools, teachers and students engage in collective sensemaking (e.g., Tracey & Morrow, 2012; Vaughn, 2019), which shapes how students understand the texts they discuss and how students activate their language skills, background knowledge, and cognitive skills and strategies in the future. For multilingual learners who use language fluidly across social contexts, opportunities to bring all of their linguistic resources to talking about and making sense of text may be especially generative for supporting reading comprehension (García & Kleifgen, 2020).

THE LANGUAGE–READING COMPREHENSION CONNECTION

The relationship between language proficiency and reading comprehension is intricate and multidimensional. In our research, we have highlighted how language components contribute to comprehension and what that means for students who speak more than one language. These explorations began with vocabulary knowledge, which has received outsized attention in explorations of the connections between language and reading comprehension. This is arguable due to the reality that if one does not know at least 98% of the words on a page, then comprehension will suffer (Hu & Nation, 2000). Consider the following passage with a single pseudoword:

> Favorable conditions are necessary to do this activity. That is you have to have enough *rouche.* If there is too much *rouche,* the object might break. But if conditions are too calm, you will have problems because the *rouche* makes the object go up. If there are obstacles, a serious problem can result because you cannot control the *rouche.* Usually, the *rouche* is most favorable during the spring.

Of the 68 words in this paragraph, *rouche* is used five times or 7.4% of the time. If one does not know what the word *rouche* means, it is difficult to comprehend the text without considerable metacognitive and metalinguistic strategy use. If we "translate" the word from *rouche* to *wind,* then the "activity" in question becomes much more apparent to a larger number of readers.

In 2008, when we started our work together, most research in reading comprehension that addressed language kept the focus squarely on vocabulary in terms of the quantity of known words. So, we started with this kind of vocabulary, which we called "vocabulary breadth," but we wanted to expand on breadth by thinking about other dimensions of language that might be better characterized as "vocabulary depth." We were guided by Nagy and Scott's (2000) conceptualization of vocabulary as multidimensional. We thought of vocabulary depth as including knowledge of semantics (i.e., relationships among words), morphology (i.e., how word parts affect meaning), and syntax (i.e., the syntactic functions of a word). This work simply asked whether these depth constructs (semantics, morphology, and semantics) predicted reading comprehension among groups of elementary school-age Spanish–English bilingual students and their English monolingual peers beyond the usual suspect of vocabulary breadth (Proctor et al., 2012; Silverman et al., 2015). This line of work clearly showed that while vocabulary breadth was indeed important for reading, so were word relations, morphology, and syntax, and the relative effects of these linguistic constructs on reading comprehension were the same for bilingual as well as monolingual students.

THINKING CROSS-LINGUISTICALLY

In this earlier work, we were eager to underscore the reality that language for bilingual students was more than just English because bilingual students bring other languages to bear on the comprehension of text. We were influenced by earlier work with Spanish–English children around cognate awareness for supporting English reading comprehension. Cognates are words that share similar meanings, spellings, and pronunciations across languages. For example, *rapid* and *rápido* share similar spellings, pronunciations, and meanings that could be leveraged should a Spanish–English bilingual encounter the word *rapid* in an English language text (see Jiménez et al., 1996; Nagy et al., 1993; Proctor & Mo, 2009). We were also interested in broader applications of Cummins's (1979) notion of *linguistic interdependence,* which rather vaguely hypothesized that, among bilingual learners, increasing levels of proficiency in one language should be associated with increasing levels of proficiency in another. Some early research had shown that this type of interdependence was predictable when it came to decoding in languages that used the same alphabet, like Spanish and English (see August & Shanahan, 2006; Bialystok et al., 2005), but when it came to vocabulary, morphology, and syntax, there was little cross-linguistic research to draw upon.

Given the lack of research, we specifically asked if, in addition to cognate connections, whether students' Spanish syntax might have cross-linguistic relevance for English reading. Spanish and English syntax share some overlaps in terms of sentence ordering (subject, verb, object), especially if the syntax is relatively simple. Consider the sentence *the children are running very fast.* Its Spanish translation, *Los niños están corriendo muy rápido,* is syntactically identical to the English, but is quite different in terms of vocabulary, save for the lone cognate (*rapid/rápido*). We reasoned that understanding how syntax works in Spanish might be predictive of reading comprehension in English. In a longitudinal prospective study with 156 bilingual Latinx children in grades 2–5 (Proctor et al., 2017), we found that Spanish syntax did, in fact, predict bilingual children's English reading comprehension in grades 2–5, suggesting that attention to language knowledge and skills across languages may be relevant for multilingual learners' reading outcomes.

DOES TEACHING ABOUT LANGUAGE IMPROVE STUDENTS' READING?

The findings detailed above clearly showed that English vocabulary, morphology, and syntax all predicted English reading for bilingual learners and also that Spanish syntax showed cross-linguistic effects on English reading. It is important to note that we chose to study the effects of these particular language indicators because we considered them to be "instructionally malleable" skills (i.e., skills that teachers could directly teach). So we theorized that if teachers taught these language components, then students' language and reading skills would improve.

We decided to test this theory through an observational study (Silverman et al., 2014). While we were collecting data for the studies detailed in the previous sections, we were spending a lot of time in the classrooms of the participating students. With permission from the students, their parents, and their teachers, we recorded the language arts instruction of 33 different third- through fifth-grade teachers at three different time points (Fall, Winter, Spring) during one academic year. We audio-recorded all instructions and transcribed all classroom talk. We coded teacher utterances (e.g., questions, comments, prompts) as vocabulary (or language) instruction, comprehension instruction, decoding/fluency instruction, other instruction, or non-instruction. We identified five different types of vocabulary (or language) instruction (providing definitions, focusing on word relations, supporting application across contexts, focusing on morphology and/or syntax, and teaching about context clues) and four types of comprehension instruction (focus on literal comprehension, focus on inferential comprehension, focus on comprehension strategies, and focus on features of text). We then calculated the average frequency of each instructional code per 60 minutes of language arts instruction observed. We wanted to know how much teaching about language and comprehension took place in the participating classrooms. We also wanted to know whether students who were in classrooms with more language instruction performed better on our measures of language and reading at the end of the year.

We found that teachers more often provided definitions of words and talked about how words could be used in different ways across contexts, but they much less often made semantic connections between words, taught about morphology and syntax, and taught about using context clues to figure out unknown words. Relatively speaking, teachers focused on comprehension instruction (literal comprehension, inferential comprehension, comprehension strategies, and features of text) much more often than they focused on language instruction. We also found that teacher talk, typically in whole group instruction, dominated classroom airtime. Specifically, teacher utterances made up 75% of total classroom talk. We observed very little student talk and very little pair and small group work.

Most importantly, however, we found that the students in those classrooms where teachers did more of the various types of language instruction noted above showed stronger reading comprehension outcomes than their counterparts who were in classrooms where teachers did less of this type of instruction. In addition, we found that focusing on comprehension strategies (predicting, summarizing, clarifying, questioning) was particularly beneficial to the reading comprehension outcomes of the bilingual children in our sample.

ADDITIONAL INSIGHTS ABOUT LANGUAGE AND ITS USE

Up to this point, we had been focused on measuring language using psychological tools that reduce language to its component parts: vocabulary, morphology, and syntax. Having spent a good deal of time in this pursuit, we noticed that the measures we were using required students to be able to actively manipulate language. For example, our morphology assessment provided students with a focal word, like *farmer,* and asked students to derive a morphologically related word by filling in the blank of the following sentence: *My uncle works on a* _____. Here, students had to manipulate the word *farmer* to get to *farm*. For syntax, students were given a sentence like *I sure happy am to be going home today* and were asked to determine if this was grammatically correct, and if not, how it could be changed to be more syntactically accurate. Like the morphology measure, this activity required analysis and manipulation of language to arrive at the correct response.

We noted that these and other measures like them were tapping into students' *metalinguistic awareness,* or their ability to manipulate language for distinct purposes, and that this metalinguistic awareness was predicting reading comprehension beyond simple breadth of known vocabulary words. What's more, we were influenced at the time by the fact that psychological research in the realm of bilingualism had shown evidence that bilingual learners showed aptitudes with respect to metalinguistic control (e.g., Bialystok, 2001), which suggested leveraging metalinguistic awareness in service of reading comprehension could be a particularly effective approach for multilingual learners.

In addition to the realization that metalinguistics might be a fruitful avenue for planning instruction, our time observing in the classroom made us realize that the relationship between language and reading comprehension could not just be relegated to knowledge about language reflected in the cognitive capacities of children. We recognized that language was being used all the time by teachers and students and that the language use itself was something we needed to attend to more specifically.

Having noticed that teachers were doing most of the talking in whole group contexts in our research, we decided to explore ways in which we could get students more engaged in authentic conversations about text in service of developing both language and comprehension. We became particularly interested in collaborative reasoning (CR), a small-group discussion approach to promoting discourse around text, first popularized by Richard Anderson and his colleagues (Clark et al., 2003; Waggoner et al., 1995). Zhang and Stahl (2011) describe CR as follows:

> In CR, students read a text that raises an unresolved issue with multiple and competing points of view. The selected texts contain multilayered issues such as friendship, family obligations, justice, fairness, duty, equality, honesty and integrity, winning and losing, or environmental policy. Students then gather in groups of five to eight to deliberate on the *big question* raised by the text. (p. 257)

In CR, the teacher's job is to talk less and facilitate more, ideally sitting back and letting the students themselves lead the discussion around text, talking with each other to make sense of it. We began piloting CR work with students in the upper elementary grades. To promote conversation, we turned to texts that focused on social studies themes (e.g., human-environment interactions), which tended to be engaging for teachers and students. In this early instructional work, we realized that integrating discussions, not just about text but also about language itself, could promote synergies between metalinguistic awareness and reading comprehension.

One of our concerns with CR, however, was that it did not include reading instruction, per se. In CR, the goal was to simply have a reasoned discussion in the service of promoting argumentation and reasoning skills. In order for us to effectively address reading comprehension, we needed to situate these discussions within reading instruction. Influenced by work on reciprocal teaching (RT; Palinscar & Brown, 1984) and collaborative strategic reading (CSR; Klingner & Vaughn, 2000), two instructional approaches that encouraged small groups of students to use comprehension strategies to comprehend and discuss text, we combined CR with teacher support for students to use reading comprehension strategies (summarize, clarify, question, predict). We also included explicit attention to language (vocabulary, morphology, and syntax) and how understanding language can support reading comprehension.

We worked with teachers of multilingual students to develop an approach, which we called dialogic reasoning (Ossa Para et al., 2016), that incorporated collaborative discussions, support for reading comprehension strategy use, and, importantly, explicit attention to language. Like CR, in dialogic reasoning, teachers are facilitators of authentic student talk that promotes text comprehension and knowledge building. Dialogic reasoning takes a three-pronged approach to promoting text comprehension and language. First, it includes teacher support for students to use reading comprehension strategies to understand and be ready to talk about text. Additionally, similar to RT and CSR, dialogic reasoning includes discussions about main ideas and concepts within and across texts (Ossa Parra et al., 2016). Finally, dialogic reasoning includes explicit instruction targeting components of language (vocabulary, morphology, syntax; Proctor, 2011) and encourages teachers to facilitate talk around the language of texts and develop metalinguistic awareness. We found this straightforward approach developmentally and sociolinguistically flexible, and over time it has been applied in preschool (Bolt et al., 2019), early elementary (Leighton et al., 2021), mid-elementary (Ossa Parra & Proctor, 2021), and upper elementary (Proctor et al., 2020) school contexts.

PUTTING OUR FINDINGS TO THE TEST

Having completed our exploratory work, we next set out to further develop and test the direct instruction of language plus dialogic reasoning approach through a program we called CLAVES. At first, CLAVES, which means *keys* or *clues* in Spanish, was an acronym that stood for Comprehension, Linguistic Awareness, and Vocabulary in English and Spanish. Over time, we began working with non-Spanish-speaking multilingual learners (e.g., initially Portuguese-speaking students and later students who spoke a range of languages including Mandarin, Cantonese, and Hmong) and changed the name to Cultivating Linguistic Awareness for Voice and Equity in Schools, keeping the CLAVES acronym for continuity. Over the course of two grants, one from 2014 to 2018 and the other from 2020 to 2025, we worked with teachers to iterate on the curriculum and test it out in a wide range of schools.

In the first grant (2014–2017), we used a longitudinal, sequential, mixed-methods approach to develop and evaluate CLAVES for evidence of its potential efficacy. The first two years (2014–2016) had us embedded in eight schools, working with a total of 40 teachers and 96 multilingual students in third through fifth grade. We used an iterative, design-based case study approach. Each of the eight participating schools constituted its own case, for which a narrative was ultimately constructed (see Proctor et al., 2021 for details). At the unit and lesson plan design stage, our research teams (one in the Northeast and one in the mid-Atlantic region of the United States) collaborated to select texts and draft lesson plans. Then, these collaboratively developed lessons were brought to teachers in our partner schools for feedback. Based on this feedback, we made revisions and edits. Then, we returned to our partner schools, where doctoral research assistants taught the lessons to small groups of multilingual students. We video-recorded all instructions, and we developed case narratives for each school site that detailed how students responded to instruction. We used these case narratives to guide final revisions and edits for units and lessons for the CLAVES program to be used in a quasi-experimental study (a study with schools, classrooms, and students that are assigned to condition but not completely at random).

We conducted the quasi-experimental study in the final year of the three-year project. In this study, we handed the CLAVES curriculum over to a new group of 22 fourth- and fifth-grade teachers. In these teachers' classes, multilingual learners were assigned to a treatment or a control group. Teachers taught the CLAVES program to students in the "treatment" group (n = 119), and they taught their typical curriculum to students in the "business as usual" (BAU) control group (n = 120). The CLAVES and BAU students performed similarly on initial measures of reading and language, so one group was not already stronger in terms of their literacy achievement at the beginning of instruction. At the end of instruction, our analyses showed that CLAVES students outperformed their BAU counterparts on measures of reading comprehension and linguistic awareness (Proctor et al., 2020) as well as on features of argumentative writing (e.g., evidence, reasoning; Silverman et al., 2021).

In the second grant (2020–2025), our goal was to test the CLAVES program on a larger scale. We spent the first year of the grant, which happened to coincide with the COVID-related school closures, refining the CLAVES curriculum based on our experience and teachers' feedback from the 2014–2017 project. We replaced some of the original books that teachers and students found less engaging or potentially problematic and revised the lesson plans to be less dense and more usable for classroom teachers. Building on work we have done that illustrated the power of using multimedia to support language learning (e.g., Silverman et al., 2019), including engaging activities in instruction (Ritchey et al., 2017), and connecting reading and writing (Silverman et al., 2015, 2021), we also included new multimedia texts and additional opportunities for students to write in response to text throughout the program. We then implemented a cluster-randomized trial with propensity score matching of students in treatment and control schools. In other words, we assigned schools to either the treatment or control condition, we had teachers in the treatment schools implement CLAVES with their multilingual learners (and, sometimes, peers who would benefit from support in language and reading comprehension), and matched these students with similar students in the control schools who received business as usual or typical instruction.

Over the course of three years, we worked with over 40 schools, 150 teachers, and 800 students in Northern California. We pretested students on word recognition, vocabulary, comprehension, and writing, and we post-tested students on core analytic language skills, comprehension, and writing. At the time we are writing this chapter, analyses are still underway, but initial analyses suggest implementing the program was challenging given all of the competing priorities in schools. Importantly, despite the vast challenges teachers faced in the wake of the COVID pandemic, many teachers felt the program was effective at supporting multilingual students' language and reading comprehension and was more systematic and engaging than the typical curricula they used for English language arts and English language development instruction.

KEY FEATURES OF THE CLAVES PROGRAM

In an article we published in *The Reading Teacher* (Proctor et al., 2021), we outlined the four principles that are at the heart of the CLAVES program:

1. Focus on language and metalinguistic awareness.
2. Enact dialogic approaches to engage students.
3. Use multimodal texts and scaffolds to support comprehension and expression.
4. Take a multilingual perspective.

Three additional principles grounded our subsequent iteration of the program:

5. Activate and build on background and content knowledge.
6. Foster reading for understanding and encourage the use of comprehension strategies.
7. Leverage connections between reading and writing.

See Table 11.1 for further description of each principle. These principles are woven across three units, each of which focuses on a social studies-related theme (i.e., Human–Nature Interactions in Unit 1, Rights and Freedoms in Unit 2, and Language, Race, and Identity in Unit 3).

In each CLAVES unit, there are two cycles that focus on two aspects of the theme. For example, in the first unit, the first cycle focuses on whether wolves should be integrated into national parks, and the second cycle focuses on whether water should have rights (like humans) and whether it should be protected from

TABLE 11.1. Seven Principles at the Heart of the CLAVES Program

Principle	Description
1. Focus on language and metalinguistic awareness	Target semantics, syntax, and morphology through explicit instruction and encourage reflection on, and manipulation of, language
2. Enact dialogic approaches to engage students	Encourage student talk. Step back and facilitate discussion about language and text that generates meaning and understanding
3. Use multimodal texts and scaffolds to support comprehension and expression	Go beyond print into video, gesturing, acting, and movement to allow students to make sense across different modes and functions of language and text
4. Take a multilingual perspective	Encourage students to use their full linguistic repertoire to compare languages and make insights into language use for power and exclusion
5. Activate and build on background and content knowledge	Encourage students to think about what they already know and provide opportunities for students to gain content knowledge to support comprehension
6. Foster reading for understanding and encourage use of comprehension strategies	Support students in making meaning of text by actively using comprehension strategies (e.g., previewing, monitoring, summarizing)
7. Leverage connections between reading and writing	Encourage students to write about what they read as writing supports students in thinking about and making meaning of texts

human interference (e.g., oil pipelines that run through indigenous lands). See Table 11.2 for a snapshot of one cycle from one unit of the CLAVES program. At the end of each unit, after two cycles on related topics, we also asked students to use what they had learned and discussed in the unit to write in response to a related big question. See Table 11.3 for an outline of an end-of-unit writing cycle.

For the purposes of testing out the program in research studies, we created semi-scripted lessons that teachers could use to teach the program. These lessons included questions teachers could ask before, during, and after reading to support students in using comprehension strategies they had learned in their English language arts instruction (e.g., activating background knowledge and summarizing); explicit wording to introduce vocabulary, morphology, and syntax and particular activities teachers could use to engage students in learning words, word parts, and sentence structures; and specific prompts for discussion and writing. We also included slide decks for teachers to use with the lessons and student workbooks in which students could take notes or complete activities during the lessons. All of these resources can be accessed for free on our website: *www.clavescurriculum.net.*

However, we do not view CLAVES as a boxed and immutable curriculum but instead as a framework with instructional practices that teachers can apply to their own texts and topics to supplement the curricula they are using for language arts or English language development instruction. In fact, throughout our implementation of CLAVES, we witnessed teachers adapting CLAVES lessons to meet the needs of their students outside of CLAVES instruction. For example, teachers added scaffolds, such as sentence starters, when students needed them, and they read aloud some texts that they thought were above students' decoding level so that students could access the content of the texts. Also, while we intended for CLAVES to be used with small groups of multilingual students in order to provide them with additional opportunities to talk about text, some teachers, particularly teachers with large numbers of multilingual learners, taught all or parts of the lessons to their whole class and had students turn and talk with partners or small groups for the dialogic parts of the lessons. Though these adaptations were "off script," they were aligned with the principles of CLAVES and allowed teachers to be optimally responsive to their students' needs. To support teachers in applying the instructional practices embedded in CLAVES, we now turn to discussing the seven CLAVES principles and illustrate how we put these into practice. We provide examples from the first unit on Human-Nature Interaction.

Focus on Language and Metalinguistic Awareness

As we found in our early exploratory work, vocabulary, morphology, and syntax are key contributors to reading comprehension. In CLAVES, we use a multifaceted approach to supporting these aspects of language and reading comprehension

TABLE 11.2. An Outline of One Cycle for One Unit of the CLAVES Program

Day 1	Day 2	Day 3	Day 4	Day 5	Day 6
• Activate background knowledge • Introduce vocabulary • Facilitate reading and noticing language in a picture book	• Facilitate reading and noticing language • Focus on vocabulary and semantic relations	• Activate background knowledge • Watch and discuss a video • Focus on morphology	• Activate background knowledge • Facilitate reading and noticing language on a news article • Focus on morphology or syntax	• Activate background knowledge • Introduce vocabulary • Facilitate reading and noticing language • Focus on syntax	• Activate background knowledge • Introduce vocabulary • Facilitate reading and noticing language

TABLE 11.3. An Outline of an End-of-Unit Writing Cycle in the CLAVES Program

Day 1	Day 2	Day 3
• Introduce writing prompt • Facilitate reading and analyzing a mentor text	• Facilitate a prewriting discussion of the writing prompt • Support students in drafting their writing	• Support students in revising or editing their drafts • Facilitate students sharing their writing with their peers

development. We explicitly taught words that were important to the content and high-leverage words that students could use outside of the program across content areas. For example, in Unit 1, we taught the words *restore, exterminate, depopulate,* and *reintroduce.* We provided clear, student-friendly definitions of the words, highlighted the use of the words in context, and provided pictures to help students visualize the words. We also guided students to use word learning strategies, such as using context clues to figure out unknown words, and encouraged students to notice vocabulary use in the texts they encountered. We further taught students to attend to morphological word parts (e.g., *re-, de-, ex-*). We taught them the meanings of these word parts and facilitated students' engagement in gamified activities that encouraged students to recognize how these word parts are used in other words. Additionally, we focused on syntax and how the order of words and their parts of speech contribute to meaning-making. For example, we explored how to identify what pronouns, such as *they,* refer to and how verb tenses, such as past, present, and future, affect our understanding of when something in a text occurred. Importantly, we did not focus on these aspects of language in isolation but rather as they occurred in the texts students were reading.

Enact Dialogic Approaches to Engage Students

Throughout each unit, we asked students to discuss texts and language. Talking about texts with each other, students were able to build a deeper understanding, drawing from the various contributions of students in the group. As mentioned, we intended this to be done in small groups to maximize the opportunity for students to talk, but some teachers set up discussions of texts in a whole group format and then used student-led small groups or pairs to give students chances to discuss texts. Then, at the end of each cycle, we devoted a whole session to student discussion so that students could use, integrate, and build on what they had been talking about in previous lessons. For example, in the first unit, after reading and discussing texts about wolf reintegration from different perspectives (e.g., farmers, Indigenous people, national park workers) across several days, students discussed the question, "Should wolves be introduced to Yellowstone National Park?" Teachers tried to step back and turn the mic over to students, so to speak, though they did jump in to facilitate discussion if the conversation stalled or was going off track.

Use Multimodal Texts and Scaffolds to Support Comprehension and Expression

Multimodal texts and scaffolds support all learners, particularly multilingual learners, in comprehending and talking about new content. In CLAVES, we included picture books with rich language and detailed illustrations, along with videos and student-friendly news articles to learn about various aspects of a particular subject or different perspectives on a topic. For example, in the first unit, students read a poetic picture book, *The Wolves are Back* by Jean Craighead George and Wendell Minor (2008); they watched a CBS video on the debate about wolf reintroduction between farmers and conservationists; and they read a student-friendly news article on the relationship between the Nez Perce tribe and wolves. We also included a graphic organizer to support students in taking notes to compare and contrast across these multimodal texts. Engaging with various kinds of content, perspectives, and forms of communication supported students in developing a deeper understanding of the complexity of the debate around the issue of wolf reintroduction.

Take a Multilingual Perspective

First and foremost, we encouraged teachers to invite students to use their full linguistic repertoire throughout the CLAVES program. Teachers asked students what words represent specific meanings in the other languages they knew, and they encouraged students to use shared languages other than English in their discussions. The curriculum also provided translations and highlighted cognates in other languages (e.g., *exterminar, reintroducir, despoblar*). Unfortunately, we found that teachers and students were so ingrained in the typical English-only mode of instruction found in most classrooms that students rarely used their other language knowledge without prompting. The exception to this was in bilingual classrooms in which instruction is delivered in English and another language. While teachers and students in these classrooms were much more attuned to a multilingual approach, even here, students relied primarily on English, perhaps because the texts were primarily in English. To fully implement the principle of taking a multilingual perspective, teachers need to regularly invite, encourage, and acknowledge students' use of multilingualism and provide positive feedback when students use all of their languages. Also, students need practice taking up opportunities to use their multilingualism so that multilingualism becomes more common and the use of multiple languages becomes more comfortable in English-medium classrooms.

Activate and Build on Background and Content Knowledge

Recognizing that students already bring a vast wealth of knowledge from their lived experiences to the classroom, encouraging students to use that knowledge to understand texts and build on that knowledge as they encounter new texts gives students a strong foundation for meaning-making. For example, in discussing wolf reintroduction in Yellowstone National Park, teachers in CLAVES asked students to think about what they know about parks and taught them new information about where Yellowstone is located and how it may be similar to or different from parks they have visited. Encouraging students to activate their background knowledge reminds them that they have a lot to bring to each reading experience and that they can build on what they bring as they read, comprehend, and learn from texts in school.

Foster Reading for Understanding and Encourage Use of Comprehension Strategies

Acknowledging that reading requires decoding and fluency, it is important to remind students that the ultimate goal of reading is not to spit out words or even to sound good reading them. The ultimate goal is to understand (and learn from) texts. Reading comprehension is not a passive process. Students cannot just read words and expect them to make sense without thinking about them. Therefore, teachers should focus on meaning-making and encourage the active use of comprehension strategies, including inferring, monitoring, and summarizing. Practicing reading for understanding and using comprehension strategies with teachers and peers will help students internalize an active stance toward reading. In the first unit in CLAVES, for example, teachers asked students to summarize what they read (e.g., "Based on what you read today, how do wolves help keep Yellowstone National Park in balance?") and infer the meaning of figurative language (e.g., *The broken parts of the wilderness were tumbling into place*) based on what they had read in the text so far. Encouraging students to stop and answer such questions will help them ask themselves these questions as they read for understanding, develop metalinguistic awareness, and learn from texts in the future.

Leverage Connections between Reading and Writing

Research has highlighted the reciprocal relationship between reading and writing, both of which are grounded in language (Fitzgerald & Shanahan, 2000; Kim, 2020). As students talk about language in text and learn about how language works to make meaning, they can reinforce what they are learning and extend their thinking through writing. Though teachers noted that there never seemed to be enough time to fit writing in, ensuring students have opportunities to write about what they are reading can support language and reading development as well as new learning. As noted, at the end of every unit in CLAVES, students wrote about a topic that spanned the two cycles of the unit. At the end of the unit on Human–Nature Interaction, after they engaged with texts related to wolf reintroduction in Cycle 1 and the debate over placing pipelines in or near bodies of water in Cycle 2, students wrote in response to the question, "Should humans be responsible for solving problems such as animal extinction and environmental issues?" Writing about the topic they had engaged with across units allowed students to further their understanding and use the language they had been studying to communicate about the topic they had been learning. Connecting reading and writing and underscoring that language is at the core of both of these processes will help students grow as readers and writers in school.

CONCLUSION

In reviewing the principles and core instructional practices of the CLAVES program, you may be wondering if these principles are relevant only to multilingual learners. In fact, we believe that designing instruction to leverage the linguistic strengths of multilingual learners and support them in language and reading comprehension development should serve as a model for supporting the language and reading comprehension of all students. It is not coincidental that many of the principles and core instructional practices of the CLAVES program align with Universal Design for Learning, a framework to improve teaching and learning for *all* students (CAST, 2024). We have shown through our work that these principles and core instructional practices are the keys or clues to supporting language and reading comprehension for multilingual learners, and we think that if we support language and reading comprehension for multilingual learners, we improve literacy education for all.

Reflection Questions

1. How can principles and core instructional practices of the CLAVES program be incorporated to align with or supplement English language arts instruction for multilingual learners in elementary school?
2. Though the CLAVES program was designed with multilingual learners in mind, how are the CLAVES principles and core instructional practices relevant to all students?

ACKNOWLEDGMENTS

The work presented here was funded by the Institute of Education Sciences, U.S. Department of Education, through Grants R305A090152 (PI: Silverman), R305A140114 (PI: Proctor), and R305A240114 (PI: Silverman), awarded to the University of Maryland, Boston College, and Stanford University, respectively.

REFERENCES

August, D., & Shanahan, T. (2006). *Developing literacy in second-language learners: Report of the national literacy panel on language minority children and youth*. Erlbaum.

Bialystok, E. (2001). Metalinguistic aspects of bilingual processing. *Annual Review of Applied Linguistics, 21*, 169–181.

Bialystok, E., McBride-Chang, C., & Luk, G. (2005). Bilingualism, language proficiency, and learning to read in two writing systems. *Journal of Educational Psychology, 97*(4), 580–590.

Bolt, M., Rodriguez, C., Wagner, C. J., & Proctor, C. P. (2019). Can we talk? Creating opportunities for meaningful academic discussions with dual language learners. *Young Children, 74*, 40–47.

CAST. (2024). Universal design for learning guidelines version 3.0 [graphic organizer]. Author.

Clark, A. M., Anderson, R. C., Kuo, L. J., Kim, I. H., Archodidou, A., & Nguyen-Jahiel, K. (2003). Collaborative reasoning: Expanding ways for children to talk and think in school. *Educational Psychology Review, 15*, 181–198.

Cummins, J. (1979). Linguistic interdependence and the educational development of bilingual children. *Review of Educational Research, 49*(2), 222–251.

Deng, Q., Kiramba, L. K., & Viesca, K. M. (2021). Factors associated with novice general education teachers' preparedness to work with multilingual learners: A multilevel study. *Journal of Teacher Education, 72*(4), 489–503.

Fitzgerald, J., & Shanahan, T. (2000). Reading and writing relations and their development. *Educational Psychologist, 35*(1), 39–50.

García, O., & Kleifgen, J. A. (2020). Translanguaging and literacies. *Reading Research Quarterly, 55*(4), 553–571.

Hattan, C., & Kendeou, P. (2024). Expanding the science of reading: Contributions from educational psychology. *Educational Psychologist, 59*(4), 217–232.

Hoover, W. A., & Gough, P. B. (1990). The simple view of reading. *Reading and Writing, 2*(2), 127–160.

Hu, M., & Nation, I. S. P. (2000). Vocabulary density and reading comprehension. *Reading in a Foreign Language, 13*(1), 403–430.

Jiménez, R. T., García, G. E., & Pearson, P. D. (1996). The reading strategies of bilingual Latina/o students who are successful English readers: Opportunities and obstacles. *Reading Research Quarterly, 31*(1), 90–112.

Kim, Y.-S. G. (2020). Interactive dynamic literacy model: An integrative theoretical framework for reading–Writing relations. In R. A. Alves, T. Limpo, & R. M. Joshi (Eds.), *Reading–Writing connections* (Vol. 19, pp. 11–34). Springer International.

Klingner, J. K., & Vaughn, S. (2000). The helping behaviors of fifth-graders while using collaborative strategic reading during ESL content classes. *TESOL Quarterly, 34,* 69–98.

Leighton, C., Ford-Connors, E., Proctor, C. P., & Wyatt, J. (2021). Teacher talk that supports young multilingual students' participation in exploratory discourse. *Reading Psychology, 42,* 1–20.

Mancilla-Martinez, J. (2023). Prioritizing dual language learners' language comprehension development to support later reading achievement. In S. Q. Cabell, S. B. Neuman, & N. P. Terry (Eds.), *Handbook on the science of early literacy* (chapter 3). Guilford Press.

Nagy, W. E., García, G. E., Durgunoglu, A. Y., & Hancin-Bhatt, B. (1993). Spanish–English bilingual students' use of cognates in English reading. *Journal of Reading Behavior, 25,* 241–259.

Nagy, W. E., & Scott, J. A. (2000). Vocabulary processes. In M. L. Kamil, P. B. Mosenthal, P. D. Pearson, & R. Barr (Eds.), *Handbook of reading research* (Vol. 3, pp. 269–284). Erlbaum.

National Center for Education Statistics. (2024). English learners in public schools. *Condition of Education.* U.S. Department of Education, Institute of Education Sciences. Retrieved February 4, 2025, from *https://nces.ed.gov/programs/coe/indicator/cgf*

Ossa Parra, M., & Proctor, C. P. (2021). Translanguaging to understand language. *TESOL Quarterly, 55,* 766–794.

Ossa Parra, M., Wagner, C., Proctor, C. P., Leighton, C. M., Robertson, D. A., Paratore, J. R., & Ford-Connors, E. (2016). Dialogic reasoning: Supporting emergent bilingual students' language and literacy development. In C. P. Proctor, A. Boardman, & E. Hiebert (Eds.), *Teaching emergent bilingual students: Flexible approaches in an era of new standards* (pp. 119–137). Guilford Press.

Palinscar, A. S., & Brown, A. L. (1984). Reciprocal teaching of comprehension-fostering and comprehension-monitoring activities. *Cognition and Instruction, 1*(2), 117–175.

Proctor, C. P. (2011). "Get starting in English": Teaching for vocabulary depth with bilingual learners. In R. L. McCormack & J. R. Paratore (Eds.), *After early intervention, Then what? Teaching struggling readers in grades 3 and beyond* (pp. 42–65). International Reading Association.

Proctor, C. P., Harring, J. R., & Silverman, R. D. (2017). Linguistic interdependence between Spanish language and English language and reading: A longitudinal exploration from second through fifth grade. *Bilingual Research Journal, 40,* 372–391.

Proctor, C. P., & Mo, E. (2009). The relationship between cognate awareness and English comprehension among Spanish–English bilingual fourth grade students. *TESOL Quarterly, 43*(1), 126–136.

Proctor, C. P., Silverman, R. D., & Jones, R. L. (2021). Centering language and student voice in multilingual literacy instruction. *The Reading Teacher, 75,* 255–267.

Proctor, C. P., Silverman, R. D., Harring, J. R., Jones, R. L., & Hartranft, A. M. (2020). Teaching bilingual learners: Effects of a language-based reading intervention on academic language and reading comprehension in grades 4 and 5. *Reading Research Quarterly, 55*(1), 95–122.

Proctor, C. P., Silverman, R. D., Harring, J. R., & Montecillo, C. (2012). The role of vocabulary depth in predicting reading comprehension among English monolingual and Spanish-English bilingual children in elementary school. *Reading and Writing, 25*(7), 1635–1664.

Ritchey, K. D., Palombo, K., Silverman, R. D., & Speece, D. L. (2017). Effects of an informational text reading comprehension intervention for fifth-grade students. *Learning Disabilities Quarterly, 40,* 68–80.

Rosenshine, B., & Meister, C. (1994). Reciprocal teaching: A review of the research. *Review of Educational Research, 64*(4), 479–530.

Silverman, R. D., Artzi, L., McNeish, D., Hartranft, A. M., Martin-Beltran, M., & Peercy, M. M. (2019). Effects of different media on vocabulary learning in kindergarten and fourth grade. *Contemporary Educational Psychology, 56,* 106–116.

Silverman, R. D., Proctor, C. P., Harring, J. R., Doyle, B., Mitchell, M. A., & Meyer, A. G. (2014). Teachers' instruction and students' vocabulary and comprehension: An exploratory study with English monolingual and Spanish–English bilingual students in Grades 3–5. *Reading Research Quarterly, 49*(1), 31–60.

Silverman, R. D., Proctor, C. P, Harring, J. R., Hartranft, A. M., Doyle, C. B., & Zelinke, S. B. (2015). Language skills and reading comprehension in English monolingual and Spanish-English bilingual children in grades 2–5. *Reading and Writing: An Interdisciplinary Journal, 28,* 1381–1405.

Silverman, R. D., Proctor, C. P., Harring, J. R., Taylor, K. S., Johnson, E. M., Jones, R. L., & Lee, Y. (2021). The effect of a language and literacy intervention on upper elementary bilingual students' argument writing. *Elementary School Journal, 122*(2), 208–232.

Tracey, D. H., & Morrow, L. M. (2012). *Lenses on reading: An introduction to theories and models* (2nd ed.). Guilford Press.

Vaughn, M. (2019). Adaptive teaching during reading instruction: A multi-case study. *Reading Psychology, 40*(1), 1–33.

Waggoner, M., Chinn, C., Yi, H., & Anderson, R. C. (1995). Collaborative reasoning about stories. *Language Arts, 72,* 582–589.

Zhang, J., & Dougherty Stahl, K. A. (2011). Collaborative reasoning: Language-rich discussions for English learners. *The Reading Teacher, 65*(4), 257–260.

12

"What If I Don't Speak Their Languages?"

Engaging Educators and Multilingual Learners in Collaborative Exploration of the Language for School Literacy

Emily Phillips Galloway

Guiding Questions

1. How do I use all my multilingual students' language resources to comprehend text if I don't speak their languages?
2. What aspects of the language in school texts should I introduce to support my students in becoming skilled readers and writers?
3. Can these two objectives—honoring what youth know and teaching new language—be achieved simultaneously?

In 2018, these guiding questions brought me (Emily)—an education researcher and former middle-grade teacher—and a group of 3 fourth- and fifth-grade educators (Janet, Rosina, and Manny) together in a teacher-learning community (TLC). We collectively envisioned classrooms as vibrant spaces where diverse voices converge—the voices of students, teachers, and even those of the authors of the texts with which we engage. We imagined classrooms could become richer meaning-making and learning sites when these many voices were in productive dialogue.

However, we also recognized that this sort of instruction was not always available to all students, especially multilingual learners receiving their education in classrooms located in U.S. states (like our own in the U.S. Southeast) that had legislated English-only instruction. Indeed, like in most U.S. states (Shin, 2017), English-medium instruction was the only instructional format available to multilingual learners in the district where we worked. In addition, we saw how policies and ideologies that privileged "academic" English over the dynamic linguistic repertoires students brought from their homes and communities further silenced student voices and foreclosed opportunities for equitable participation (Aukerman, 2007; Cole et al., 2012; Emily Phillips Galloway et al., 2015). Like educators across the United States, my TLC partner educators, who all identified as not multilingual themselves, grappled with how to access and fully leverage the linguistic resources youth brought to the classroom. A common refrain was "What if I don't speak their languages?"—a question stemming from a place of care, but one the field has been reticent to address with concrete guidance.

In our TLC, we sought to address this question together. We were motivated by the belief that linguistically permeable instruction, while challenging to implement, is of great importance for supporting the academic thriving of language-minoritized youth, such as multilingual learners who are subject to the systemic exclusion of their language resources in schools. Literacy research has demonstrated the powerful affordances of leveraging students' complete linguistic resources for meaningful sensemaking, particularly during language-mediated tasks like reading comprehension (García & Li Wei, 2014; Li Wei, 2018; Makoni & Pennycook, 2007).

Translingual pedagogies, which aim to intentionally utilize all learners' language resources toward particular instructional goals, have been shown to be effective in expanding learners' conceptual knowledge and scaffolding their literacy participation (Daniel et al., 2019; Ridley & Rowe, 2024). These translingual pedagogies include inviting students to use languages other than English as they work with classmates, creating opportunities to engage with texts written in a range of languages, and on the use of collaborative translation activities in which students work together to create their own translations of text (García et al., 2017).

Yet fewer studies have examined how such asset-oriented approaches could be used by educators who identify as monolingual to cultivate students' dynamic, socially situated knowledge *of* language and *about* language—how it works and can be used. As a result, we know little about how pedagogies could be utilized to inform middle-grade instruction that aims to both honor and expand students' skills to engage in *languaging* or the dynamic social process of shaping knowledge and making meaning using language (Swain, 2006), particularly in the context of English language arts classrooms.

Box 12.1. Translingual Pedagogies

Translingual pedagogies intentionally utilize all learners' language resources toward well-specified instructional goals (David et al., 2019). Examples include activities like the collaborative translation of text, the creation of bilingual dictionaries, or inviting students to use all language resources when explaining concepts to classmates (García et al., 2017).

This chapter is the outcome of this productive, year-long TLC collaboration. We aimed to co-design approaches for (1) supporting students to develop knowledge of the language for school literacy and (2) placing these language resources in dynamic conversation with youths' home linguistic repertoires. Recognizing the language of schooling as socioculturally situated rather than neutral, this work sought to make visible its power dynamics (Louie, 2020; Paris, 2012). This chapter is rooted in teacher reflections on embracing what we call "syncretic language instruction" and shares the products of this collaboration, a four-phase instructional routine designed to foster equity-oriented pedagogy around the language for school literacy.

We were inspired by the work on syncretism by Gutiérrez (2014), which illustrated how the literacy practices used by Spanish-home-language migrant youth brought together the powerful literacies common in their communities with those dominant in schools, revealing the possibility of bringing together distinct language communities in ways that lead to hybridization rather than subsummation. An initial concern of educators in our TLC was that teaching the *language for school literacy*—or the word, sentence, and discourse structures that commonly co-occur with reading and writing activities at school (Uccelli et al., 2020)—left little room for students to use and to continue to develop their home language literacy skills. This chapter documents how we created an instructional activity that made this hybridization possible.

Below, I first introduce the concept of classrooms as points of contact between diverse language communities and enumerate the linguistic features that typically track with reasoning and knowledge-sharing practices in academic ones. As a result of their usefulness for scholarly communication, these language features are also prevalent in school texts and talk. To advance the efforts of teachers hoping to adopt this approach, I share a four-phase instructional routine designed by our TLC to facilitate syncretic language instruction. Indeed, I envision the readers of this chapter to be educators and teacher educators. This four-phase routine outlines the instructional steps from the educators' perspective to enable its use in their own classroom. Then, by drawing on the reflections of my three collaborating educators, I examine the potential affordances of this syncretic instructional routine in classrooms where educators hope to teach the language for school literacy while simultaneously teaching youth to draw on their vast stores of linguistic and metalinguistic skills as part of textual sensemaking.

Box 12.2. Language for School Literacy

Language for school literacy refers to the word, sentence, and discourse features commonly co-occurring with knowledge generation and transmission activities in classrooms and other academic and professional communities. It is the language frequently found in school texts and used for communicating ideas in writing.

CONCEPTUAL UNDERPINNINGS

Classrooms: Points of Contact between Diverse Language Communities, Each with distinct Ways of Languaging

Language learning is not simply about learning language forms; it is also about learning how these language forms are marshaled to construct knowledge in different communities (Gee, 2004; Schleppegrell, 2004). Classrooms represent places of contact between the language communities of students and teachers. For some learners, these language communities mostly overlap with those of their classmates and teachers. For others, however, there is little overlap in the language resources used across the outside-of-school communities in which they are participants and those commonplace in classrooms. In some instances, students speak languages—Spanish, Tagalog, Arabic—that educators and peers do not speak. In other cases, students are speakers of language varieties, such as Southern American English or Black English, not known by their teachers. Inevitably, students and teachers are members of different generations, separated by differences in speech that track with youth culture and participation in various special interest communities.

In our TLC, we drew on the theoretical lens provided by translanguaging that offers the central understanding that each individual's communicative resources exist as a unified whole (Wei, 2018). In linguistics, we sometimes call this an idiolect. The basic idea driving translanguaging theory is that for each of us, all of our language resources, as well as the additional tools available for meaning-making, like gestures and facial expressions, are always available to be assembled in novel ways to support communication (Li Wei, 2018). For multilingual learners, translingual theory casts language meshing, where, for example, English and Spanish are used seamlessly within conversation, as an everyday practice (García et al., 2017). For example, Orellana and García-Sánchez (2023) document how multilingual youth serving as language brokers routinely develop languaging practices for supporting Spanish-speaking family members to communicate in English-dominant settings. These experiences mean that multilingual learners enter classrooms with a vast array of strategies for making meaning between and across language communities.

Texts, too, are the products of distinct language communities, produced by writers who bring significant experience in reading, writing, and using the language common in academic and literacy communities. As members of academic communities, these authors bring knowledge of ways of communicating that reflect the norms of scholarly inquiry and knowledge production (Gee, 2004; Halliday, 2006). They are familiar, for example, with ways of using language to assert authority and establish the veracity of their claims. This is what we call a register of English—language designed for completing a particular activity in a specific community (Biber & Conrad, 2009). For example, explaining the relationship between concepts or a stepwise scientific process is more manageable when language resources aid us. While academic registers generally share some language features with standardized language varieties, they are conceptually distinct, given that registers develop around tasks and language varieties around groups of people (Biber & Conrad, 2009). The challenge, however, is that this language has also operated historically to exclude the participation of people of color, women, and other minoritized groups in the work of academic communities, a phenomenon that continues in the present (Janks, 2010; Paris, 2012). While this language, which was tailor-made for communicating the types of concepts that dominate academic inquiry, is functional, it also carries the potential to operate as a tool for exclusion and for perpetuating racism, sexism, and other deeply problematic patterns of social interaction within our broader society and in our own classrooms.

Some students and their teachers may be embedded in the same language communities as the writers of school texts and so share knowledge of a common set of language features (Phillips Galloway et al., 2020). Yet, as students enter the middle grades, few have had much extended opportunity to participate in communities of mathematicians or literary scholars. So, accessing texts by authors writing from within these communities for an imagined audience of others who share this disciplinary orientation requires mastering new language resources. The challenge, though, rests in how to provide this instruction in ways that acknowledge multilingual learners' vast experience moving across and within linguistic communities.

In this chapter, I offer an instructional approach that aims to invite students into the language for school literacy. However, in contrast to approaches that do not invite students' own languaging resources to coexist with those taught at school, the routine outlined here aims to combat the exclusionary ways that this language can be taught in school settings. However, we must first understand the sorts of language used by readers and writers of academic texts.

Unpacking the Language Used within Academic Communities and Its Role in Literacy Processes

The *language for school literacy* consists of language features—words, sentences, and discourse structures—and has been the focus of my prior research and the research of many others. Indeed, decades of research have demonstrated the significance of these language resources and ways of languaging for literacy development and academic performance (Bailey, 2007; Bailey & Heritage, 2014; Berman, 2007; Christie & Derewianka, 2008; Nagy & Townsend, 2012; Schleppegrell, 2004, 2007; Schleppegrell et al., 2023).

Some of the language that students need to learn to access the language of the text is disciplinary, comprised of the vocabulary of a content area, the sentence structures used predominately in a single discipline, and the language for argumentation, which studies reveal differs somewhat by field (see, e.g., Schleppegrell, 2004 for insight into discipline-specific language features). However, learning the language used across disciplines is equally essential for middle graders. My work with colleagues has sought to make visible the language features commonly used by academic writers regardless of their content area, which must be learned to ensure students' equitable access to the concepts and content contained in school texts. We refer to the skills needed to navigate these language features as *core analytical language skills* (CALS; Phillips Galloway et al., 2020a; Uccelli et al., 2015). CALS includes a set of cross-disciplinary language skills that members of academic communities routinely use because they are useful. These include not only knowledge of cross-disciplinary language features but also an awareness of when to use these features to achieve one's own communicative goals. Yet, CALS skills are often overlooked in curricula and instruction despite being essential for students' equitable and meaningful participation in school learning activities.

CALS includes six skills that readers must develop to effectively comprehend and make meaning of texts in school: unpacking dense information contained in complex words and sentences, connecting ideas logically using information provided by connective words, tracking participants and ideas, understanding how analytic texts are organized, understanding metalinguistic vocabulary, and understanding a writer's viewpoint. See Table 12.1 for examples of each of these skills. In addition, CALS includes a seventh skill that is much more metalinguistic: recognizing when texts are written in an academic register. Strategic readers must apply the skills outlined in Table 12.1, but recognizing that these skills are needed is a requisite first step. Middle-grade readers bring vast stores of language knowledge and experience to a reading task, so they have to determine which skills are more appropriate to use on the fly.

Our research has explored how CALS relates to reading and writing. Extensive work with teachers and thousands of monolingual and multilingual students in grades 4–8 has documented substantial individual differences in students' understanding of the language for school literacy, as operationalized by the CALS construct. Our studies and those of others that examine CALS have shown strong associations between CALS and students' reading comprehension and writing quality across different languages and contexts (Barr et al., 2019; Cardoso et al., 2020; Meneses et al., 2018; Phillips Galloway et al., 2019, 2020a; Proctor et al., 2020; Uccelli et al., 2015, 2020; see also Cervetti et al., 2020). Furthermore, as we have found in our other studies with middle schoolers in dual-language programs, CALS proficiency in students' first and second languages affects their English reading comprehension, highlighting the interconnected nature of multilingual students' language systems (Aguilar et al., 2020; Phillips Galloway et al., 2019). For instruction, this finding offers the vital insight that students entering the classroom with literacy skills in a language other than English can be supported to access this linguistic knowledge to facilitate their engagement with school texts in English. CALS also contributes to students' productive language use, with studies demonstrating strong associations between receptive CALS and the quality of their expository and persuasive writing (Hsin et al., 2024; Phillips Galloway et al., 2020a, 2020b; Uccelli et al., 2020).

These findings are not particularly surprising if we imagine that text understanding is a language-mediated task that demands engaging with the language of the text and, as outlined above, with that of the author (Phillips Galloway et al., 2020a). To this task, readers bring existing linguistic and cultural knowledge, which informs their text understanding, and seek to integrate this with the new information and language in the text (Kintsch, 2005). Readers who share the conceptual and linguistic knowledge of the author have an advantage. Ensuring that all students can access this language is an urgent matter of equity. Yet, educators often wonder how to do so in ways that allow space for the languages of all—students, texts, and teachers themselves—to be in generative conversation.

TABLE 12.1. Examples of CALS Skills Commonly Used across Texts at School

CALS skills used when reading texts at school	Examples of how this language appears in the text
Unpacking dense information contained in complex words and sentences	*Science textbook example:* The rapid deforestation of the Amazon rainforest has resulted in the disruption of the delicate ecological balance within the region, leading to a significant decrease in biodiversity and the potential loss of numerous undiscovered plant and animal species. *Social studies textbook example:* The ratification of the United Nations Universal Declaration of Human Rights in 1948 represented a pivotal moment in the global effort to enshrine fundamental individual freedoms and liberties, providing a framework for the promotion of justice, equality, and human dignity across nations. These examples include nominalized forms *(deforestation, ratification),* embedded clauses *(that has resulted in. . ., that provide a framework for. . .),* and expanded noun phrases *(the delicate ecological balance, the global effort to enshrine fundamental individual freedoms and liberties)* to facilitate concise and precise communication of complex concepts.
Connecting ideas logically using information provided by connective words	*Math textbook example:* *Consequently,* if the perimeter of a square is 16 units, then the length of each side must be four units. *English language arts textbook example:* *On the one hand,* the protagonist in the story faced many obstacles, *but on the other hand,* they remained determined to overcome them.
Tracking participants and ideas	*Social studies textbook example:* *The Roman Empire* was one of the most powerful civilizations in ancient history. *It* stretched across Europe, North Africa, and the Middle East. Known for *their* advanced engineering, *the Romans* built impressive architectural feats, and sophisticated legal system. *Science textbook example:* *Photosynthesis* is the process by which plants convert sunlight, water, and carbon dioxide into glucose. *This chemical reaction* occurs in the chloroplasts of plant cells.

(continued)

TABLE 12.1. *(continued)*

CALS skills used when reading texts at school	Examples of how this language appears in the text
Understanding how analytic texts are organized according to its conventional academic structure (e.g., thesis, argument, counterargument, conclusion) and paragraph-level structures (e.g., compare–contrast; problem–solution)	*Social studies textbook excerpt:* The industrial revolution that swept through Europe in the 18th and 19th centuries had a profound impact on the lives of ordinary citizens. *On one hand*, the factory system provided new economic opportunities and a more reliable source of income for many people. *However*, the working conditions in these factories were often harsh, with long hours, unsafe environments, and minimal worker protections. *While* the industrial revolution fueled economic growth, it also created new social tensions and inequalities that governments had to grapple with. *Ultimately*, the industrialization of Europe transformed society in complex ways, with both benefits and drawbacks for the general population. *Math textbook excerpt:* Mathematical models can be a powerful tool for understanding and predicting real-world phenomena. *For example*, population growth models can help us forecast changes in a city's demographics over time. These models rely on factors like birth rates, death rates, and net migration to project future population size. *At the same time*, real-world systems are often complex, with many interdependent variables. A simple mathematical model may overlook important nuances and uncertainties. *Additionally*, the reliability of a model depends on the accuracy of the data used to construct it. *While* mathematical models offer valuable insights, they should be considered as one input among many when making important decisions that affect people's lives.
Understanding metalinguistic vocabulary that makes thinking and reasoning visible, known as metalinguistic vocabulary (e.g., hypothesis, generalization, argument)	*Science lab report example:* In *this experiment*, we will *test the hypothesis* that increasing the amount of fertilizer applied to a plant will lead to faster growth. *We will observe* the plants over time and *record our data* to see if the results support or *refute this hypothesis*. *English language arts assignment example:* Cummins's use of specific rhetorical devices, such as metaphor and hyperbole, conveys the central message. *Explore* how these linguistic choices contribute to the *author's overall argument* in a short essay.

(continued)

TABLE 12.1. *(continued)*

CALS skills used when reading texts at school	Examples of how this language appears in the text
Understanding a writer's viewpoint, especially "epistemic stance markers," those that signal a writer's degree of certainty in relationship to a claim (e.g., *Certainly, It is unlikely that*)	*Social studies textbook example:* *It is clear that* the ancient Roman Empire was one of the most influential and long-lasting civilizations in human history. *Undoubtedly*, the Roman Empire's military prowess, advanced infrastructure, and sophisticated system of governance played a significant role in its expansion and dominance across the Mediterranean world. However, *it is unlikely* that the empire's success was solely due to these factors. *Mathematics textbook example:* In mathematics, *it is unlikely* that there is a single, universal approach to solving complex problems. However, *we can say with confidence* that breaking down problems into smaller, more manageable steps is often an effective strategy.

SUBSUMMATION OR HYBRIDIZATION?!: THE ROLE OF SYNCRETIC INSTRUCTIONAL DESIGN IN IMAGINING SPACES WHERE DIVERSE LANGUAGE COMMUNITIES ARE IN CONVERSATION

Designing instruction that leverages these parallels between students' everyday languaging practices and the linguistic demands of school literacy is a crucial challenge—and opportunity—for educators. Necessary for designing this instruction, though, are robust conceptual frameworks that empower teachers to reason about, design for, and navigate the complexities of creating more expansive, equitable learning environments that honor and amplify the full range of students' linguistic resources.

Gutiérrez and Jurow's (2016) notion of a "syncretic approach" offers one such conceptual framework that enables educators to think about how these diverse language resources coexist. Drawing on sociological accounts of how Samoan American families create hybrid literacies (Duranti & Ochs, 1997), syncretic approaches in teaching aim to bring the literate practices of nondominant learners into productive dialogue with those of academic communities to create new, more expansive, and equitable forms of hybridized knowledge (Gutiérrez, 2014; Vogelstein et al., 2023). For example, while we sometimes understand the contact between two distinct cultures' language and literacy practices—such as those of home and of school—leading deterministically to the total subsumption of one by the other, syncretic theories introduce the possibility for fluid coexistence. Particularly powerful are the ways in which syncretic literacies can be learned by educators from students. As Souto-Manning (2013) highlights through her analysis of narratives elicited from an Afro-Latino child, students who have developed the know-how to navigate across normative boundaries for language use established in schools are often "syncretic natives." Teachers, in contrast, often occupy the role of "syncretic immigrants." Souto-Manning argues that because of both the ideologies commonly circulating in schools about language and the lack of professional learning opportunities to learn to transgress norms that exclude students' languaging resources, educators often rely on familiar pedagogical practices. There is much to be learned from children, who, as syncretic natives, can model the creation of new hybrid language and literacy practices.

Yet, syncretic approaches in classrooms have more often been explored in work involving STEM educators. For example, Vogelstein and colleagues (2023) show, for example, how a middle school STEM educator engaged her students in melding their everyday knowledge of candy and of their classmates' love of sweets in combination with data literacy skills taught in the classroom to write claim–evidence–reasoning paragraphs. This combining of sensemaking resources acquired across two social worlds offers a vision of hybrid instruction. Relatedly, Pierson and colleagues (2021) worked with an educator in an English-dominant sixth-grade STEM classroom to implement a nine-week ecology unit with multilingual learners. They found that canonical scientific modeling practices could incorporate students' home languages via translanguaging, expanding what was considered legitimate participation in the disciplinary learning taking place.

This chapter examines one approach to syncretic language instruction designed in our TLC, which brought together a group of five English language arts educators. We meet monthly over the course of one school year. From this initial group, 3 fourth- and fifth-grade educators (Janet, Rosina, and Manny) agreed to serve as focal participants, designing language-focused lessons and reflecting on the process. We were initially brought together through a partnership with the district office for English language learners. The basic premise driving our shared work was that students enter classrooms as skilled languagers in home and community settings, adept at using language for a variety of social functions (Heath, 2012). However, the specific ways of using language to make meaning from academic texts that are encompassed by CALS often need to be clarified. For example, students may be skilled in argument-making but still learning the linguistic skills needed to clearly articulate stances and perspectives in school-based genres (Hsin et al., 2024). Similarly, multilingual youth who serve as language brokers for their families possess valuable metalinguistic and communicative skills but understandably have little experience applying these to academic text comprehension (Orellana & García-Sánchez, 2023). In the following sections, I share the approach we designed to bring multiple language communities into conversation.

DESIGNING SYNCRETIC LANGUAGE INSTRUCTION: A ROADMAP TO PRACTICE

In our TLC, a common source of instructional challenge was supporting students to access grade-level text. These texts, which provide vital content knowledge, can be challenging for students with less accumulated experience reading and writing at school. However, students must have access to these developmentally appropriate texts to develop the requisite background knowledge needed to comprehend future texts and fully participate in the learning taking place in the classroom.

In designing an approach to tackle this complex text, we looked to two sources: *collaborative translation protocols* and *instructional approaches originating in applied linguistics research*. First, *collaborative translation protocols* have been shown to support text comprehension in multilingual youth (Jiménez et al., 2015). In particular, we drew on the work my colleagues and I have conducted over two decades to develop a collaborative translingual pedagogical approach as part of Project TRANSLATE (Teaching Reading And New Strategic Language Activities To English-learners) (e.g., Cole et al., in press; Cole et al., 2012; David & Cole, 2021; Jiménez et al., 2015; Puzio et al., 2013; White et al., 2023). The TRANSLATE protocol provides a routine for classroom use that engages students, working in pairs and small groups, in the translation of short, purposefully chosen segments of English text. Post-translation, students, guided by educators, reflect on what they have learned about language and the texts' meaning (Cole et al., in press). Second, we looked to *instructional approaches originating in applied linguistics research* focused on helping students recognize and use the linguistic features of text to comprehend texts, including disciplinary texts (Gebhard, 2019; Schleppegrell, 2004; Schleppegrell et al., 2023). Most relevant to our work was the so-called 3Ls protocol pioneered by Lily Wong-Fillmore and Maryann Cucchiara (see Cucchiara, 2018). This lesson flow protocol utilizes six essential elements that build on each other to foster multilingual learners' literacy development: (1) framed motivation; (2) wordplay; (3) reading closely; (4) juicy sentences; (5) differentiated tasks; and (6) closure/wrap-ups (Cucchiara, 2018). During the juicy sentence moment in the lesson, the students and teacher mine a single sentence from the text read that day, examining vocabulary, phrases, and clauses in order to answer the essential questions (Cucchiara, 2018).

After examination of these protocols and iterative cycles of application in TLC participants' classrooms, we designed a hybrid approach that included features of the collaborative translation protocol and applied instructional approaches informed by linguistics used in classrooms described above. For example, while collaborative translation activities generally placed no focus on the explicit teaching of the CALS needed to navigate linguistic features contained in English texts, this was a core component of those instructional routines designed by applied linguists. Similarly, while collaborative translation activities placed a heavy emphasis on encouraging students to make metalinguistic connections—an activity that called for negotiating the selection of words, phrases, and sentence structures in a language other than English with peers—this focus on students' home languages was generally absent from those designed by applied linguists. Combining these led to the four-phase syncretic approach for supporting text understanding (Figure 12.1) described below.

Similar across existing approaches (collaborative translation; the Juicy Sentence Activity within the 3Ls) is a focus on a short segment—two to three sentences—of meaningful text abstracted from a larger text to which students have previously been introduced. This represented a significant instructional shift for the TLC educators. Typical comprehension lessons in partner teachers' classrooms focused on large segments (about 10–15 pages) of young adult fiction novels in English, which were often read aloud. However, after piloting, we elected to design lessons that focused on short text segments abstracted from the novel being read in each classroom. These lessons were designed to augment the discussion-based read-alouds already occurring. After the pilot phase, we settled on three guidelines to drive the selection of two- to three-sentence text segments. First, segments should relate to a central theme in the larger text and be worth discussing at length as part of developing comprehension. Second, the selected text segment should contain English language features that will be highly useful for accessing future texts. These include many CALS features—morphologically complex words that can

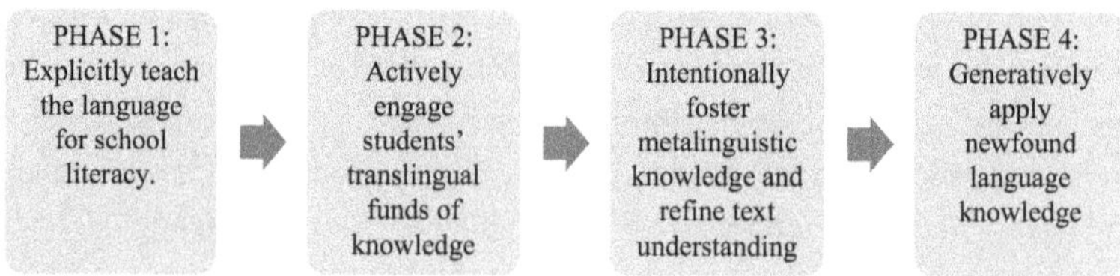

FIGURE 12.1. The four-stage syncretic approach for supporting text understanding.

be unpacked, participants and ideas that can be tracked through text, or complex sentence structures such as those that contain embedded clauses or noun phrases. Third, the text should contain features that make it interesting to translate and likely to generate rich debate and discussion among students. Often, this demanded selecting text that captured emotions, ideas, or concepts that could not be readily translated word-for-word from English.

The Four-Phase Instructional Routine

Below, I outline the teacher activities and rationale for each phase of the protocol designed by our TLC. The protocol is designed to be adapted for any text and group of students so that educators can use it flexibly across contexts. Within the lesson flow, this four-phase instructional routine occurs after students have read along as their teacher reads aloud a larger segment of text, often multiple pages. After teaching some essential vocabulary and engaging students in answering comprehension questions to assess basic comprehension, the teacher returns to a short segment of the text (one to three sentences) in order to foster students' deeper comprehension. This segment of text should contain essential information—that is, it offers an answer to the most central comprehension questions guiding the lesson. In addition, the segment should contain CALS language features that are worthy of teaching because they are quite likely to appear in future texts.

Box 12.3. Why Focus on a Sentence or Two?

While comprehension lessons often focus on multiple pages of content, this four-phased instructional routine engages students in purposeful study of a text segment (one to three sentences) selected because it contains essential information needed to comprehend the overall text.

Phase 1: Explicitly Teach the Language for School Literacy

Begin by reminding students that the purpose of attending to language in the text is to make meaning. Reread the English text segment aloud, then explicitly teach one or two CALS skills that could be used to navigate the CAL feature of the text segment. The CALS skill selected for teaching could be, for example, tracking a person mentioned by the author using anaphoric references within the text (e.g., *Pinochet* was known for *his* policies. *He* was a cruel *dictator*.). With a focus on anaphoric reference (what we call the *CALS feature focus*), this lesson would underscore that authors typically vary the language used to refer participants to reduce repetition and support concise communication. The associated text navigation routine would teach students to engage in participant tracking by drawing lines to all subsequent references to "Pinochet" within the text. An alternative approach would be to highlight in a single color all references to a single person or ideas, which is a particularly useful approach when a text contains references to two or more people, movements, or ideas. While the *CALS feature focus* (anaphoric references to Pinochet) is specific to the text itself, the *text navigation routine* (participant tracking) is designed to be transferable to future texts. These lessons equip students with knowledge of why authors employ this CAL feature and support students in taking an active stance as readers.

After teaching the CALS feature focus and text navigation routine, work with the students to generate a student-friendly paraphrase of the text in English. This can be done collaboratively until students have developed enough familiarity with the text type. The paraphrase activity places the language of students in juxtaposition to that of the text's author. Having unpacked the contents of the focal text segment in the prior step, students are generally equipped to create a paraphrase. However, in classrooms with larger numbers of multilingual learners at the beginning stages of English language development, educators may provide a series of statements that students assemble to create this paraphrase.

Phase 2: Actively Engage Students' Translingual Funds of Knowledge

Request that students work with a partner who shares knowledge of the same first or additional language to generate a translation of the text into a language other than English. Remind students that they may not be able to translate the text word-for-word, but their translation should capture the feeling or mood of the text segment. You can invite students to transliterate (use English script to record words phonetically) as well as use invented spelling. Students can also work with dictionaries or online tools. In hyper-linguistically diverse classrooms, where students speak multiple home languages, some students may lack a partner who shares a common home language. In these instances, invite students to attempt a translation and then to generate one using an online tool, serving in the role of a bilingual buddy. Monolingual English-speaking students can be asked to shift the register of the text, rewriting it for another audience in language that students might use outside of school settings (e.g., rewriting as a text message or using Black English to communicate with peers).

As students translate, circulate and pose questions that support metalinguistic inquiry—for example:

- "I notice that your Arabic translation has fewer words than the English version. Why is that?"
- "That Spanish word looks like the English word. Is that a cognate?"
- "When you translated, could you keep the word order the same?"
- "Your translation and the one generated by ChatGPT contain different words. Did this cause you to make any revisions? Why or why not?"
- "Online tools like ChatGPT are not often aware of regional differences in language. Do you think this is why your translation contains some different vocabulary words?"

You may not speak students' languages, so the goal is to assume the role of an engaged and interested language learner—this positions youth as experts in their own languages. The goal is not to produce a perfect translation. Instead, the focus is on carefully examining the text's language, which is unavoidable when generating a translation.

After students have generated their translations, ask them to join another pair of students to form a group of four. Working together, students should create a translation that draws on the prior translation they created with their partner. The goal is to negotiate the meaning together, which calls for making thinking visible through language. Students should be paired into groups with a shared language other than English, for example, a group of four Spanish–English speakers or four monolingual English speakers who are users of Black English.

Phase 3: Intentionally Foster Metalinguistic Knowledge and Refine Text Understanding

Engage students in sharing their translations, highlighting their linguistic choice-making—for example:

- "I noticed that you used this word while Miguel's group used this other word in your translations. Are these words synonyms?"
- "How did you decide which word best captured the authors' meaning?"
- "Were there words that you could not translate word-for-word? What strategies did you use when that happened?"

This makes visible strategies that multilingual learners use to make sense of the unfamiliar language of English text against the backdrop of their knowledge of languages other than English. This resonates with a view of language systems in English and in languages other than English as interconnected.

Then, to highlight the importance of metalinguistic noticing, return to the paraphrase generated at the start of the lesson and revise together, adding any newfound understandings of the text's meaning gained through translation. The aim is to help students see how engaging in translingual activities, like translation, can support them in school-relevant tasks.

Phase 4: Generatively Apply Newfound Language Knowledge

To cement students' knowledge of the CAL feature introduced in Phase 2 of the lesson, engage them in applied practice. This may involve, for example, presenting students with a discussion question and accompanying response frames that contain the target CAL feature. In a lesson involving participant tracking, you may share a student essay containing unclear chains of reference that students can discuss and revise collaboratively. This final phase aims to move knowledge of a language feature from students' receptive to productive repertoire, enabling them to use the language feature when speaking or writing. Frequently, phase 4 spans multiple lessons across a given week.

KEY LEARNINGS FROM TLC EDUCATORS

As we designed and refined the instructional activity above over one academic year, the three English language arts educators (identified by the pseudonyms Manny, Janet, and Rosina) offered their written reflections (often recorded using speech-to-text capabilities) in a dialogue journal within a shared Google Doc. Here, I share segments of their responses highlighting three prominent learnings educators had taken from the experience. Each educator worked with all multilingual students (Manny and Janet in fourth-grade classrooms and Rosina in a fifth-grade classroom), who were speakers of Spanish, Arabic, and Kurdish. Each teacher provided daily instruction during a personalized learning block during the school day.

Learning 1: Moving Beyond Vocabulary Can Be Transformative

A common reflection from TLC participants was that preparing lessons to teach CALS created opportunities to conceptualize language more broadly. After six months of engaging in weekly lessons with students, Manny wrote:

> At first, I was preteaching so much vocabulary. This had been the focus of the PL [professional learning] provided by central [the district central office administration], and I took that advice. The problem was that we were barely getting to the text, and I wasn't teaching any other aspects of language—syntax—within the text. I would sometimes teach syntax through worksheets. This instructional activity helped me move beyond this focus on vocabulary and teach things like connectives and embedded clauses in ways that were really embedded in understanding text. I also had never thought much about explaining why to use these features. I guess to me, it felt obvious. I realize now that my students didn't always understand that part, and this was probably part of why they didn't use the features.

As Rosina responded to Manny, she further underscored the role of teaching a more comprehensive array of language features in supporting students to apply this knowledge when reading and writing:

> "Manny, I can really relate to what you're saying. I was in a similar boat—I had become so laser-focused on just teaching vocabulary, but my students needed so much more than that. It was a real breakthrough moment for me when I realized that.
>
> "Like you, I had been relying a lot on those grammar worksheets, trying to cover all the language features my students were supposed to know based on the WIDA standards. But the problem was, it just didn't seem to be clicking for them. All that grammatical knowledge was just kind of floating out there in this vacuum, disconnected from the actual reading and writing we were doing in class. They weren't able to apply it as a tool for understanding the texts or for improving their own writing.
>
> "But then I started seeing these really promising signs of transfer, just like you experienced. I'll never forget this moment when one of my students, M., was working on a writing piece. She had these two sentences that were related, but they needed to be connected better. I asked her, 'What can you do here to join these ideas?' And without hesitation, she said, 'However!' It was like a light bulb went off—she had internalized the purpose and function of those connective devices, and she was able to apply that knowledge in the moment to communicate her ideas more effectively.
>
> "Experiences like that really made me feel like, yes, this shift towards teaching more than just vocab is making a meaningful difference. My students are starting to see how all these [CALS] linguistic features can be powerful tools for expressing themselves. It's been so gratifying to witness."

Box 12.4. A Quote from Rosina

This shift toward teaching more than just vocab is making a meaningful difference. My students are starting to see how all these [CALS] linguistic features can be powerful tools for expressing themselves. It's been so gratifying to witness.

—Rosina

As these segments of Manny and Rosina's dialogue journal illustrate, the teachers appreciated the move to focus on more than vocabulary in their text-focused language instruction. For each, teaching language forms, as linked to their purposes, supported students in using this language as a communicative resource.

Learning 2: Valuing Students' Languages Doesn't Require Speaking Them

For the teachers in our TLC, an initial concern about engaging their students in translation was how they would evaluate the quality of students' translations, as none were speakers of the multiple languages spoken in the classroom. Indeed, Manny and Rosina both brought experience learning Spanish as high school students, but none of the three focal teachers identified as bilinguals. Each was interested in learning a new language, however. After the first translation activity in his classroom, Manny puzzled over how to support his students:

> I'm unsure what to do as students are translating. I don't speak Spanish, Arabic or Wolof, so I feel less helpful. My students are actually the real experts, and it's strange for me as a teacher to just stand back. I'm also finding myself wanting to evaluate what they've written down as a translation. This isn't the point, right?

Later, after seven weeks of teaching using the four-phase protocol, Manny seemed to grow more comfortable in his newly defined teacher role, which placed him in the position of a learner and his students as experts:

> "You know, in my class I've been really trying to incorporate more metalinguistic questions as part of my instruction. In our last lesson, I asked the students, 'What did you have to think about as you were translating, since word-for-word translations don't always work?' The responses I got were so fascinating. My Spanish-speaking students started commenting on how the adjective placement is different between Spanish and English. But then my

Wolof speakers had even more to say—they shared that they'd never had to write down their home language before, so they had to really think through how to express those words using the English alphabet. It was just really cool to see them grappling with those language differences.

"I've got to admit, at first, it felt a little strange to be releasing that responsibility to the students, you know? I'm so used to being the one guiding the discussion. But I'm starting to see how powerful it can be to position them as the experts on their own linguistic knowledge. They have so much to teach me, and I'm learning that my role is more about facilitating that collective exploration, rather than lecturing. It's a shift, for sure, but one that I think is really paying off in terms of engaging my multilingual students in deep, meaningful discussions about language."

Box 12.5. A Quote from Janet

But what I'm really starting to learn through all of this is that my students have so much valuable knowledge to share with me. The more I open myself up to learning about their languages, the better I'm able to anticipate and understand some of the challenges they might face.

—Janet

Janet responded to Manny, offering her own experiences as evidence of how she continues to develop into the role of language learner:

"You know, Manny, I totally relate to feeling that initial sense of discomfort when students started using their home languages in the classroom. At first, I wondered if they were talking about me or veering off-topic as they engaged in those translations. It was just such an unfamiliar experience, because our classrooms are usually these spaces where English is the dominant language, you know?

"But what I'm really starting to learn through all of this is that my students have so much valuable knowledge to share with me. The more I open myself up to learning about their languages, the better I'm able to anticipate and understand some of the challenges they might face. I guess on some level I knew that students' first languages played a big role in how they engage with English, but that was just kind of a theoretical idea for me. Now, as my students teach me about the nuances of their home languages, I find myself making observations like 'Ah yes, that makes sense—English and Spanish handle adjectives in really different ways, don't they?'"

Box 12.6. A Quote from Manny

I'm starting to see how powerful it can be to position them as the experts on their own linguistic knowledge. They have so much to teach me, and I'm learning that my role is more about facilitating that collective exploration, rather than lecturing. It's a shift, for sure, but one that I think is really paying off in terms of engaging my multilingual students in deep, meaningful discussions about language.

—Manny

Across the participants, including translation in the instructional routine shifted their positions within the classroom. Manny's and Janet's comments also underscored that incorporating students' linguistic knowledge in instruction required educator curiosity—rather than linguistic expertise. This offers the potential for classrooms to be places of both educator and student language learning.

Learning 3: Viewing Reading Comprehension as a Conversation Can Empower Students

A final learning from implementing this instructional routine was the observation that comprehending text could be about placing the language of students, teachers, and texts in conversation. After completing 10 weeks of instruction using this instructional routine twice weekly, the focal teachers reflected:

JANET: "One of the key things I've taken away from this experience is that my own voice and the language used in the texts have been the primary focus of my teaching up until now. While my students' voices were present, my instruction was largely centered on unpacking the language and vocabulary in the assigned readings. The paraphrase activity that places the language that makes the most sense to my students right alongside the original text was really valuable for helping me realize the importance of elevating all languages as equal. The translation work also highlighted this for me—my classroom has been very English-dominant, not by design, but I didn't have any consistent activities where students could use their home languages, like Spanish, in an academic context."

MANNY: "In one of our TLC meetings, we discussed this idea of 'languaging' and the different communities students belong to. That conversation really got me thinking about how I can intentionally bring students' languages into the classroom so that we're all genuinely communicating across these diverse linguistic backgrounds. Like Janet mentioned, I've always told my students they're welcome to use their home languages, but I didn't have any specific lesson activities that made it clear to them that I truly value those linguistic resources."

ROSINA: "The journal entries that have been shared really resonate with me and my own experience. I'm still working on conceptualizing these interactions as more of a back-and-forth conversation rather than a one-way transmission of knowledge. I find myself posing questions like 'If you were to rephrase this idea in your own words, how would you say it?' I appreciate this framing of meaning-making as a collaborative process. It's also helped me recognize that there are multiple valid ways to convey the same concept—the translation activity in particular drove that point home for me."

Box 12.7. Another Quote from Manny

In one of our TLC meetings, we discussed this idea of "languaging" and the different communities students belong to. That conversation really got me thinking about how I can intentionally bring students' languages into the classroom so that we're all genuinely communicating across these diverse linguistic backgrounds.

—Manny

Across the participants' reflections, there was a common consensus that the activity of teaching the language for school literacy alongside the language of students profoundly disrupted the language hierarchies in classrooms that typically place the English language of texts above those of students themselves. This reshuffling of languaging resources by placing increased value on the language known and produced by students impacted how educators came to view text understanding as a discursive and conversational activity.

CONCLUSIONS

The four-phase instructional routine presented in this chapter represents one approach to syncretic language instruction—a flexible framework for designing lessons that place students' linguistic resources in productive dialogue with the language demands of academic texts. By intentionally incorporating opportunities for students to leverage their full linguistic repertoires, including their home languages and ways of languaging, alongside explicit instruction on the language features prevalent in school texts, this approach aims to make visible the connections between diverse ways of using language and the language skills needed for full participation in academic reading and writing.

The reflections of the participating teachers highlight several key learnings from their implementation of this syncretic approach. First, moving beyond a sole focus on vocabulary instruction to also target syntactic and discourse-level language features supported students in applying this knowledge flexibly when reading and writing. Second, the teachers recognized that valuing students' linguistic knowledge did not require them to be proficient in those languages—instead, adopting a stance of curiosity and positioning students as language experts opened up new avenues for learning. Finally, the teachers came to conceptualize text comprehension as a "conversation" between the language resources of the text, the teacher, and the students, disrupting typical hierarchies that privilege the language of academic texts.

Ultimately, this four-phase instructional routine offers an example of a syncretic approach that seeks to honor the rich linguistic assets that all students bring to the classroom while supporting the development of the specific language skills needed to thrive in academic settings. By positioning students as active agents in the meaning-making process and by making visible the connections between students' everyday languaging and the language of school literacy, this instructional routine holds promise as a tool for fostering more equitable and inclusive learning environments. As educators continue to grapple with the challenge of engaging multilingual students, models like this can serve as springboards for reimagining classroom instruction in ways that value the dynamism and diversity of language.

Reflection Questions

1. How does the syncretic approach described in this chapter aim to position students' linguistic resources in relation to the language demands posed by academic texts? What are the critical components of this instructional routine that you might adopt in your own lessons?
2. The chapter highlights several key learnings that emerged from the participating teachers' implementation of the syncretic approach. Which of these learnings resonates most with you and your own instructional context? Why?
3. The chapter suggests that this approach conceptualizes text comprehension as a "conversation" between the language of the text, the teacher, and the

students. How might this view of reading reshape typical classroom practices around supporting students' engagement with academic texts? What are some implications for your own instruction?

4. How might you adapt or build upon the instructional routine described in this chapter to better address the needs of the multilingual learners in your own classroom context? What modifications or additional supports might you incorporate?

ACKNOWLEDGMENTS

Thank you to my collaborating teachers and their students, who generously allowed me to join their classrooms. Also, thank you to the Spencer Foundation for the generous funding to support this collaboration. All perspectives are my own.

REFERENCES

Aguilar, G., Uccelli, P., & Galloway, E. P. (2020). Toward biliteracy: Unpacking the contribution of mid-adolescent dual language learners' Spanish and English academic language skills to English reading comprehension. *TESOL Quarterly*, *54*(4), 1010–1036.

Aukerman, M. (2007). A culpable CALP: Rethinking the conversational/academic language proficiency distinction in early literacy instruction. *The Reading Teacher*, *60*(7), 626–635.

Bailey, A. L. (2007). *The language demands of school: Putting academic English to the test.* Yale University Press.

Bailey, A. L., & Heritage, M. (2014). The role of language learning progressions in improved instruction and assessment of English language learners. *TESOL Quarterly*, *48*(3), 480–506.

Barr, C. D., Uccelli, P., & Phillips Galloway, E. (2019). Specifying the academic language skills that support text understanding in the middle grades: The design and validation of the core academic language skills construct and instrument. *Language Learning*, *69*(4), 978–1021.

Berman, R. A. (2007). Developing linguistic knowledge and language use across adolescence. In E. Hoff & M. Shatz (Eds.), *Blackwell handbook of language development* (pp. 347–367). Blackwell.

Biber, D., & Conrad, S. (2009). *Register, genre, and style.* Cambridge University Press.

Cardoso, W., Paulet, C., & de Laboratório Educação, P. U. C. (2020). Vocabulary and academic literacy: An analysis of texts used by young learners of English. TESL-EJ, *24*(2), n2.

Cervetti, G. N., Pearson, P. D., Palincsar, A. S., Afflerbach, P., Kendeou, P., Biancarosa, G., et al. (2020). How the reading for understanding initiative's research complicates the simple view of reading invoked in the science of reading. *Reading Research Quarterly, 55,* S161–S172.

Christie, F., & Derewianka, B. (2008). *School discourse: Learning to write across the years of schooling.* Continuum.

Cole, M. W., Puzio, K., Keyes, C. S., Jiménez, R. T., Pray, L., & David, S. (2012). Contesting language orientations: A critical multicultural perspective on local language policy in two middle schools. *Middle Grades Research Journal, 7*(2), 129.

Cucchiara, M. (2018). *3Ls™ learning, language, and literacy.* Council of the Great City Schools.

Daniel, S. M., Jiménez, R. T., Pray, L., & Pacheco, M. B. (2019). Scaffolding to support English learners' language development and content learning. *The Reading Teacher, 72*(6), 711–718.

David, S. S., & Cole, M. W. (2021). Jostling Isaac: dynamic configurations of bodies and objects during a language problem solving event. *Classroom Discourse, 12*(1–2), 101–120.

Duranti, A., & Ochs, E. (1997). Syncretic literacy in a Samoan American family. In L. B. Resnick, R. Säljö, C. Pontecorvo, & B. Burge (Eds.), *Discourse, tools and reasoning: essays on situated cognition* (pp. 169–202). Springer Berlin Heidelberg.

García, O., & Li, W. (2014). *Translanguaging: Language, bilingualism and education.* Palgrave Macmillan.

García, O., Johnson, S. I., Seltzer, K., & Valdés, G. (2017). In *The translanguaging classroom: Leveraging student bilingualism for learning* (pp. v–xix). Caslon.

Gebhard, M. (2019). *Teaching and researching ELLs' disciplinary literacies.* Routledge.

Gee, J. (2004). Learning language as a matter of learning social languages within discourses. In M. Hawkins (Ed.), *Language learning and teacher education: A sociocultural approach* (pp. 13–32). Multilingual Matters.

Gutiérrez, K. D. (2014). Integrative research review: Syncretic approaches to literacy learning. Leveraging horizontal knowledge and expertise. In P. Dunston, L. Gambrell, K. Headley, S. Fullerton, & P. Stecker, (Eds.), *63rd literacy research association yearbook* (pp. 48–61). Literacy Research Association.

Gutiérrez, K. D., & Jurow, A. S. (2018). Social design experiments: Toward equity by design. In M. Cole, W. Penuel, & K. O'Neill (Eds.), *Cultural-historical activity theory approaches to design-based research* (pp. 79–112). Routledge.

Halliday, M. A. (2006). *Language of science* (Vol. 5). Bloomsbury.

Heath, S. B. (2012). *Words at work and play: Three decades in family and community life.* Cambridge University Press.

Hsin, L. B., Galloway, E. P., & Snow, C. E. (2024). Supporting social strengths amid emerging bilingualism: Effects of Word Generation on social perspective taking in English learners' writing. *International Journal of Bilingual Education and Bilingualism, 27*(6), 854–869.

Janks, H. (2010). *Literacy and power.* Routledge.

Jiménez, R. T., David, S., Fagan, K., Risko, V. J., Pacheco, M., Pray, L., & Gonzales, M. (2015). Using translation to drive conceptual development for students becoming literate in English as an additional language. *Research in the Teaching of English*, 248–271.

Kintsch, W. (2005). An overview of top-down and bottom-up effects in comprehension: The CI perspective. *Discourse Processes, 39*(2–3), 125–128.

Kris D. Gutiérrez & A. Susan Jurow (2016): Social design experiments: Toward equity by design. *Journal of the Learning Sciences*, DOI: 10.1080/10508406.2016.1204548

Phillips Galloway, E., McClain, J. B., & Uccelli, P. (2020). Broadening the lens on the science of reading: A multifaceted perspective on the role of academic language in text understanding. *Reading Research Quarterly, 55*(S1), S331–S345.

Louie, B. (2020). Centering cultural knowledge: Decolonizing and indigenizing academic literacy instruction. *Journal of Adolescent & Adult Literacy, 64*(1), 7–15.

Makoni, S., & Pennycook, A. (Eds.). (2007). *Disinventing and reconstituting languages* (Vol. 62). Multilingual Matters.

Meneses, A., Uccelli, P., Santelices, M. V., Ruiz, M., Acevedo, D., & Figueroa, J. (2018). Academic language as a predictor of reading comprehension in monolingual Spanish-speaking readers: Evidence from Chilean early adolescents. *Reading Research Quarterly, 53*(2), 223–247.

Nagy, W., & Townsend, D. (2012). Words as tools: Learning academic vocabulary as language acquisition. *Reading Research Quarterly, 47*(1), 91–108.

Orellana, M. F., & García-Sánchez, I. (2023). Language brokering and immigrant children's everyday learning in home and community contexts. In H. Pinson, N. Bunar, & D. Devine (Eds.), *Research handbook on migration and education* (pp. 173–188). Edward Elgar.

Paris, D. (2012). Culturally sustaining pedagogy: A needed change in stance, terminology, and practice. *Educational Researcher, 41*(3), 93–97.

Phillips Galloway, E., McClain, J. B., & Uccelli, P. (2020a). Broadening the lens on the science of reading: A multifaceted perspective on the role of academic language in text understanding. *Reading Research Quarterly, 55*, S331–S345.

Phillips Galloway, E., Uccelli, P., Aguilar, G., & Barr, C. (2020b). Exploring the cross-linguistic contribution of Spanish and English academic language skills to English text comprehension for middle-grade dual language learners. *AERA Open, 6*(1), 1–20.

Phillips Galloway, E., & Uccelli, P. (2019). Examining developmental relations between core academic language skills and reading comprehension for English learners and their peers. *Journal of Educational Psychology, 111*(1), 15.

Phillips Galloway, E., Stude, J., & Uccelli, P. (2015). Adolescents' metalinguistic reflections on the academic register in speech and writing. *Linguistics and Education, 31*, 221–237.

Pierson, A. E., Clark, D. B., & Brady, C. E. (2021). Scientific modeling and translanguaging: A multilingual and multimodal approach to support science learning and engagement. *Science Education, 105*(4), 776–813.

Proctor, C. P., Silverman, R. D., Harring, J. R., Jones, R. L., & Hartranft, A. M. (2020). Teaching bilingual learners: Effects of a language-based reading intervention on academic language and reading comprehension in grades 4 and 5. *Reading Research Quarterly, 55*(1), 95–122.

Puzio, K., Keyes, C. S., Cole, M. W., & Jiménez, R. T. (2013). Language differentiation: Collaborative translation to support bilingual reading. *Bilingual Research Journal., 36*(3), 329–349.

Ridley, J., & Rowe, L. W. (2024). Translanguaging and early childhood literacy: Themes and possibilities for theory, pedagogy, and policy. *Journal of Early Childhood Literacy, 24*(3), 511–522.

Schleppegrell, M. J. (2004). *The language of schooling: A functional linguistics perspective*. Routledge.

Schleppegrell, M. J. (2007). At last: The meaning in grammar. *Research in the Teaching of English, 42*(1), 121–128.

Schleppegrell, M. J., Sun, S., & Monte-Sano, C. (2023). The value of models to support students' voice in middle school social studies argument writing. *Journal of Second Language Writing, 61*, 101043.

Shin, S. J. (2017). *Bilingualism in schools and society: Language, identity, and policy*. Routledge.

Souto-Manning, M. (2013). On children as syncretic natives: Disrupting and moving beyond normative binaries. *Journal of Early Childhood Literacy, 13*(3), 371–394.

Swain, M. (2006). Languaging, agency, and collaboration in advanced second language proficiency. In H. Byrnes (Ed.), *Advanced language learning: The contribution of Halliday and Vygotsky* (pp. 95–108). Bloomsbury.

Uccelli, P., Phillips Galloway, E., Barr, C. D., Meneses, A., & Dobbs, C. L. (2015). Beyond vocabulary: Exploring cross-disciplinary academic-language proficiency and its association with reading comprehension. *Reading Research Quarterly, 50*(3), 337–356.

Uccelli, P., Galloway, E. P., & Qin, W. (2020). The language for school literacy. In P. Afflerbach, P. Enciso, E. B. Moje, & N. K. Lesaux (Eds.), *Handbook of reading research* (Vol. 5, pp. 155–179). Routledge.

Vogelstein, L., McBride, C., Wilkerson, M., Vogel, S., Barrales, W., Ascenzi-Moreno, L., et al. (2023). Storytelling "in theory": Re-imagining computational literacies through the lenses of syncretism and translanguaging. In *Proceedings of the 17th International Conference of the Learning Sciences-ICLS 2023* (pp. 800–807). International Society of the Learning Sciences.

Wei, L. (2018). Translanguaging as a practical theory of language. *Applied Linguistics, 39*(1), 9–30.

White, H., Galloway, E. P., & Jiménez, R. T. (2023). Bridging theory to practice: Exploring the role of an educative translingual curriculum to support linguistically diverse classroom practices. *TESOL Quarterly, 58*(2), 802–829.

Index

Note: Page numbers followed by 'n' indicate note number(s).